BURGON SOCIETY HISTORICAL REPRINTS 2

THE HISTORY OF LAMBETH DEGREES
SOURCES AND STUDIES

EDITED BY

WILLIAM GIBSON

THE BURGON SOCIETY

2019

CONTENTS

INTRODUCTION

The purpose of this volume is to bring together a selection of material on the history, nature and academical dress of 'Lambeth degrees' – the degrees which the archbishops of Canterbury can legally confer under the statute of 1534 (25 Henry VIII cap 21). This law removed the authority of the pope in England and Wales and reserved to the sovereign the right to hear ecclesiastical appeals. It was held that the previous power of the popes to confer degrees had now become the prerogative of the archbishops of Canterbury. There was of course much debate about whether this was a spiritual authority or a temporal right. The archbishops of Canterbury possessed this right as primates of the Church of England. It follows that the northern primate and Irish primate might have also exercised the right to confer degrees. So in theory there could have been 'Ebor' or 'Armagh' degrees. It seems likely that, in the case of Armagh, the archbishops used that right to nominate the award of a degree by Trinity College, Dublin.

This volume is divided into two sections. The first brings together a group of sources on Lambeth degrees. Foremost among these is the celebrated 1717–25 case of Francis Gastrell against Samuel Peploe. The appointment of the Latitudinarian Whig Peploe to the wardenship of Manchester was an affront to the Bishop of Chester, Francis Gastrell, since he was a Tory High Churchman. Undoubtedly Peploe's appointment was with the intent that he would sort out the Tory Jacobite leanings of some of the prebendaries of the Manchester Collegiate Church. Gastrell's means of opposing Peploe's appointment was to challenge his right to hold the post (the holder of which was required by the statutes to be at least a bachelor of divinity) since Peploe held a Lambeth BD, rather than a BD from a university. So to impugn the right of the archbishops to award full degrees was a political act. Gastrell's fifty two page attack on Lambeth degrees is reproduced in full together with an introduction which establishes the context and content of the attack. Gastrell's legal claim failed, so from the 1720s it had been clear that in law the degrees awarded by the archbishops are full degrees, equivalent to those awarded in the universities and with the same status. Lambeth degrees are often confused with honorary degrees, but they are not.

The next item is a list of the principal manuscript holdings relating to Lambeth degrees in British archives. This has been derived from the National Archives catalogue. As might be expected, the majority of the items are in Lambeth Palace Library. The papers are extensive and would clearly repay some detailed investigation. However one feature of them which stands out is the ways in which, in the nineteenth century, Lambeth degrees were conferred on colonial clergy and bishops, who for the most part had no access to universities or their degrees. In this respect, the archbishops of Canterbury were an early example of an 'open' university –conferring awards on those who did not have access to the universities. It is clear that there was some process of examination undertaken for clergy who applied for degrees. Other matters are interesting. For example, the correspondence in 1881–2 of Archbishop Tait and others on the question of whether Lambeth degrees might be conferred on Protestant Nonconformists and Roman Catholics. Similarly, the correspondence in 1938 on the issue of stamp duty on Lambeth degrees and its abolition is important, not least because a number of writers both in the twentieth century and before had complained of the heavy fees payable for the award of the degrees.

I am grateful to Lambeth Palace Library for permission to reproduce their list of Lambeth degrees awarded in chronological order, compiled by Melanie Barber using the Faculty Office fiats and the Vicar-General Act Books. The list is available on the Lambeth Palace Library website[1] together with a similar list organised by the degree awarded to the individual. Besides the list of names, it is interesting to note that these degrees include some no longer awarded, including the BA, LLB, BCL and MB. The list includes the MA conferred on Owen Jones which was awarded in 1699 and subsequently revoked.

There follows then some interesting snippets from the *Gentleman's Magazine*, *Notes and Queries* and other

---

[1] http://www.lambethpalacelibrary.org/

journals and publications from the 1860s to the 1930s. Some of these are attempts to record information on Lambeth degrees and the people on whom they were conferred. Others relate to the opinions of scholars, churchmen and physicians on the character of Lambeth degrees.

The second section of this book is a series of articles, already published elsewhere, which examine aspects of Lambeth degrees and their academical dress. First is a precis of chapter thirteen of Charles A H Franklyn's *Academical Dress From the Middle Ages to the Present Day including Lambeth Degrees* (1970, Lewes: W E Baxter). In it, Franklyn outlines a distinct view of Lambeth degrees –that they were in effect state degrees awarded by the sovereign – this view was rejected unanimously by contemporary legal opinion. That did not, however, prevent Franklyn from regarding his own opinion as correct and unassailable. It is an example of Franklyn at his most opinionated and obdurate. He was, of course, wrong.[2]

The other items in this section, by Noel Cox and Graham Zellick are more focused on Lambeth degrees and their legal status, the ceremony of awards and the academical dress to which they are entitled. Of particular interest is the Zellick article which addresses the issue of whose academical dress is worn. The convention that Lambeth degree holders used the robes of the university that the archbishop had attended only worked when only two universities existed. By the time that Zellick wrote, the first archbishop who was a London graduate, rather than a graduate of either Oxford or Cambridge, had been appointed. Zellick, as Vice-Chancellor of the University of London corresponded with Lambeth Palace on whether the convention meant that London robes would now be used for Lambeth degrees. It is a fascinating discussion.

This collection does not adopt an opinion on the issues that exercised Gastrell, Franklyn and Zellick as to the origins, validity, nature and dress of Lambeth degrees. It does, however, seek to make more widely available sources and studies which illustrate this fascinating subject. It is perhaps also worth noting that the Archbishop of Canterbury is included as an institution authorised to award degrees in a Statutory Instrument made under the 1988 Education Act.

William Gibson

---

[2] The form of the presentation of Franklyn's views is in a precis rather than direct quotation so that the issue of copyright is not raised.

SOURCES

1 'What Kind of Hood doth he use?': The Challenge to the Validity of Lambeth Degrees in 1717–25

William Gibson

On 1 July 1717 Samuel Peploe was nominated to the post of warden of St Mary's collegiate church, Manchester. Peploe's was not a popular appointment. He was a Low Churchman and since 1705 had been an outspoken anti-Catholic vicar of Preston, which was a centre of Catholicism in Lancashire.[1] He had moreover been friendly with Presbyterians in Lancashire and this made fellow Anglicans suspicious of his churchmanship. Peploe had come to the attention of ministers by his heroic action against the Jacobite invasion of 1715. As the rebels entered Preston, Peploe entered his pulpit and preached to the town that they should remain loyal to King George I and resist the rebels. It was a courageous act and one which deserved a reward. So two years later he was appointed to the wardenship of Manchester collegiate church, which lay in the gift of the King. The appointment did not find favour with the Bishop of Chester, Francis Gastrell. This was for two reasons. Firstly, Gastrell was the final episcopal appointment made in April 1714 during the extreme Tory government which held power for the last four years of Queen Anne's reign. Gastrell represented an inflexible and stern wing of High Church Toryism. Peploe's Whig Low Churchmanship was far distant from Gastrell's ideal. Secondly, before Peploe's nomination, Gastrell had sought to annex the wardenship of St Mary's, Manchester to the bishopric of Chester as a way of raising the meagre income of the see.[2] For Gastrell, Peploe's nomination was unacceptable, and he thought he had a means to obstruct the appointment.

The statutes of St Mary's collegiate church in Manchester required the warden to hold the degree of bachelor of divinity, which Peploe did not — he had taken his MA from Jesus College, Oxford but had not progressed to the BD.[3] The simple expedient was found that Archbishop William Wake would award Peploe a Lambeth BD and this would qualify him to be appointed to the wardenship.[4] However, Bishop Gastrell refused to induct Peploe to the wardenship on the grounds that the Lambeth degree of bachelor of divinity was not a valid university qualification. The refusal to admit Peploe to the wardenship sparked a lengthy legal battle.

Archbishop Wake was certain that the statute forbidding papal dispensations allowed him to award degrees in the way the pope had. It was such an unchallenged right that even during a vacancy in the see of Canterbury in 1677 the dean and chapter of Canterbury had used the right to award two degrees. Wake awarded forty seven degrees during his primacy.[5]

From the start, Peploe thought that the Bishop was acting from political motives. He wrote to Archbishop Wake in April 1722 that, 'I believe … that this has been made a Party Cause on one side from the beginning.'[6] There was other evidence that Gastrell allowed political prejudice to influence his episcopal functions. It was claimed that in 1720 Gastrell rejected a candidate for holy orders, on the grounds that he had argued for 'the King's title against one who advanced certain propositions which manifestly subverted it'.[7]

---

[1] P. G. Green, "Samuel Peploe and the ideology of anti-Catholicism among the Anglican clergy in early Hanoverian England", *Transactions of the Historic Society of Lancashire and Cheshire* 145 (1995) 75–94; C. M. Haydon, "Samuel Peploe and Catholicism in Preston, 1714", *Recusant History* 20 (1990–91) 76–80.

[2] S. W. Baskerville, "Gastrell, Francis (1662–1725)", in: *Oxford Dictionary of National Biography*, Oxford University Press (2004).

[3] S. W. Baskerville, "Peploe, Samuel (bap. 1667, d. 1752)", in: *Oxford Dictionary of National Biography*, Oxford University Press (2004).

[4] http://www.lambethpalacelibrary.org/files/lambeth_degrees_date.pdf

[5] N. Sykes, *William Wake, Archbishop of Canterbury, 1657–1737*, Cambridge University Press (1957), volume 1, page 210.

[6] *Christ Church Wake MSS, Arch. W. Epist.* 9/182.

[7] ibid., 8/296, *Peploe to Wake, 13 September 1720*.

The legal case was complex and fraught, being passed between the ecclesiastical and temporal courts. Altogether the battle took seven years to resolve, in part because Gastrell's tactics seem to have been to delay the action coming to court for as long as possible. Equally, Peploe refused attempts at resolutions in 1718 which included the prospect of a royal dispensation from the need for a BD and the possibility of the University of Oxford awarding him a BD.[8] Archbishop Wake, assisted by Richard Chicheley and Thomas Tanner, combed through precedents and evidence and were supported in their determination to defend the right to award degrees by the attorney-general, Sir Richard Raymond. In August 1722, the case was finally heard in court at the assizes in Lancaster. The hearing took fifteen hours and the jury deliberated for two hours. Finally the judgement was given to Wake and Peploe.[9] But Gastrell again refused to admit Peploe. Gastrell's counsel sought a bill of exception to the assize decision, and appealed the case to the King's Bench, which in May 1725 ruled definitively against him.[10] The judgement was clear: the archbishop of Canterbury was empowered to confer degrees and such 'Lambeth degrees' were of equal value to those granted by the universities. Certainly they met the criteria of the legal qualification to hold certain offices. The case ended within a few weeks of Gastrell's death. To the dismay of his supporters, Gastrell's successor in the see of Chester was Samuel Peploe.

The purpose of this article is to examine the arguments that Gastrell presented to the public in 1721 in his Bishop of Chester's Case.[11] Gastrell's 'case' was in fact a series of claims and assaults on the right of the Archbishops to award Lambeth degrees and a challenge to the assertion that such degrees were the equivalent of university degrees. Gastrell opened his claim with the 1636 charter of St Mary's, Manchester, reciting the 1578 charter, which required the warden to hold the degree of bachelor of divinity from a university and that Peploe had only been granted a degree by Archbishop Wake. However this was an opening preliminary, Gastrell went on to argue that the 1534 Act (25 Henry VIII cap 21) did not actually allow the archbishops to grant degrees, only 'licences, dispensation and faculties' as formerly conferred by the pope. He argued that the Act sought to restrain papal powers and grant them to the king, not to create new powers. Gastrell then examined the first use of the Lambeth powers, by which Archbishop Cranmer dispensed with the requirements for George Broke to be awarded the degree of BA. He argued that there was a distinction between dispensing someone from the requirements of a degree and actually awarding one.[12]

More directly, Gastrell argued that when, under Elizabeth I, the Reformation legislation was restored, one of the provisions referred to 'degree of learning in any University within the Queen's realm.' And by a law of 1610, graduates were required to swear oaths 'before the Vice-Chancellor of the University in the Congregation-House' -- which Gastrell took to mean that degrees could not be granted elsewhere.[13] He also cited the draft statutes of Archbishops Whitgift and Laud which said that 'no degrees, but such as were taken regularly, and according to due form, in the Universities, were proper Qualifications for such as were admitted Canons in any Cathedral.' In comparing the statutes of Hereford Cathedral, which included the reference to university degrees, and those of Manchester, Gastrell claimed there was no difference.[14]

---

[8] *Christ Church Wake MSS, Arch. W. Epist.* 8, Canterbury III, f. 36.

[9] Sykes, *William Wake, Archbishop of Canterbury, 1657–1737*, volume 1, page 211.

[10] Baskerville, "Gastrell, Francis (1662–1725)"; W. Stubbs, "Lambeth Degrees", *The Gentleman's Magazine* 1 (1864) 633–635.

[11] The full title of which was *The Bishop of Chester's Case With Relation to the Wardenship of Manchester, in Which is Shewn that No Other Degrees But Such As Are Taken in the Universities Can Be Deemed Legal Qualification for Any Ecclesiastical Preferment*, Oxford, 1721. An identical version was also published by the University Press in Cambridge also in 1721. Clearly both were designed to mobilise the Universities in his support. The case is briefly mentioned in passing in the principal legal examination of Lambeth degrees, Noel Cox, "Dispensations, Privileges, and the Conferment of Graduate Status: With Special Reference to Lambeth Degrees", *Journal of Law and Religion* 18.1 (2002–2003) 249–274.

[12] F. Gastrell, *The Bishop of Chester's Case*, Oxford (1721), pages 1–21.

[13] ibid., page 22.

[14] ibid., page 37.

Gastrell also used the evidence of Matthew Parker's ordination articles of 1564. These required ordinands to indicate their parish of birth 'except such as shall be of Degrees in the Universities'. And the articles required graduates to wear their 'side gown with sleeves … and tippets of sarcenet, as is lawful for them…' and others who have 'taken their Degrees in some University' to wear their proper apparel.[15] Parker also did not appear to have conferred any degrees, claimed Gastrell. He listed the fees payable to the Lambeth Faculty Office in the second half of the sixteenth century and did not find any evidence that there was a fee payable for the award of a degree.[16] Gastrell reproduced the list of Archbishop Grindal's Faculty Office dispensation fees to prove that there had been no arrangement for payment of fees for Lambeth degrees under his archiepiscopate either.[17]

A central plank in Gastrell's claim, which he recited at length, were the articles of enquiries issued at archbishops, bishops and archdeacons visitations. In all, he quoted from nineteen of these from the seventeenth century. In each case the articles asked whether the clergy wore the appropriate hood of their degree from their university. For example, Archbishop Bancroft asked in 1606 'whether … doth he weare upon his surplice, during the times aforesaid, such whood (sic) as by the orders of his University is agreeable to his Degree?' Matthew Wren in Norwich diocese asked in 1636 'is your minister, parson, vicar or curate a graduate in either of the Universities? And, if he be a Graduate, of what Degree is he? And what kind of Hood doth he use to wear in Church?' And Nicholas Stratford of Chester asked in 1692 in visiting the Cathedral whether each prebendary was at least an MA 'and we presume each will upon demand give evidence of his University Degree.'[18] This emphasis on university degrees seemed to Gastrell to point to the fact that bishops did not regard degrees awarded by the archbishop of Canterbury as equivalent to those from the universities. He also pointed out that the same restriction applied to the College of Physicians which in 1688 limited membership to those who had obtained the degree of doctor of physic in one of the universities.[19]

Gastrell also listed cases in which the universities had awarded what he called 'honorary degrees' –by which he meant degrees awarded other than by the usual regulations. For example, in 1593 Sir John Mason, Chancellor of Oxford, was permitted 'to wear the habit of a Doctor, tho' he was only Master of Arts.' Gastrell included in his list, awards to graduates when they were absent, instances of clergy supplicating for degrees though they had not formally qualified for them and being awarded them, degrees granted ad eundem, degrees granted by diploma, judges made doctors of laws on their appointment to the status of chief justice and awards made at the request of chancellors, the speaker of the House of Commons and the monarch.[20]

Gastrell also cited the case of Simon Lowth, appointed dean of Rochester in November 1688. The statutes of Rochester, like those of Manchester, required the dean to hold a specific degree, in this instance a doctorate, which Lowth did not possess. However, Archbishop Sancroft did not award Lowth a DD, he wrote to the University of Cambridge from which Lowth held an MA saying 'I desire you (it being also the Desire of his Diocesan) that you would grant him the Degree of Doctor of Laws, that he may be qualified to enjoy his Majesty's Favour…' In this instance, however Gastrell's use of evidence is questionable. He conceded that throughout James II's reign Sancroft did not exercise his powers of awarding degree.[21] Moreover there is evidence that Sancroft regarded James II with sufficient caution and reservation not to engage with his rule

---

[15] ibid., page 25.
[16] ibid., page 28.
[17] ibid., page 31.
[18] ibid., pages 37–39.
[19] ibid., page 43.
[20] ibid., pages 40–42.
[21] ibid., page 46.

at all, certainly this was the case by November 1688.[22] In Lowth's case the delay in obtaining a doctorate cost him the deanery. He did not obtain the degree until January 1689, by which time James II had fled and William III ignored Lowth's nomination and installed Henry Ullock as dean of Rochester. Lowth refused the oath of allegiance to William and Mary and was dispossessed of all his church livings in August 1689.

Although he could not find an instance of it, Gastrell claimed that Archbishop Thomas Tenison had granted many Lambeth degrees but refused to allow them to be used as a qualification for some status, because he said 'it would make a noise.' Gastrell also claimed that Tenison had told him privately of his own opinion of 'the invalidity of his degrees.'[23] This seems implausible: Gastrell and Tenison were not close and the latter was dismayed at Gastrell's appointment as bishop of Chester. Tenison was also dead, so Gastrell's suggestion could not be tested.[24] Moreover Tenison had awarded thirty two Lambeth degrees during his primacy, which does not suggest scruples about their validity.[25] In his conclusion, Gastrell claimed that whether the archbishop had the right to grant degrees or not – which he doubted – the issue was also whether such degrees could be used to qualify anyone for an appointment under charters such as that of Manchester collegiate church. He argued that they were not. He ended his argument with an appropriately partisan flourish, hoping 'that an old popish abuse, long since exploded, and banished from all parties in Europe, will not now be adjudged a convenience and necessary practice here in England.'[26] In some respects Gastrell's case was always likely to fail, and in part this explains his tactic of delay and temporising.

Gastrell's case was influenced in part by the circumstances of the day. Since Gastrell had spoken in the House of Lords in defence of the Jacobite bishop, Francis Atterbury, he was regarded with suspicion by many.[27] Moreover there were rising anxieties about the dangerously Jacobite tone of the clergy in Manchester's collegiate church, hence Peploe's appointment was so important. By 1726, when Peploe was Bishop of Chester, he sought to hold a visitation of the collegiate church to inquire why the chaplain, Richard Assheton, refused to say prayers for the King.[28] On that occasion a satirical tract had been produced in which, in answer to a question of whether Assheton was properly qualified to be chaplain, the author wrote: 'Not duly qualified? Why let him go to Lambeth then; he may be duly qualified there. Whatever other good qualifications he may be possessed of.'[29]

By 1725 therefore, nearly two centuries after the passage of the Act which granted the right, the King's Bench endorsed the power of the archbishops of Canterbury to award degrees and for those degrees to have the same validity and legal qualification as university degrees.

---

[22] W. Gibson, *James II and the Trial of the Seven Bishops*, Palgrave Macmillan, Basingstoke (2009).

[23] Gastrell, *The Bishop of Chester's Case*, pages 46–47.

[24] E. Carpenter, *Thomas Tenison*, SPCK, London (1948), page 186.

[25] Sykes, *William Wake, Archbishop of Canterbury, 1657–1737*, volume 1, page 210.

[26] ibid., volume 1, page 52.

[27] G. V. Bennett, *The Tory Crisis in Church and State, 1688–1739*, Clarendon Press, Oxford (1975), pages 273–274.

[28] P. K. Monod, *Jacobitism and the English People, 1688–1788*, Cambridge University Press (1993), pages 151–152.

[29] *The Bishop of Chester's Case Against Mr Richard Assheton*, [1726]. This item is often catalogued as published in 1720 as part of Gastrell's case against Peploe, but it is clear that it relates to Peploe's period as bishop of Chester and therefore is after 1725.

2 The Bishop of Chester's Case With Relation to the Wardenship of Manchester, in Which is Shewn that No Other Degrees But Such As Are Taken in the Universities Can Be Deemed Legal Qualification for Any Ecclesiastical Preferment

Francis Gastrell

THE
BISHOP of *CHESTER's*
C A S E,

With Relation to the

WARDENSHIP of *MANCHESTER*.

In which is fhewn,

That No Other DEGREES

But fuch as are taken in the

U N I V E R S I T Y,

Can be deemed

L E G A L   Q U A L I F I C A T I O N S

For any

Ecclefiaftical Preferment in *ENGLAND*.

O X F O R D,
Printed at the THEATER, MDCCXXI.

THE

PREFACE.

*W*HEN I drew up the following Case, I never imagined that I should have been engaged in any Controversy with the Crown about it. Because, whatever I have offered in maintenance of that Ancient and Noble Privilege, claimed by our Universities, to confer Degrees, is urged in Defence of the King's Prerogative also; from whence only that Power can be derived; and in support of Royal Charters, the true meaning and intention of which was certainly, in the Opinion of those Princes that granted them, and of all the Lawyers that ever read them, the same that I contend for.

'Twas a great while before it was judged proper to interest the Crown in this Affair. And, when a Suit was ordered, I appeal to all the Officers concerned in the Prosecution of it, whether, in all the Steps I took, I did not shew a just regard to the Crown, and a great desire to avoid such an unhappy Contest by any reasonable Expedients; tho' I was very ready to try the Cause upon any other foot. And at last, when a publick Decision was thought necessary, and it could not be expected that the Universities should freely give up what they look'd upon to be their undoubted Right; it was with great uneasiness, and not till after assurance given that a Legal Defence in this case should not be construed as an instance of Un-
dutifulness

The PREFACE.

dutifulnefs *or* Difaffection *in thofe* Learned *Bodies*; *that I undertook to prove in a* Court of Juftice *what I have here offered to the confideration of Men of* all Profeffions.

As to the Archbifhop of Canterbury; *I have no defign to rob his See of any Privileges belonging to it.* He may give *as many* Titles, *and beftow as many* Honours *as the* Pope *himfelf does, provided they are not admitted into the fame rank with thofe conferred by the Favour of the* Crown, *and they do not challenge any place in the conftruction of* Charters *and* Acts of Parliament. *Nor is it my intention to deny the* prefent Archbifhop *any thing that his Predeceffors enjoyed, having always been defirous to treat Him with a particular Refpect. Only in this thing, wherein I am perfuaded that He has exceeded former Examples, I think my felf obliged to prove it, and I have* his Grace's *leave fo to do.*

I muft defire likewife to fet my felf right in the opinion of the World, with regard to that Gentleman *who has been the occafion of this Difpute; and I cannot do it more effectually than by telling them what I told him when I firft fcrupled to admit the* Archbifhop's Degree *for a* Qualification, *viz.* "*That, being in all refpects qualified to take his Degree re-* "*gularly in the* Univerfity, *he might proceed that way,* "*without any fear of being denied; but, if he defired any* "*Favour, ufually indulged to other Perfons, that I would en-* "*deavour to obtain it for him; and I did not doubt but the* "*Univerfity would readily grant it*". *Upon what Views and Motives* Mr. Peplo *declined taking his* Batchelor of Divinity's Degree in Oxford, *when he had actually prepared the beft part of the* Exercife *required in order to it, I cannot tell; but fure I am that he might have done it without hurting the* Archbifhop's Pretenfions; *becaufe there are living Precedents of Perfons who have taken the fame Degrees in* Oxford, *which had been given them before at* Lambeth.

I have nothing farther to add in relation to the Cafe now publifhed, *but that it has been approved by fo many eminent Men of* Learning *and* Judgment, *feveral of which have great skill in* Antiquities, *and others great* Knowledge *and* Experience in the Laws of the Realm, *that I am fure the Caufe now depending cannot be adjudged* Frivolous, *or* Litigious, *whatever other fentence may be pafs'd upon it.*

THE

THE

BISHOP of *CHESTER*'s

C A S E,

With Relation to the

WARDENSHIP of *Manchester*, &c.

The laſt CHARTER of Foundation of *Man-chester College*, granted by *Charles* the Firſt, bears date *Oct.* 2. *A. D.* 1636. in which are theſe Words, *viz.*

OLUMUS, Concedimus, & Ordinamus, quòd virtute harum Literarum Patentium in perpètuum ſit & erit in Villâ de Manchester —— *Unum Collegium perpetuis futuris temporibus duraturum —— Ac Collegium illud de uno Guardiano, Presbytero, & ſacræ Theologiæ ad minus* Baccalaureo, *vel Legum Canonicarum & Civilium* Baccalaureo ; *& quatuor Sociis, Presbyteris,* Artium *ad minus* Magiſtris, *vel* Legum (*ut prædicitur*) Baccalaureis —— *erigi, ordinari, & ſtabiliri decrevimus —— Volumus etiam, conſtituimus, & ordinamus per præſentes, quòd quandocunque & quotieſcunque Officium & Locum Guardiani in poſterum vacare contigerit, in Locum ejus concedat & ſit Guardianus quicunque Presbyter, & ad minus ſacræ* Theologiæ, *vel Ju-*

B   *rium*

rium (*ut prædicitur*) Baccalaureus: *Qui à Nobis, Hæredibus, &c. —— per Literas, magno Sigillo nostro, Hæredum, &c. munitas nominabitur —— Præsentatione factâ* Episcopo Cestriensi —— *Qui statim curabit Clericum à Nobis sic nominatum canonicè institui, & installari —— & quandocunque Locum alicujus Sociorum vacare contigerit, Volumus & ordinamus, quòd in Locum ejus concedat —— quicunque Presbyter, ad minus* Artium Magister, *vel* Legum (*ut dicitur*) Baccalaureus —— *Ulteriùs volumus & constituimus, quòd duo sint in perpetuum in prædicto Collegio Capellani, seu Vicarii, ad minus* Artium Baccalaurei, *& Clerici —— Volumus etiam & concedimus, quòd* Episcopus Cestriensis *& Successores sui habeant potestatem & licentiam visitandi dictum Collegium.*

In the Charter granted by Queen *Elizabeth, Anno* 1578, (from whence this is, for the most part, transcribed) the first incorporating Clause runs thus: (*viz.*) *Collegium illud de uno Guardiano, Presbytero, & sacræ Theologiæ ad minus Baccalaureo ; & quatuor Sociis, Presbyteris —— ad minus* Artium Baccalaureis —— *fundari & stabiliri decrevimus.*

Sam. Peplo, Master of Arts of Oxford, having obtained a Grant of the Wardenship of this College, in order to qualify himself for it according to the Charter, procures a *Faculty* from *the Archbishop of Canterbury* for *the Degree of Batchelor of Divinity ;* the Tenour of which Faculty is as follows ; *viz.*

GULIELMUS, &c. —— *Ad infra scripta Autoritate Parliamenti Angliæ legitimè fulcitus ——* Sam. Peplo, *Clerico, & in Artibus Magistro Salutem & Gratiam.*
Quum in Scholis ritè institutis laudabilis iste mos & consuetudo inoleverit, ut qui in aliquâ Scientiâ liberali cum laude & profectu desudaverint, insigni aliquo Dignitatis gradu decorarentur : Quum etiam Cantuarienses Archiepiscopi (*publicâ Legum autoritate muniti*) *prædictos Gradûs & Honoris titulos in homines benemerentes conferendi potestate gaudeant, & jamdudum gavisi sint, (prout ex Libro authentico de Taxandis Facultatibus, Parliamenti autoritate confirmato, pleniùs apparet) Nos igitur prædictâ autoritate freti, & exemplum Antecessorum nostrorum imitati, Te —— sacræ Theologiæ Baccalaurei gradu & titulo insigniri decrevimus, & quantum in nobis est, juraque regni patiuntur, Tenore præsentium, Te in sacrâ Theologiâ Baccalaureum actualem creamus, paritérque in numerum Baccalaureorum sacræ Theologiæ hujus regni aggregamus, Juramentis infrà scriptis priùs per Nos, vel Magistrum Facultatum, de Te exactis, & à Te juratis ——*
Ego Sam. Peplo, *&c.*
[Here follow the Oaths of Allegiance and Supremacy in *English.*]
Proviso autem, quod hæ Literæ tibi non proficiant, nisi registrentur, & subscribantur per Clericum —— in Cancellariâ.

At the Head of this Faculty, and sewed to it with Thread, is a distinct Piece of Parchment, in which are these Words ; *viz.*

Cùm Seren. Princeps, &c. —— Sam. Peplo *Artium Magistrum, Vicarium de* Preston, *propter inconcussam in se fidem, insignemque contra Rebelles præstitam ibidem operam, Guardianum Collegii apud* Manchester —— *constituere dignatus sit : Cúmque Provisum sit per ejusdem Collegii statuta*

tuta

(3)

tuta ut ——— Guardianus fit ad minus gradu Baccalaureatûs in facrâ Theologiâ vel Jurium infignitus ; *Nos, ut erga Regiam Majeftatem officium & pietatem, & in viros de Repub. & Ecclefiâ bene meritos favorem teftatum faceremus,*

GULIELMUS, &c. ——— *Salutem & Gratiam* ———

By *the Authority of Parliament* infifted upon in this Inftrument, is underftood an *Act made 25 H. 8. cap. 21.* But, there being no mention at all of *Degrees* in this Act ; nor any thing that, upon a careful Perufal of the Act, can lead any one to think of Degrees ; the Power now challenged by the *Archbifhop*, of conferring Degrees, muft be couched under the *General Powers* there conveyed to him, which are ranked under thefe two Heads, *viz.*   *25 H. 8. cap. 21.*   *s. 3.*

    1. "All manner of Licences, Difpenfations, Faculties, &c. as heretofore hath been *ufed and accuftomed to be had at the See of* Rome ——— " or of any Perfon by Authority of the fame ———
    2. " All *other* Licences, Difpenfations, &c. ——— For all fuch Caufes and " Matters as fhall be *convenient* and *neceffary* to be had, for the Honour " and Surety of the King, and the Wealth and Profit of the Realm.

Under which of thefe Heads *the Power of conferring Degrees* is to be placed, it is not eafy to conjecture from the Words of the Act ; but, fpecial Reference being had in the Body of the Faculty to a *Tax-Book*, faid to be confirmed by Parliament, that neceffarily confines it to the *Firft* Head of fuch Faculties, &c. as had been ufed and accuftomed to be had and obtained at the See of *Rome* : For it is Enacted, "That there fhall be " two Books made and drawn of one Tenour ; in which fhall be con-"tained the Taxes of all *cuftomable* Difpenfations, Faculties, Licences, "and other Writings wont to be fped at *Rome*." ——— And Bifhop *Gibfon* in his Notes upon this Act founds the Archbifhop's Right of conferring Degrees of all kinds wholly upon this: "That in the faid Book " of Taxation, among the other Heads in which Faculties had been cu-" ftomarily grantable, and were now made grantable by the Archbifhop, " in virtue of this Act, are found the Two that follow, *viz.*   *s. 11.*   Cod. Jur. Ecclef. p. 106.
    " *Creatio Doctorum in quâcunque facultate,* 4l.
    " *Creatio aliorum Graduatorum in quâcunque facultate,* 4l.   [It fbould be 3l.]

And that a *Faculty for a Degree* (if any fuch be made grantable by this Act) muft be reckoned among the *cuftomable* Faculties, is plain from another Part of the Act, where the Archbifhop is reftrained from granting any Faculty in any Cafe *not accuftomed*, without *Licence from the King, or Council.*   *s. 5.*

This being then the *fole* Ground and Foundation of *the Archbifhop's Power* ; in order to clear up the Matter in difpute, it will be proper to confider *the Nature and Defign of the Act* ; to examine *the Authority of the Tax-Book* referred to in the Faculty ; to enquire what *the Practice* has been with relation to *Degrees* fince the making of this Act ; and to fee of what *Value and Effect* Degrees conferred by the Archbifhop are.

With

(4)

With relation to *the Nature* and *Design* of this Act, these Observations occur to me.

1. The only Reasons alledged for making the Act are;

Preamb. "To deliver his Majesty's Subjects from *Intolerable Exactions* claimed "by the *See of Rome*, and from grievous and exceffive Charges in obtain- "ing such Licences, Dispensations, &c. as they *wanted*:

§. 3. "And to vest a Power in some Person residing *within this Realm*, to "grant all such Dispensations, Faculties, &c. as were *convenient* and *ne-* "*ceffary* to be had, for the Honour and Surety of the King, and the "Wealth and Profit of the Realm.

These Words, *convenient* and *neceffary*, are proper to be noted; be- cause, by the whole Tenour of the Act, it appears, that *all manner of Dispensations*, whether such as had been *customable*, or such as should be granted *hereafter*, were to come under these Characters.

§. 17. Now *the beftowing Degrees in Learning* could never be reckoned a- mong *the Impositions and Exactions of the Pope*; nor were *Degrees* such *Licences* and *Dispensations*, as His Majesty's Subjects *wanted* to obtain from *the See of Rome*; because no body ever had any *good, just*, or *rea- sonable Cause* to have recourse to *Rome* for them; there being always a standing Power *within this Realm*, from whence they might be obtained: Whereas no other Faculties, &c. granted by the Archbishop, in virtue of this Act, could then be procured *any other* way than by *the Authority of the See of Rome*. And it was not likely that any Persons would be at an *exceffive Charge* to obtain Degrees from *Rome*, which they might take at a cheaper rate here *at home*.

Neither can I persuade my self, that *the Pope's* Power of conferring De- grees ever was, or *the Archbishop's* can now be thought, *convenient and neceffary for the Honour and Surety of the King, and the Wealth and Profit of the Realm*, when such regard has been constantly paid to *Aca- demical* Degrees, by All our *Kings*, *Parliaments*, and *Convocations*. And when, as far as my Enquiries have reached, there is no Footstep to be found in any *Law Book* whatever, of the least Esteem, or Allowance, of any Degrees taken any other way than in some *University*.

And that I have here given a true Account of *the Meaning* and *Design* of the Act, is further manifest from the Title under which it is repealed by the 1ˢᵗ and 2ᵈ of *Phil.* and *Mary*, and revived 1 *Eliz.* 1. *viz. An Act concerning the Exoneration of the King's Subjects from Exactions and Impositions before that time paid to the See of* Rome, *and for having Licences and Dispensations within this Realm, without suing further for the same*; which I find to have been the ancient Title of the Act, as it was printed immediately after that Session of Parliament in which it was made.

§. 7. 2. It is Enacted, That if *the Archbishop* shall *refuse* to grant any Dif- pensations, Faculties, &c. —— which he is authorized to grant by Virtue and Authority of this Act —— he shall be liable to be *punished* for such Refusal —— From whence it is very obvious to infer, that he is not au- thorized by this Act to *confer Degrees*; because there is hardly any Case supposable, where a Person can have such a *Right* to a Degree by Faculty from the Archbishop, as that the Archbishop shall render himself obnoxi- ous to Punishment for refusing to grant it.

3. It

(5)

3. It is likewife provided by this Act, that no Difpenfation, Faculty, &c. ——— which was charged 4l. or above, at *Rome*, fhall be put in Execution, till the fame Difpenfation, Faculty, or other Writing, of what Name or Nature foever it be, fhall be *confirmed under the Great Seal*, and inrolled in Chancery. §. 6.

And it is farther Enacted, That all *Fees* for cuftomable Difpenfations, Faculties, &c. which were wont to be fped at *Rome*, fhall be paid according to fuch *Tax-Books* as are by the faid Act ordered to be made; and that all fuch Difpenfations, Faculties, &c. which are taxed at 4l. or more, in thefe Books, *fhall be confirmed under the Great Seal*. The neceffary confequence of which is, that thofe Faculties for Degrees granted by the Archbifhop, which are taxed at 4l. and are not confirmed under the Great Seal, can receive no Authority from *this Act*, or from *the Tax-Books* made by direction of this Act. §. 11, 12.

As to the *Tax-Books* mentioned in the Act; neither of the *Original* Books, (if any fuch were ever made) is now to be found; But *Bifhop Gibfon*, in his Notes before quoted, fays, that *One Copy at leaft of this Book is ftill remaining*. This is now kept in the *Faculty Office*, and was, about forty Years ago, tranfcribed by Mr. *Taylour*, then a Clerk in the Office, from an ancient Paper MS. in the cuftody of Sir *Charles Hedges*, and (as Mr. *Taylour* himfelf affured me) exactly tranfcribed, without the Omiffion, or Alteration, of any one Word, to the beft of his skill and remembrance. But that this *ancient MS.* (the Copy of which I have carefully perufed) was not an *Original Tax-Book*, made according to the direction of the Act of Parliament, or *a Copy of fuch Original*, will plainly appear from the following Confiderations. Cod. Jur. Ecclef. p. 106.

For in the firft place it feems very probable, that, if any *Tax-Books* had been made according to the direction of the Act, they would have been drawn *in Englifh*; becaufe they were defigned for the ufe of all fuch as *were Suiters for any Difpenfation or Faculty*, who were to *have recourfe to them* whenever *they required* it. But, if they had been drawn *in Latin*, the *Titles* of them would certainly have been *in Latin* too, and would have expreffed by what *Authority* or *Direction* the Books were made: Whereas the Book now remaining is *in Latin*, with this *Englifh Title* to it, viz. *A Book of Taxations concerning the Act of Difpenfations.* §. 11.

In the next place it is to be obferved, that this Book is not *figned*, or *fubfcribed*, by any Body; whereas the Act pofitively orders, that *every Leaf of thofe Books*, (which were Enacted to be drawn and made of one Tenour) *and both fides of every Leaf, fhould be fubfcribed by the Archbifhop* of Canterbury, *the Lord Chancellor* of England, *the Lord Treafurer, and the two Chief Juftices of both Benches for the time being*. And fuch Subfcription was abfolutely neceffary to render the faid Books *authentick*. Neither is there any *Date* to this Book; fo that we cannot tell, whether it were *later* than *the Act of Parliament*, or whether it were *earlier*, and adapted to it afterwards, (as from the following Remark it appears to have been) for, §. 11.

Another thing obfervable in this Book is; that, in the Margin, juft over againft feveral Sums at which certain Difpenfations are taxed, it is faid, *vel arbitretur fecundum provifionem Statuti*; over againft many others, *vel arbitretur ut fupra*; and fometimes *arbitretur fecundum provifionem Statuti*,

C

(6)

tuti, without any Tax; (but the Taxes for *Degrees* have no such Note annexed) Which marginal Entries must have been made by way of accommodation to the Statute, before any Tax-Books were drawn in pursuance of it; because, if such *Authentick* Books had been made, the Rates for all manner of Dispensations and Faculties would have been there fixed and determined, and not left to the discretion of the Officers concerned to regulate, as they saw fit.

But that which puts this matter beyond all doubt, is; that several Faculties and Dispensations, with the Taxes of them, are entred in this Book, which were *not grantable by the Archbishop*, or by any other Power whatsoever, *by virtue of this Act*. These therefore could not be inserted in those Books, which were to contain the Taxes of such Dispensations and Faculties *only* as were made grantable by the Act; and, if they had been put in by those who were appointed to *draw* these Books, they could not have been allowed by those great Persons, who, upon a strict Perusal and Examination, were to *subscribe* them.

This will be made out by the following Instances.

The Statute of the 21 *H. 8. cap. 13.* was made on purpose to regulate the Abuses introduced by the Court of *Rome*, with relation to *Pluralities* and *Non-residence*, and to prohibit all Dispensations from that Court, or

S. 21. elsewhere, contrary to this Act: And in the 25 *H. 8.* which translates the Power of Dispensing from the *Pope* to the *Archbishop*, there is a particular Proviso, that *nothing contained in that Act, nor any License or Dispensation thereafter to be made by Virtue and Authority thereof,* shall any way alter the Statute of the 21 *H. 8. cap. 13.* which was made *for Reformation of Pluralities and Non-residence*.

Gibson's Cod. And yet, notwithstanding *the former Statute*, which *sets Dispensations*
Jur. p. 109. *on a new foot*, and the *Proviso* made in the *latter*, to *confirm the Limitations in the said Statute contained*, we find, in the *Tax-Book* now remaining, all the same extravagant Dispensations for Pluralities and Non-residence as had been granted by *the See of Rome* before the making of the
Cod. Jur. Statute of the 21. to restrain them. For (as Bishop *Gibson* observes in
p. 946. his Notes upon this Act) " in the Catalogue of Faculties, which were
" grantable at *Rome* in the Times of Popery, were the Three following.
" *Dispensatio ad quæcunque & quotcunque Beneficia incompatibilia.*
" 1. *Ad valorem* 500 l. *per Annum.*
" 2. *Ad valorem* 1000 l. *per Annum.*
" 3. *Absque ullâ restrictione.* Which Dispensations were called *Tot Quot.*
P. 199. " And Dispensations were granted heretofore for such a number of Be-
" nefices without specification, and sometimes with an additional Power
" to exchange and take others, only keeping within the number." All which Dispensations for Pluralities are particularly specified in the aforesaid Book; and one of them runs in this Form: *Dispens. ad quæcunque & quotcunque Beneficia incompatibilia, cum clausulâ non residendi ——— absque quâcunque restrictione.* So that, if this *Tax-Book* be allowed to be authentick, neither *the Practice*, nor *the Law*, with regard to *Pluralities*
Ibid. and *Non-residence, was altered by the Statute of* 21 *H. 8. from what it was while the Right of Dispensation rested in the Pope* (as Bishop *Gibson* in his Notes before cited asserts it was.)

There are likewise several other matters mentioned, and taxed in that Book, which, tho' they had been, in some Form or other, executed, or
dispatched

(7)

difpatched by *the Court of Rome*, yet did not come within the Meaning and Intention of the Statute of 25 *H*. 8. fo as to be paffed by the Archbifhop in his Faculty Office eftablifhed by this Act. *E. G.*

Difpenfatio ad contrahendum Matrimonium, non obftante quocunque impedimento publicæ Honeftatis, Juftitiæ, &c.

Becaufe this was a Matter *repugnant to the Law of Almighty God*, in which cafe *the Archbifhop could in no manner of wife grant any Difpenfation:* S. 3.

Indulgentia decem annorum.

Indulgentia plenaria:

Becaufe thefe were Privileges allowed by all *Catholicks* to be fo appropriate to the Perfon of the *Pope*, that they could not be exercifed by *any other* Perfon whatever, without an *immediate* Authority from him.

Abfolutio ab Excommunicationis fententiâ,

Commutatio ultimæ voluntatis,

Declaratio Juris in cafibus dubiis:

Becaufe thefe were Matters tranfacted in the *Confiftory Court*, and could not be done merely by a *Faculty*, or any fuch Inftrument, without a *Judicial Procefs.*

Several other Obfervations might be made; but thefe are fufficient to demonftrate, that *the Tax-Book now remaining* in the Faculty Office cannot be *a Copy* of any fuch *Original* as was made, and *fubfcribed, according to the Direction of the Act*; but is rather (as it feems to me) a loofe Collection of various Matters, taken out of feveral different Books, relating both to the *ordinary*, and *extraordinary* Jurifdiction of the *Court of Rome*, put together with a defign to compofe out of it fuch a *Tax-Book* as the Act of Parliament directed to be made, and which, I believe, was never made.

How thefe two Titles, relating to *Degrees*, came to be inferted, I cannot tell; for, having fearched all the *Original Office-Books* belonging to the *Court of Rome* in the time of *Leo X.* about the Year 1514. (now preferved entire in the *Harley-Library*) in which are contained all forts of Matters difpatched by *the Datary, Penitentiary, Confiftory Court, Secretary's Office, Chancery*, and *Chamber Apoftolical*, no fuch Bulls or Faculties as thefe appear. Under the Head *De Creationibus*, where it was moft likely to find them, there are no other than what follow, *viz.*

Creatio in Notarium Apoftolicum.

Creatio in Comitem Palatinum.

Creatio in Accolytum Capellanum Papæ.

Creatio in Protonotarium.

Creatio in Canonicum alicujus Ecclefiæ.

There is indeed in thefe Books, but in what Office I could not well diftinguifh, (it feems to me to be a feparate Head of it felf) this Title, *De Licentiâ Doctorandi.*

This Licenfe is defcribed, in the firft Claufe, to be *a Power granted to fome Prelate, together with two or three Doctors of the Faculty, to inveft a Perfon with the Enfigns belonging to a Doctor's Degree.* Several Directions are afterwards given for the proper Exercife of this Power in different cafes, without any mention of *Taxes*, or of *lower Degrees*. This feems to have been the common Method in which the *Pope* himfelf conferred Degrees; and, when he empowered any others by *Bull* to make *Doctors*, it was by giving them Authority to grant fuch *Licenfes* as thefe;

(8)

these; which is very different from the Method of *Creation* now ufed by *the Archbifhop*.

The next thing to be confidered, is, what *the Practice* hath been with relation to *Degrees* conferred by *the Archbifhop*, fince this Statute 25 *H*. 8. was made.

It is faid indeed, in the Faculty granted to Mr. *Peplo* —— *Exemplum Anteceforum noftrorum imitati* —— But (as I have good reafon to believe) there are very few Inftances to be found of fuch Faculties, granted *before the Reftauration*: None, upon the beft fearch I could make, appeared to me, in either of *the Offices* where fuch Faculties ought to be regiftred; and all the Faculties, which did appear there were manifeftly built upon the miftaken Authority of *the Tax-Book* before mentioned, having no other Foundation to fupport them.

But I have been fince informed, that, in an old Book, remaining in the *Archbifhop's Faculty-Office*, (which I did not fee) entituled, *Facultates expeditæ & figillatæ Anno Dom.* 1543. (which Book contains the Entries of all Difpenfations and Faculties to the Year 1548.) is the following Entry, *viz.*

1544. *fexto die Decemb. prædict. Difpenfatio conceffa* Georgio Broke, *Filio naturali & legitimo Domini* Georgii Broke, *Domini de* Cobhin, *Venetiis jam ftudenti; quâ dictus* Georgius Broke *ad Gradum Baccalaureatûs in Artibus promotus exiftit; & quòd ipfe omnibus & fingulis Privilegiis, & Prebeminentiis, & Prerogativis quibufcunque, ubique locorum, uti, frui, quatenus Jura & Statuta hujus Regni non adverfantur, gaudere valeat & poffit, quibus alii ad Gradum hujufmodi in Univerfitatibus Studiorum Generalium promoti, uti, frui, & gaudere valeant & poffint, in formâ communi.*

Now, as to this *ancient Faculty for a Degree* (which we are fure, from the Account given of the Book in which it is found, is the only one that was granted during the fpace of 5 or 6 Years) there are feveral Remarks to be made, which feem to me of great ufe for determining the prefent Controverfy.

1. In the firft place then I obferve, that the Inftrument, by which *Broke* was promoted to the Degree of *Batchelour of Arts,* is called a *Difpenfation;* for the ufe of which Word no other Reafon can be given, but that it was thereby intended to cover the Practice of conferring Degrees under the fhelter of *an Act of Parliament,* which was known to extend only to *Difpenfations.* For *the Creation of a Graduate* hath nothing of the Nature of a *Difpenfation* in it; fo that, had the Archbifhop any power of *Difpenfing* in this cafe, it could not be by *giving a Degree;* but by granting a *Faculty* to fupply *the want of a Degree,* where fome *Canon,* or *Local Statute* required it; which fort of *Difpenfation* was never granted fince 25 *H.* 8. by any *other* Authority but that of *the Crown.*

2. The next thing to be taken notice of, is, *the Extent of thofe Privileges,* which are here granted to *Broke; viz. all manner of Privileges,* which any other Graduates of the fame Rank, in *any Univerfity* throughout the World, did, or might enjoy: For thus much do thefe Words, *ubique locorum,* and *in Univerfitatibus Studiorum Generalium,* import; there being no Reftriction of them expreffed, or implied, either

to

(9)

to *the King's Dominions*, or to *the Universities of this Realm*. Now these are such *extravagant* Privileges, as no *Archbishop of Canterbury* (whose Jurisdiction was confined to *England*) had any Colour or Pretence of Authority to grant: But all these *general* Expressions are manifestly taken out of Faculties granted by virtue of *the Pope's Authority*, which he claimed to exercise in all this part of the World. For in this very Style did the Instruments of *Counts Palatine* run; who were empowered by *Bulls from the Pope* to give Degrees; tho' 'tis very well known, at the same time, that even *such Faculties* as these (in whatever Terms they were conceived) were never regarded in any other *Popish* Country besides *Italy*: and particularly as to *England*, we are sure that none of the Full Powers granted to *Counts Palatine*, viz. to *confer Degrees, make publick Notaries, Legitimate*, and *bestow Arms*, were ever permitted to take place in this Kingdom; and abundance of Instances may be shewn, where every one of these Powers have been denied here, excepting that of *giving Degrees*; and it does not appear that That was ever attempted.

It is farther to be observed upon this Head, that *Broke* was actually resident at *Venice*, when he was made *Batchelour of Arts*; and therefore the chief Design of the Faculty must have been, to enable him to enjoy all the Privileges of that Degree in *foreign Countries*; which 'tis certain he could not do by any Authority of an *English Parliament*; and consequently it was absurd to found the Power of granting *such a Faculty* upon any *Law* or *Statute of this Realm*: and that softening Clause of *quatenus Jura & Statuta hujus Regni non adversantur*, did not only imply a Distrust of the *Legality* of what was granted; but was, with relation to the *ubique locorum*, and the other general Terms made use of, highly *improper*.

3. There is another Expression in the Entry now before us, which deserves to be considered, because some Stress may probably be laid upon it, and that is, *in formâ communi*. Upon which I beg leave to observe, that in the old *Tax-Book* (as it is called) after several Heads or Kinds of Faculties, these Words are added: E. G. *Creatio Notariorum in formâ communi*; *Literæ Dimissoriæ in formâ communi*: But after *Creatio Doctorum*; and *Creatio aliorum Graduatorum*; no such Words are found. From whence it plainly follows, that, where these Words occur, there were some *known Forms* of granting such *Faculties* or *Dispensations* before that Book was compiled; and, where they are not added, the Framers of that Book, whoever they were, could not tell in what manner such Faculties were to pass, nor consequently whether they were *grantable* by the Act or not; and therefore, very probably, these *Faculties for Degrees* were not within the Meaning of the Statute; because, if they had been *customable* before the Act, *the Form* in which they were granted would have been well known at the Time of making the aforesaid *Tax-Book*.

What then can be meant by this Expression, *in formâ communi*, at the close of the Entry in 1544? There had been, 'tis likely, some Instances of Degrees given before this, tho' not many, I presume, in the nine Years which had passed, from the making of the Act to the Date of the Book in which this Entry is found, since in the five following Years there was but one: And a *few Instances*, during so small a space of Time, cannot well justify the Expression of *Forma communis*, had the Instruments been all drawn in the same Form (as I can hardly persuade my self they were.) The *Form* therefore here meant (if these Words were not added

D   by

(10)

by the Clerk at random, as I fufpect they might, becaufe they were ufed in the Entries of other Difpenfations) muft be fome *common Form* of conferring Degrees at *Rome*, which had not yet obtained in *England*; and could be (as I judge) no other than the *Licentia Doctorandi* mentioned in the Books of *Leo* X. before taken notice of; that being the only Form of granting Degrees, which we meet with in the *Roman Office-Books*: but *the Power of creating Doctors*, and other *Graduates* (if any fuch Power was lodged in the *Archbifhop* by the Statute) is *perfonal*, and muft be exercifed (as all the other Powers there granted are) by fome *immediate* Act of his own; and he can have no Authority from the Statute to *delegate* this Power to another, as is done by a *Licentia Doctorandi*. If therefore it fhould be found, that this was the Form in which *Archbifhop Cranmer* conferred Degrees, it muft have been derived from fome other *Original* than the *Act of Parliament* now fet up.

4. The laft Obfervation I fhall make upon this Entry, is, That there is no mention of it in any *Act of Parliament*, or *Tax-Book*, or of *the Example of Predeceffors*, or indeed of any particular Authority, upon which the Faculty referred to was granted; and therefore nothing can be concluded from hence in favour of a Power now claimed upon thofe feveral Grounds.

But to fpeak freely upon this Subject; after the 28th of *Hen.* 8. when *the Pope's Authority* was entirely *abolifhed* (before which time I have reafon to think *no Faculty for a Degree* was granted here by any body) *the Papal Powers* were exercifed in a *very arbitrary* and *extravagant* manner, without any regard to *Acts of Parliament*; not only by *the King* himfelf, but by all others who were *commiffioned, fupported,* or *encouraged* by him.

About the time that the Act before mentioned had paffed, *Cromwell* was made *Vicegerent in Ecclefiaftical Affairs*, and, whilft he continued in this Office, he did (as it is well known) exercife *as great*, and in fome cafes *greater*, Power than the *Popes* ever did in *England*. For (as we find in *Strype's Life of Cranmer*) *the Archbifhop* himfelf took a *Licence* from him to vifit his *own Diocefs*. *Difpenfations* and *Faculties* were then granted by *his* Authority, he having (as the fame Learned Writer tells us) *a Mafter of the Faculties* as well as the *Archbifhop*, tho' by 25 *Hen.* 8. the Power of granting Difpenfations, and appointing Officers for that purpofe, is lodged *folely in the Archbifhop*; and therefore *Cromwell* might, in all probability, begin the Cuftom of *conferring Degrees*.

And, as *Cromwell*, by virtue of his *extraordinary Commiffion*, might imitate *the Pope* in this particular; fo the *Archbifhop* afterwards might take upon him to do the fame upon the ftrength of his *Legantine Power*. For 'tis well known that, after *the Pope's Authority* was *reftrained*, and even after it was *extinguifhed* by Parliament, the Archbifhop continued to ufe the Style of *Apoftolicæ Sedis Legatus*, and was fuppofed to do many things *by the Pretext or Colour of that Name of Legate*, tho' (as it was argued in the Difpute againft his *Court of Audience*) no longer *Bifhop of* Rome *Lord here*, *no longer his Vicar* [or Legate.] And fo 'tis probable his *Power of conferring Degrees* might be what he claimed as *Legate*; tho' he was willing to have *that*, as well as his *Court of Audience*, fcreen'd by the Act of 25 *H.* 8. But, as it was then alledged, that *this Act of Parliament could not be drawn with twenty Team of Oxen to ftretch to the continuance of the Court of Audience*; fo may it now with as much reafon

P. 55.

Ibid.

App. to Life of Cranm. p. 22, 30.
Ibid. 29.

Life of Cranm. p. 39.
App. p. 29.

(11)

reafon be afferted, that it cannot be *ftretched to the continuance* of that *Power of giving Degrees* in the *Archbifhop*, which *Legates* only pretended to; and confequently *Archbifhop Cranmer* might be miftaken in pleading this Statute upon either occafion. For the Notion which at that time feems to have prevailed was, that *whatever the Pope could do in any Countrey fubject to his Jurifdiction*, (which was not contrary to the Law of God) *that might be done*, after the Abolition of his Power here, by *fome other Authority in England*: but none of our Lawyers have ever interpreted that Act in fo extenfive a *Senfe*, as far as appears from any Comments upon the Act now extant; tho', if they had, it would not ferve the prefent purpofe, becaufe there always was *another Authority in England*, by which *Degrees* were granted. Whether therefore *Archbifhop Cranmer* ufed the Style of *Legate*, when he gave *Degrees* or not, it may be as well affirmed in *this* cafe, as it was in *the other*, concerning his *Court of Audience*; that no *Archbifhop can exercife this Authority, except he implieth to all the World* (*though he fpeak it not nor write it not*) *that he is a Legate of the See of Rome*; or at leaft, that he derives this Power from his Predeceffors, *as Legates*, and not *as Archbifhops*.

Thus ftood matters in the Reign of *Hen.* 8. but in *Edw.* 6[th's] time, when not only *the Pope*, but *Popery* alfo, was laid afide, there are no Traces to be difcovered of fuch a *Power*, as is now claimed, *of conferring Degrees by Faculty*. Nay, fo far were our *firft Reformers* from favouring any thing that look'd like it, that *beftowing Degrees regularly in the Univerfities* was hardly fuffered by the *Vifitors* of thofe Places, as being a Practice of *Popifh Original*, tho' inftituted to very wife Purpofes.

When Queen *Mary* came to the Crown, this Act of 25 Hen. 8. was repealed; and after the Revivour of it by Queen *Elizabeth*, in the firft Year of her Reign, (from whence the Plea of *Practice* in relation to the *Archbifhops* giving *Degrees* ought to bear date) till *Laud* came to be *Archbifhop*, it does not appear that this Power was ever exercifed or pretended to. But He (as there's fome ground to believe from the Accounts given by *A. Wood*) did confer one or two Degrees in *his own Family*; and, upon his Authority alone (as I take it) *Juxon*, after the *Reftauration*, granted a few Faculties, for Degrees, of *different Kinds*; after which, from *Sheldon's* Succeffion to the See of *Canterbury* till this time, *Degrees by Faculty* have been multiplied *without diftinction*.

This is a full and impartial Account of *the Exercife of this Power of conferring Degrees by Faculty* ever fince 25 *Hen.* 8. From whence it feems very evident, that no fuch *Cuftom* of conferring Degrees can be pleaded, as will eftablifh *the Right* now claimed by *the Archbifhop*; becaufe *Cuftom* muft be *certain, uniform, conftant*, and *uninterrupted*; whereas *the Practice* in this cafe has been *various*, both as to *Form* and *Authority*, with a long Intermiffion of at leaft 80 Years, after a very confiderable Change made in the *firft Ground* and *Foundation* of the Pretence.

The Reafon given why fo *few ancient Faculties* for Degrees are to be found is; that *the Office-Books are loft*. Which of them are loft, and how they came to be loft, I cannot tell. But this is certain, that fome of thefe Books have furvived the Calamities both of *War* and *Fire*; and I wifh they had all been preferved with more care, for then I am confident, it would have appeared more plainly that *the Practice of giving Degrees* was extinguifhed together with *Popery*.

But

(12)

But fuppofing there was *a Power of conferring Degrees* of all Kinds granted to the Archbifhop by *25 Hen. 8.* and fuppofing this Power had been *continually exercifed* by Archbifhops of *Canterbury* ever fince; notwithftanding this, it may be fafely affirmed, that Degrees fo conferred could never be reputed or taken to be any more than *bare Titles of Honour*, which were attended with no *Legal* or *Canonical Effect* whatfoever.

The Truth of all which, and efpecially of this L A S T Point (which I fhall chiefly infift upon) will, as I am firmly perfuaded, be very evident from the following Extracts.

STATUTES *and* CONSTITUTIONS *made before* 25 H. 8. *and other Hiftorical Paſsages relating to* Degrees.

Inter Petitiones Parliamenti de Anno 9. Hen. 5. in Turri Londin. remanent.

—— "Plefeth to your Excellents Wifdomes to ordeyne —— that no "Man practife in Fyfick fro this time forwarde, but he have long time y "——ufed the Scoles of Fyfick within fome Univerfitee, and be *gra-* "*duated* in the fame; that is to fay, but he be *Batcheler*, or *Doctour of Fy-* "*fick*, having Letters Teftimoyalz fufficiente of on of thefe Degrees of "*the Univerfitee* in which he took his Degree ——

The Act in Anfwer to this Petition ordains, "That the Lords of the "King's Council fhall have Power to punifh, as they fee fit, fuch as "fhall Practife the Arts of Phyfick or Surgery, *& ne font ny habilez ne* "*approurez en ycelles comme appent as mefmes les Arts, ceft affavoir ceux de* "*Fifick en les Univerfitees, & les Surgeons entre les Meftres de celle Art.*

"The King by the Affent, &c. —— hath ordained and eftablifhed, "that all People born in *Ireland* fhall be voided out of the Realm within "a Month after Proclamation made, except *Graduates in the Schools*, and "Men having Benefice, &c. —— And that *the Graduates*, and Beneficed "Men fhall find Surety —— that the Scholars of *Ireland*, which be *not* "*Graduates*, and be of the Kings Obeyfance, fhall find Surety —— in "the fame manner as the faid *Graduates* fhould do.

In the Recital of another Act, which enforces this Law, it is faid, "Whereas it is ordained that *the Graduates* and Beneficed Men fhould "find Surety——

In an Act made for *regulating Apparel*—— "It is provided that *the* "*Scholars of the Univerfities of this Realm*, and Scholars of *any Univer-* "*fity out of this Realm*, may wear fuch Array as they may wear by the "Rule of the faid Univerfities, notwithftanding this Ordinance

It is ordained—— "That no Man under the Degree of a Gentle- "man, except *Graduates of the Univerfities*, &c. —— fhall ufe or wear any "Furres —— And that no Man under the Degree of a Knight, except "Spiritual Men and Serjeants at the Law, or *Graduates at Univerfities*, "fhall ufe any more Cloth in a long Gown than four broad Yards.

"No Man fhall practife Phyfick in *London*, or within feven Miles of it, "——unlefs he be firft approved by the Bifhop of *London* or Dean of "*Pauls*——nor in any other part of *England*, unlefs examined, and ap- "proved by the Bifhop of the Diocefs.

"Provided

(13)

"Provided always that this Act, nor any thing therein contained, be
"prejudicial to the *Universities of Oxford and Cambridge*, or either of
"them, or to any Privileges granted to them.

Another Act of Apparel, with the same Proviso's for *Graduates of the* 6 H. 8. c. 1.
Universities as in the former, *viz.* 1 *H.* 8. *cap.* 14.

The same Proviso's are repeated in a like Act made the next Year. 7 H. 8. c. 7.

In a Statute made the 14th of this Reign, it is Enacted———"That no 14 H. 8. c. 5.
"Person be suffered to exercise and Practise Physick throughout *England*
"———without being examined and approved by the College of Physici-
"ans———except he be *a Graduate of* Oxford *or* Cambridge, *which hath*
"*accomplished all things for his Form without any Grace.*

In an Act, which takes away all *Dispensations for Plurality of Be-* 21 H. 8. c. 13.
nefices, it is provided, "That all *Doctors and Batchelors of Divinity*, §. 23.
"*Doctors of Law, and Batchelors of Law Canon*, and every of them,
"which shall be admitted to any of the said Degrees by *any of the Uni-*
"*versities* of this Realm, and not *by Grace only*, may purchase Licence,
"and take, have, and keep two Parsonages or Benefices with Cure of
"Souls.

By another Act concerning *Apparel* it is declared, "That it shall be 24 H. 8. c. 13.
"lawful to all Archdeacons, Deans, and———*Doctors or Batchelors in*
"*Divinity, Doctors* of the one *Law* or of the other, and also *Doctors*
"*of other Sciences*, which have *taken their Degrees* or be admitted in *any*
"*University*, to wear Sarcenet———

"None of the Clergy under the Degrees aforesaid may wear any man-
"ner of Furres———And none of the Clergy under the Degrees afore-
"said, other than *Masters of Arts*, and *Batchelors* of the one *Law* or the
"other, *admitted into any University*, shall wear in their Tippets any
"manner of Sarcenet.

Now from all the Laws made concerning *Apparel*, in Popish Times,
'tis plain, that no *Doctor*, or other *Graduate, made by the Pope*, or any
other Person by Authority of the See of *Rome*, was allowed to wear
the same Habit that *Graduates of any University* whatever might wear;
and, if this small Privilege was not granted them, it is not likely that
they were permitted to enjoy any greater. And so in fact we find
them excluded from all other Privileges granted by Act of Parliament to
University Graduates: For they could not, by virtue of their Degrees,
practise Physick in *England*, nor *enjoy Pluralities*; nor, if *Irishmen*, were
they allowed to stay in *England* in *H.* 6th's time. From whence it evidently follows, either that there were no such *Graduates by Papal Au-*
thority here, when these Laws were made; or that no manner of Regard
was then shewn to them by *the State.*

Let us see in the next place of what account *the Pope's Degrees* were
held *in the Church.*

Ordinatio———Hen. Chichley, *Archiepisc. Cantuar. de promotione Gra-* Lyndwood.
duatorum in Academiis Oxoniæ & Cantabrigiæ, facta in Convocatione Cle- Constit. Prov.
ri———*incepta Novemb.* 6. *Anno* 1417. Ed. Oxon.
1679. p. 71.

Hen. Chichleius, *Archiepisc. Cantuar.*———*& Apostolicæ Sedis* Legatus Ann 1417.
———*Nos attendentes, Apostoli attestante Doctrinâ, laborantem Agricolam*
de fructibus oportere percipere, Ordinamus———*quod* Doctores *sacræ Theo-*
logiæ, Decretorum, Legum, & in Medicinis, promoveantur ad Beneficia curata
ad valorem———60 *Marcarum per Annum*———Licentiati *in Facultatibus*
E *prædictis,*

(14)

prædictis, at Baccalaurei *in Theologiâ ad Beneficia* 50 *Marcarum* ——— Magiſtri & Baccalaurei *prædict. ad Beneficia* 40 *Marcarum, &c. Proviſo ſemper quòd Perſonæ prædictæ Gradus ſupradictos per Gratiam non attigerint. Volumus etiam & ordinamus, quod omnes & ſinguli Patroni ſpirituales infra Cantuar. Provinc.* ——— *primum Beneficium hujuſmodi vacaturum alicui de perſonis prædictis conferre teneantur* ——— *Et quòd* Graduati *prædicti, antequam ad Beneficia promoveantur, Litteras Teſtimon. ſub Sigillo* Univerſitatis, *in quâ Gradus ſuos adepti fuerint, Patronis & Ordinariis* ——— *de* Gradibus & Lecturis *ſuis, exhibeant realiter & oſtendant.*

——— *Proviſo quòd ſi per Sedem Apoſtolicam, contra quam nullatenùs attentare intendimus, alias pro promotione* Graduatórum *prædictorum infra tempus ſtatut. (ſc. Decennium) Proviſiones Generales dudum conſuetas fieri contingat, quòd extunc omnino ceſſet Ordinatio antedicta,* Vid. Antiq. Brit. pag. 278.

Pag. 72. Ann. 1421. *Alia Ordinatio per prædictum Archiepiſcopum, pro promotione* Graduatorum *in Academiis prædictis fact. Julii* 16. *An.* 1421.

This Order contains only a Command from the Archbiſhop to all his Suffragans, that they ſhould take care to ſee the former Conſtitution ſtrictly executed in their ſeveral Dioceſes, and was obtained upon a freſh Application of the two Univerſities, as I find by Mr. *Wood*'s *Hiſt.* & *Antiq. Univ. Oxon. viz.*

Wood's Hiſt. p. 210. Anno 1421. *Hoc Anno Cancellarii utriuſque Academiæ, in Synodo jam Londini coactâ, pro utriuſque Academiæ Studioſis exorárunt, ut Decretum antè quatuor annos in Synodo latum, de conferendis Beneficiis, in eos ſolos qui* Gradibus Academicis *erant ornati, pro Beneficiorum cenſu & Graduum Dignitate, jam promulgaretur* ———

Ibid. ex Reg. Chich. *Eodem quaſi tempore ſanctionem de utriuſque Academiæ Graduatis ad Beneficia evehendis evulgare propterea maturavit Archiepiſcopus, quòd eam rem rogâſſent Ordines Parliamentarii.*

Pag. 217. An. 1438. ——— *Univ. Oxon. Alumnorum ſuorum pauciſſimos ex antedictis Synodorum conſtitutionibus ad Beneficia evectos ægre ferens* ——— ad Hen. Chichely *Arch. Cant. reliquoſque Prælatos Londini coactos* ——— *ſcripſit. Litteras haſce tradidit Cancellarius, qui miſerrimum Academiæ Statum tantâ arte enarravit, ut (ſuorum quoque diſpendia eodem tempore aperientibus Cantabrigienſ. Delegatis) Epiſcopos ad ita ſanciendum adegerit, (viz.)* "Quod quicunque Patro- "nus Eccleſ. Provinciæ Cantuar. quodcunque Beneficium Eccleſ. etiamſi "Dignitas vel Præbenda fuit ——— alicui Perſonæ alterutrius Univerſi- "tat. prædict. *Gradum Scholaſticum* habenti, Doctori (viz.) Theologiæ, "Legum, vel Medicinæ, Magiſtro Artium, Licentiatove, aut Baccalau- "reo in aliquâ Facultate prædict. offerre teneatur ———

——— *Eâdem tempeſtate deſignati ſunt* ——— *qui de conſimili Lege in Provinciâ ſuâ ferendâ cum Archiepiſcopo Eboracenſi agerent.*

Pag. 218. *Neque hâc tantùm ex parte voto potiuntur Academici, verùm Decreto Archiepiſcopali obtinent; ut Vicarii Generales, Officiales, & Commiſſarii (quorum jam muneribus fruebantur Legulei quidam imperiti) ex utriuſque Univerſitat. in Jure Civili & Canon. Graduatis deligerentur.*

This is repreſented as a Decree of the Synod made *Anno* 1430. in B. *Parker*'s *Antiq.*

Antiq. Brit. 284. *In hâc Synodo multæ contra Epiſcopos ab inferioribus Prælatis querelæ delatæ ſunt, quòd Vicarios Generales, Officiales, & Commiſſarios, ignaros & imperitos Legum in Diœceſibus ſuis ſtatuiſſent. Conſtitutum itaque eſt* "ne quis Juriſdictionem Eccleſiaſticam exerceret, niſi Juris "Civilis

(15)

" Civilis aut Canonici Gradum *à Cantab. vel Oxon. Academ.* accepif-
" fet.

From hence 'tis plain, that, in Archbifhop *Chichley's Time,* no Perfon
promoted to a Degree by *the Pope,* or any *Authority of the See of Rome,*
was capable of any *Ecclefiaftical Benefice,* or of exercifing any *Ecclefiaftical Jurifdiction in England:* And it does not appear that thefe *Canons* were ever refcinded, or any other of a contrary tendency ever made
before 25 *H.* 8. And if thefe *Canons* or *Conftitutions* were in force at
the Time of making the Act; (as there is juft Reafon to believe they
were) then *Degrees given by the Archbifhop afterwards* could not be
efteemed *Legal Qualifications* for any *Ecclefiaftical Benefice,* or *Office with
Jurifdiction;* becaufe *the Pope's Degrees* were not fo efteemed *before.* But,
whether *the Authority* of thefe *Canons* lafted fo long or not, there was certainly no *Change in the Opinion* either of *Convocation,* or *Parliament,* with
relation to *Univerfity-Degrees,* in all that Time.

And what was done in *England* in favour of *Degrees taken in the Univerfity,* will appear to be very agreeable to what paft *Abroad* about the
fame time, from the following Inftances.

Among the Regulations made by the Council of *Conftance,* with re- L'Enfant
gard to the Officers of the Apoftolick Chancery and Chamber, *An.* Hift. Conc.
1416. we find this.   Conft. l. 7.
                                                                      p. 669.

*Il s'etoit introduit un grand abus à l'egard des Docteurs. Il y en avoit
Beaucoup qui au lieu de prendre des Degrez dans les Univerfitez, apres y
avoir bien Etudié, alloient en Cour de Rome folliciter des Bulles de Do-
cteur, qu'on accordoit pour de l'argent. Par là on peut aifement Juger, que la
Science étoit fort avilie, & que la Religion étoit fort profanée par le pa-
reils Docteurs. Pour remedier à fe defordre, le College Reformatoire ordon-
ne, qu'à l'avenir le Siege Apoftolique ne donnera plus le pouvoir de faire
des Docteurs, ou Maitres aux Arts, dans quelque Faculté que ce foit, ni aux
Legats, ni aux Nonces Apoftoliques, ni aux Generaux d'Ordres; & que ce
pouvoir fera refervé aux Chanceliers de Univerfitez. A l'egard de la
Cour de Rome, qui eft cenfeé avoir les Privileges d'Univerfité, perfonne n'y
fera Gradué qui n'y ait fon cours dans la Science où il voudra être Do-
cteur, ou qu'il n'ait étudié dans quelque Univerfité; De quoi il apportera
de bons Temoignages du Chancellier & des Docteurs de l'Univerfité, auffi bien
que de fes meurs. Alors il fera receû, non par une Bulle, on par une Commiffion particuliere, mais par les Docteurs & Profeffeurs de la Cour de
Rome, aprés un rigoreux examen. De forte que les Degrez accordez par
Commiffion particuliere du Siege Apoftolique feront deformais regardez comme
nuls.*

In the *Concordata Germanicæ Nationis & Martini V. Papæ,* eftablifhed Vonder-
by the faid Council, there is this Conftitution, *viz.*   hardt. p.1055.

" *Quòd in Metrop. & Cathed. Ecclef. German. Nationis fexta pars Ca-*
" *nonicatuum & Præbendarum fit pro* Doctoribus, *aut* Licentiatis *in Sacrâ*
" *Paginâ, vel altero Jurium, vel in Theolog.* Baccal. *formatis, aut* Magi-
" *ftris in Medicinâ, qui per biennium, feu Magiftris in Artibus, qui per quin-*
" *quennium poft Magifterium, in Theologiâ, aut altero Jurium, ftuduerunt in*
Studio Generali.

About the fame time a Decree paft, *De Collationibus Beneficiorum pro* P. 1067, 1077.
Natione Anglicanâ, in which I find the following Paffages ——— " *Pa-*
" *pa pro tempore exiftens in fuis provifionibus ad prælaturas & alia Be-*
                                                                " *neficia*

" *neficia Ecclef. mentem habeat & gerat ſpecialem ad* Doctores *in Theolog.*
" *Jure Canon. & Civili.*

    " *Archiepiſcopi*, *Epiſcopi*, *&c.* —— *Beneficiorum Collatores* ; Doctores
" *in Theol. Jure Canon. & Civili, necnon* Baccalaureos *in Theol. ad quæcun-*
" *que Beneficia — conferant* —— And then, after ſeveral Rules given
with relation to the different ſorts of Benefices which were to be beſtowed upon *Graduates*, it follows ——

    " *Et ad Finem* , *ut præmiſſa effectualiter valeant* , Cancellarii, *vel* Re-
" ctores Univerſitatum *pro tempore exiſtentes de nominibus* Doctorum,
" *Licenciat. ac* Magiſtrorum, *& Baccalaur. Ordinariis locorum certificent de*
" *tempore in tempus.*

P. 926. 972.   There are likewiſe in the *Regulæ Cancellariæ* of *Joh.* XXIII. and *Martin* V. ſeveral Favours and Privileges granted to Perſons who *proceeded
regularly in Divinity, Law, Medicine,* or *Arts,* with an Exception to all
other but *Familiares D. Papæ Commenſales, Sedis Apoſtol. Officiales, &c.* without any mention of ſuch as were created *Doctors, Maſters,* or *Batchelors*
by *the Pope,* or any Commiſſion from him.

P. 1021.   And in *Martini* V. *Reformatio Curiæ Romanæ* —— theſe two Orders
were made, *viz.* " *Ad Epiſcopales Dignitates nullus eligatur niſi* Doctor, *aut*
Licentiatus, *cum rigore examinis.*

    " *Dignitates majores in Eccleſiis Cathedralibus* , *& Principales in Colle-*
" *giatis, nullis niſi* Doctoribus, *vel* Baccalaureis formatis *in Theologia, vel*
" *Doctoribus, aut Licentiatis in Jure Canonico vel Civili conferri valeant.*

Concil. Baſil.   In the Council of *Baſil, An.* 1438. the like Orders and Proviſions were
Seſſ. 31.   made for the benefit of ſuch as were *Graduates in ſome Univerſity,* the
particular Degrees and Standing of the Perſons being there ſpecified ;
and every Preſentation of a *Non-Graduate,* where a *Graduate* might have
been found, was declared null and void.

Concil. Lat. 5.   Decrees of the ſame kind were made alſo in the fifth *Lateran Council,*
Seſſ. 11.   *An.* 1516. But theſe relating only to the *French Nation,* I ſhall tranſcribe
them out of the Concordate confirmed by this Council.

    Concordat. inter Leo X. *Pap. & Franciſcum Galliæ Regem.*

    " *Præbenda & Canonicat. in quâlibet Eccleſiâ Metrop. & Cathedrali*
" *conferri debet* Theologo, Magiſtro, Licentiato, *aut* Baccalaur. forma-
" *to, qui per decennium in* Univerſitate Studii Generalis *privilegiata ſtu-*
" *duerit.*

    " *Ultra dictas Præbend. Theologales tertia pars omnium Dignitatum, Per-*
" *ſonatuum, cæterorumque Beneficiorum Ecclef. Viris Literatis,* Graduatis, *&*
" *per Univerſ. nominatis conferri debent, qui Literas ſuorum Graduum cum*
" *tempore ſtudii debitè inſinuaverint.*

    And at this Day (as I am well informed) a Degree conferred by *the
Pope* is no *Qualification* for any Benefice or Dignity whatever in *the Church
of France.*

    From theſe authentick Accounts of what paſſed in *the Romiſh Church*
before 25 *H.* 8. it plainly appears, that giving Degrees in any *other* way
or form, but in ſome *Univerſity,* was all along look'd upon as an *Abuſe* :
And that great care was taken, not only with relation to the *Church in
general,* by *Decrees of Councils* ; but with regard to divers *National
Churches,* and *the Engliſh* in particular, by diſtinct *Concordates* between
the Popes and thoſe Nations, that *no other* Degrees ſhould be admitted
as *Qualifications* for any Eccleſiaſtical Benefice, but what were regularly
taken in ſome *Univerſity.* From whence I infer, that, at the time of
               making

(17)

making the aforesaid Act, it was *not customable* for the Subjects of *England* to sue to *Rome* for Degrees; and that, if any Persons had procured *Bulls* or *Faculties for Degrees* from the *See of Rome*, they would not have been allowed as *Qualifications* for any Dignity or Benefice, contrary to what was provided by *Councils*, and *Concordates* in that behalf; and consequently, that *the Archbishop's Degrees now* (did the Act impower him to confer Degrees) cannot be esteemed *Legal Qualifications* for any Ecclesiastical Preferment. For the Act says, "That all Faculties, Dif- " pensations, &c. granted by *the Archbishop*, shall be accepted ——— and " admitted ——— *good and effectual in Law*, and *as beneficial* to the Persons " obtaining the same, *as* they should have been if they had been obtained " of the *See of Rome*, or of any other Person by Authority thereof: And therefore, since *the Pope's Degrees* were never accounted *good and effe-ctual in Law*, and *beneficial* to Persons in *England*, *before the* 25 *H.* 8. Degrees conferred by the *Archbishop*, upon the pretended *Authority of that Act*, can give no *Legal Advantages* to the Persons upon whom they are conferred; because they can have *no more* Value, Effect, or Benefit, than they would have had, if they had been obtained of *the See of Rome before the Act* was made.

But to return to what past in *England* with relation to Degrees before the Statute of 25 *H.* 8.

Clauf. 5. E. 2. m. 8. dorfo.

Rex dilecto sibi in Christo Cancellario Universitatis Oxoniæ, & Majoribus Regentibus in eâdem facultate, salutem. Religiosum & discretum Virum, No-bisque in Christo carissimum, Rogerum de Baketon, *Ordinis Prædicatorum, qui, sicut accepimus, in Universitate vestrâ prædictâ, in sacræ Theologiæ fa-cultate est in proximo incepturus, cupientes prosequi gratiosè, ipsum vobis pleno recommendamus affectu; rogantes attentè, quatenus eidem Fratri Rogero, dudum per vos licentiato, super hiis, quæ circa ipsius inceptionem requiruntur juxta libertates & consuetudines, quibus Fratres Prædicatores hactenus ibidem studentes usi sunt temporibus retroactis, non obstantibus aliquibus Ordinationi-bus contrariis per Nos factis, favorem & gratiam nostris precibus impendatis: Ita quòd pro gratiâ sibi per vos in hâc parte faciendâ, Nos invenire possitis ad Universitatis vestræ commoda de cætero promotiores. T. R. apud Eborum* 28 *Martii.*

Wood's Hift. & Antiq. Oxon. p. 194.

About the Year 1384. there arose a great Difference between the *Phy-sicians* and *Lawyers* concerning *Precedence*; and the Cause being given by the Convocation of the University in favour of *the Physicians*, the *Lawyers* intended to appeal to *Rome* ——— " *Quo intellecto, Rex causarum* " *in fraudem Universitat. aliò delatarum Decisionem irritam pronunciavit*, " *edixitque Juristis ne Regno excederent, aut aliquam pecuniæ summam in eam* " *rem transmitterent* ———

Pag. 196.

An. 1390. *Cùm Fratres nigri* ——— (*præcipuè verò quotquot pares gradui progressus haud fecerint) Examen Academicum fugientes ad exteros commea-bant, ibique Magistri titulum sibi comparabant, non sine Fratrum Doctorum infamiâ atque gravi Universitatis dispendio; super his* ——— *Nostrates & Cantabrigienses Regem fecerunt certiorem* ——— *Qui ad Priorem Provincia-lem omnesque in Angliâ Priores Conventuales, in hæc verba scripsit* ——— " *Vobis omnibus & singulis* ——— *injungimus & mandamus, inhibentes ne ali-* " *quem Fratrem* ——— *mare transeuntem, ac Gradum sibi Magisterii, ac* " *alias Gratias subdolè ac fraudulenter impetrantem* ——— *& postea in regnum* " *regressum* ——— *ad Libertates, Honores, seu Favores Doctoribus in Theo-*

F " logiâ

(18)

" logiâ per examinationem Univerfitat. debitè factis *confuetos*, *aliquâ-*
" *liter admittatis, nec ipfum in Honoribus, Favoribus, feu Libertatibus hujuf-*
" *modi pertractetis, feu pertractari, aut eifdem uti & gaudere quomodolibet*
" *permittatis* ——— *nullâ habitâ confideratione ad Impetrationes, Provifiones,*
" *feu Exemptiones hujufmodi* ———

Notwithftanding the many fevere *Statutes of Provifors*, by which all
manner of Perfons, however dignified or recommended by *the Pope*, were
excluded the Benefit of Papal Provifions for Preferment in *England*, *the
Graduates of our own Univerfities* were particularly favoured in this refpect
by the Crown : as appears by the following Licenfe, *viz. Licentia im-*
petrandi Gratias Expectativas feu Proviforias â Summo Pontifice. Graduatis
utriufque Univerfitatis conceffa, de quibufcunque Beneficiis & Officiis curatis
& non curatis.

The foregoing Paffages plainly fhew, that, as the *Univerfities* were
founded and regulated by *the King*, fo they were conftantly under the
Protection of *the Crown* ; and that *the Royal Authority* often interpofed
in fuch Matters as concerned their Intereft, even *againft the Pope* : But
efpecially with regard to *Degrees* ; the Power of conferring which, whether as *Honours*, or *Rewards of Merit*, or as *Proofs* to the Church and
Commonwealth *of Men's Sufficiency*, they received *folely* from the gra-
cious and wife Appointment of *the Crown*. And no Inftance can be given
of a *Popifh King of England*, who ever allowed *the Pope's Degrees* to be
Qualifications for any Preferment in his Gift.

Great Complaints being made by Dr. *Gafcoign* (from whom Mr. *Wood*
tranfcribes his Account) of Corruptions and Abufes in giving Degrees
by *the Regents* of the Univerfity ——— the Author adds ——— *At verò fa-*
tendum eft magnorum hâc in re virorum, immò ipfius Pontificis, veftigia fuiffe
ingreffos ——— Here one would naturally expect to find fome Complaint
of *the Pope's* giving Degrees to unworthy Perfons ——— but inftead of
that the Complaint made of *the Pope* in this place, is, of his beftowing
Bifhopricks and other Preferments in as fcandalous a manner as *the Re-*
gents then gave *Degrees*.

Cardinal *Wolfey*, in order to fill his great College at *Oxford* with Scholars, befides what he took out of other Colleges and Halls in both Univerfities, brought in fuch as practifed the Civil and Canon Law in his
Courts, who had been formerly of this Univerfity ——— *Quod ipfis pro*
formâ ceffit, hoc eft, exercitiorum ad gradus capeffendos requifitorum loco
habebatur. He did not make ufe of any Authority he had from *the See
of Rome*, tho' as great as ever *Legate* had, to give Degrees, but accepted
them as Favours from the *Univerfity*.

Hoc Anno, viz.1368. *in Congregat. Regentium conceffa eft Gratia D.* Simoni
Iflip, Archiep. Cant. *in Cardinal. jam elect. cujus fumma erat quòd vocaretur
ad incipiendum*; that is, to commence *Doctor* in *Divinity*.

It was granted to *James Stanly Bifhop of Ely*, that he might be created *Doctor of Decrees*, by a Cap put on his Head by *William Archbifhop
of Canterbury*, and *Richard Bifhop of London*, which was accordingly by
them performed at or near to *London*. And a Letter was fent by the
Bifhop to the Univerfity, to thank them for the Honour they had done
him.

Thefe two *Archbifhops* feem to have had no Value or Regard for *the
Pope's Degrees*, but a very great Efteem for *Degrees conferred by the Univerfity*.

It

Marginal notes:

Rot. Parl.
Turri Lond.
Anno 1403.
5 H. 4.

Wood's An-
tiq. p. 220.
Anno 1455.

Pag. 249. An-
no 1524.

Pag. 389.

Wood's Faft.
Part 1. p 646.
Anno 1507.

Wood's An-
tiq. Part 1.
Pag. 557.

(19)

It is affirmed by *Harpsfield*, a Popish Writer in Q. *Elizabeth's* time, Harpsfield, that *Archbishop Courtney*, who lived between these two Archbishops, had Ecclef. Hift. among other extraordinary Privileges, *the Power of making Doctors* P. 539. granted him by *Pope Urban* VI. But he cites no Authority for this ; neither does *Archbishop Parker* mention any such thing in his Life of *Court-* Parker's Antiq. p. 267. *ney*, taken out of the *Registers* at *Lambeth*, and other authentick Re-An. 1383. cords; tho' he takes notice of another extravagant Grant of the same Pope to one *Diffe*, a *Carmelite* Fryar, *viz.* to *make Chaplains to his Holiness* ; and therefore very probably this was a Mistake in *Harpsfield*. But, supposing it true, this *Urban* was but an *Antipope*, who had a Competitor claiming and exercising at the same time all the Authority belonging to the *See of Rome*. Then the Grant was only *personal* to *Courtney*, and not to his *Successors* in the See of *Canterbury* ; and to make *Doctors* only (which were the chief *Titles* of *Honour* and *Distinction*) not any *other* sort of *Graduates*. Nor is there any Instance to be found of any *Degree* given, either by *Courtney*, or any *other Archbishop of Canterbury*, before the 25 *H.* 8. and, by what was just now mentioned of *Warham*, the immediate Predecessor of *Cranmer*, (in whose Time that Act was made) 'tis very plain, that he did not pretend *to give Degrees himself*, when he condescended in such a Ministerial manner to convey an *University Degree* to one of his Brethren.

STATUTES *and* CANONS *made since* 25 H. 8. *with other Historical Passages relating to* Degrees.

In an Act Entituled, *An Act extinguishing the Authority of the Bishop* 28 H. 8. c. 10. *of* Rome, it is ordained, for stronger Defence and Maintenance of that s. 5. Act, that an Oath of Supremacy there set down should be taken by every Ecclesiastical Officer or Minister— every Temporal Judge —&c. And—by s. 6. every Person taking Orders ——— " And by every Person which shall be " promoted or preferred to any *Degree of Learning in any University with-* "*in this Realm*, or other the King's Dominions, at the Time of his Pro-" motion or Preferment.

In another Act Entituled, *An Act for the Release* (or Relief) *of such* 28 H. 8. c. 16. *as have obtained pretended Licences and Dispensations from the See of* Rome, after a Confirmation of lawful Marriages, it is Enacted, " That all who s. 2, 3, 4. " were at that time taken and reputed for Archbishops and Bishops "———for Abbots and Priors———and other Heads of Religion——all " Persons taken and reputed as Masters, Presidents, Provosts and War-" dens of Cathedral Churches and Colleges, all Priests and Clerks which " have received any of the Ecclesiastical Orders, all Archdeacons, and " Deans, and others having Offices, Cures and Dignities spiritual, may, " by Authority of this Act, and not by virtue of any foreign Power or " Authority, use and exercise all things pertaining to their Dignities, " Offices, Orders, Cures, &c. And may use all Tokens, Ensigns, and Ce-" remonies, which they have been accustomed to use in time past (so it be not expresly against the Laws of God and this Realm.)

It is likewise Enacted, That all the King's Subjects who have purchased " and obtained any Bulls, Breves, Faculties, &c. ——— from the See of
Rome,

(20)

"*Rome*, as *Pluralities*, *Unions*, *Commendams*, &c. —— may, by Au-
"thority of this Act, and not by virtue of the said Bulls, &c. enjoy all
"the Effects contained and specified in such Bulls, &c. in all such Cases
"only as may be *dispensed* with by *the Archbishop of Canterbury*, by Au-
"thority of the Laws and Statutes of this Realm; which Bulls and Fa-
"culties shall be delivered up to such Persons as the King shall appoint;
"and if, upon due Examination, it shall appear, that the Effects specified
"in them may be lawfully granted by *the Archbishop of Canterbury*, then
"the King's said Subjects, upon their humble Suit, shall obtain —— by
"sufficient Writing in due Form to be made, and to be sealed under the
"King's Great Seal, all such Effects specified in such Bulls, as may be
"granted by *the Archbishop of Canterbury*, by the Authority of the Laws
"and Statutes of this Realm.

Now this Act being plainly of greater Latitude than 25 *H.* 8. as ex-
tending not only to all such Causes and Matters as the Power there
granted to the Archbishop extends to, but to several others, it is reasonable to suppose, that some mention would here have been made of *Degrees*, had any of the King's Subjects at that time been *Doctors*, or otherwise *graduated by the Pope's Authority*; especially among *the Dignities*, *Offices*, and *Preeminences* to which the 2d and 3d Section relate, and where
all other Ranks and Orders of Men, who owed their Titles to *the Pope*,
are (as I believe) plainly named or described; in which number one
would naturally expect to find such as had been then *taken* and *reputed*
for *Doctors*, or *other Graduates*, by virtue of some *Bulls* or *Faculties* received from *the See of Rome*.

But, since there is nothing in all this Act, that can be construed to point
particularly at *Degrees*, it would be proper to enquire, whether at the time
when all manner of *Bulls* and *Faculties* were to be delivered up to the
King's Commissioners, according to the direction of this Act, in order to
their being confirmed by new Writings under the Great Seal, any *Faculties for Degrees* were brought in; and whether the Persons, who brought
them in, were allowed under the Broad Seal to enjoy the same Titles
and Honours, as had been before conferred upon them by their Faculties
from *the Pope*: Could any one Instance of this kind be produced, it would
be of weight in the present Dispute; and if there were any such at that
time, some or other might probably now be found, at least some Account
of such an Instrument; since all Persons, who had any Instruments then
granted under the Broad Seal, by virtue of this Act, would be sure to
take care to see them registred, and to preserve the Originals very
safe.

It may be likewise further observed upon this Act, that, no Persons being allowed to enjoy the Effects contained in any *Bulls*, *Breves*, or *Faculties* granted by the See of *Rome*, in any *other* Cases but such *only* as might
be *dispensed with* by *the Archbishop of Canterbury*, by Authority of the
Laws and *Statutes* of this Realm; and there being no other Law or Statute of the Realm then in force, which gave *the Archbishop* a Power *to
dispense* in any case whatever, but the 25 *H.* 8. From hence it plainly
seems to follow, that the whole Power granted by 25 *H.* 8. to the Archbishop, is properly *a dispensing Power*, and related entirely to such Matters (how various soever in their kinds) where some Stop, Relaxation,
or Change of the usual Course of the Law, is, in certain Cases, judged requisite to be made; and consequently *conferring Degrees* can never come
within

(21)

within the general Purport and Intention of this Act: But, if it gives *the Archbishop* any Power at all in relation to Degrees, it must be (as hath before been observed) *to dispense with* the want of them in such Persons, where the Law requires that they should be *Graduates*; which Power, I believe, was never yet exercised, or claimed, by any *Archbishop of Canterbury*. And, if the *Archbishop's Right* to confer Degrees is not derived from *that Act*, I know no *other* Law or Statute of the Realm that gives it him.

This Observation is entirely confirmed by *the Commission* or *Letters Patents* granted in pursuance of the Act, and lodged in the Office of the Rolls, whereby " the said King appointeth——*Tho. Budell*, Archdeacon " of *Cornwall*, *Jo. Tregumwell* and *Will. Peter*, all three Masters of the " Chancery, to receive all *Bulls, Breves*, and *Faculties*, which shall be " rendered up by any of the King's Subjects—— and to try and examine " whether the Effects of the said *Bulls, Breves*, and *Faculties* be con- " tained under the compass of such Cases as *the Archbishop of Canterbury* " *may dispense withal* by the Laws of this Realm"——And this according to *the Meaning of an Act of Parliament* held at *Westminster* 8° *Junii*. Rolls Part 1. H. 8. An. 28. Nov. 25.

For further corroboration of the Act made 28. and another made 33. of the King, in *cap*. 10. of this last Act, a new and stronger Oath is requir- ed to be taken in place of the former, by every Person that shall have any Office—— every Ecclesiastical Person taking Orders—— and every Person which shall be promoted or preferred to any *Degree of Learning* in any *University within this Realm*, &c. as in the said former Act. [35 H. 8. c. 1. §. 7. §. 8.]

In an Act of the 37ᵗʰ of this Reign, it is Enacted, " That all and singu- " lar Persons —— being *Doctors of Civil Law*, *lawfully* created and made " in *any University*——may lawfully exercise all manner of Ecclesiastical " Jurisdiction——albeit such Person or Persons be Lay, married or un- " married, so that they be *Doctors* of the Civil Law, as is aforesaid. [37 H. 8. c. 17. §. 4.]

Whether this Act does restrain the Exercise of Ecclesiastical Jurisdiction to *Doctors* or not, 'tis certain that no other Doctors were then thought of or intended, but such as were *lawfully created in some University*.

In the Repeal of this Act 1, 2 *Phil. & Mar.* and in the Revivour of it 1 *Eliz.* it is said, only *Doctors of Civil Law*; from whence it may be fairly collected, that whatever Degrees are mentioned in any Act of Parliament, without an express mention of the Universities at the same time, it ought to be understood of such Degrees as were taken in *some University*.

At the End of the *Service-Book* established by *Edw.* 6. it is said, " In all " Cathedral Churches and Colleges the Archdeacons, Deans, Provosts, " Masters, Prebendaries and Fellows may use in the Quire, besides their " Surplices, such Hoods as pertaineth to their several *Degrees*, which " they have taken in *any University within this Realm*. [2 Edw. 6. c. 1.]

In an Act made the 1ˢᵗ of Q. *Mary*, which repeals *All Statutes and Provisions made against the See of Rome*——It is provided and Enacted, That this Act shall not extend to *take away or diminish the Privileges of the Universities of* Oxford *and* Cambridge. So that even at this time, when the Pope's Power was *re-established* in its full Vigour and Extent, care was taken that it should not be exercised in any such manner as would in the least hurt *the Universities*, or diminish any of their Privileges. And therefore it may fairly be presumed, that, when this extravagant Power of the *See of Rome* was *again abolished*, the *Universities* were in no respect to be Sufferers by it. [1 Phil. & Mar. cap. 8. §. 49.]

(22)

1 Eliz. c. 2.
§. 25.
   An. 1 Eliz. it is Enacted, "That such Ornaments of the Church, and " of the Ministers thereof, shall be retained and be in use, as was in this "Church of *England* by Authority of Parliament in 2 *Ed.* 6.

1 Eliz. c. 1.
§. 19.
   In the same Year an Oath of Supremacy is appointed to be taken by all Bishops, every Ecclesiastical and Temporal Officer and Minister, &c. "and " by every Person taking Orders —— and every other Person, which shall " be promoted or preferred to any *Degree of Learning in any University* " *within the Queen's Realm* or Dominions, before he shall receive or take " any such Orders, or be preferred to any such Degree of Learning.

5 Eliz. c. 1.
§. 5.
   The same Oath is afterwards appointed to be taken by all manner of Persons expressed in the former Act, and particularly "by all that have "been or shall be promoted, preferred, or admitted to *any Degree of Learn-* "*ing in any University within this Realm,* or Dominions to the same belong- "ing —— As also all manner of Persons that have taken, or shall take any "Degree of Learning in or at *the Common Laws of this Realm* —— And " every of them shall take and pronounce the Oath aforesaid in some " *open Place* before a *convenient Assembly* to *witness* the same.

13 Eliz. c. 12.
§. 6.
   By 13 *Eliz.* it is provided, that "None hereafter shall be admitted to " any Benefit with Cure, of or above the Value of 30 *l. per Annum* in the "Queen's Books, unless he shall then be a *Batchelour of Divinity,* or —— *Vid. infra* Bonham's *Case.*

7 Jac. 1. c. 6.
§. 21.
   By 7 *Jac.* 1. an Oath is injoined to be taken by all and every Person that is or shall be promoted to *any Degree in School, before the Vicechancellor of the University in the Congregation-house,* and no Provision is made for any Persons who are admitted to Degrees (except in the Common Laws) to take the Oath *elsewhere.*

   In all the Acts concerning *Oaths,* and especially this last, there is a most particular and exact Recital of all Ranks and Degrees of Persons, who are obliged to take them; but under none of the Heads of Distinction there mentioned can those who *take Degrees by Faculty from the Archbishop* be comprehended. And no Account can be given why they should be *exempted.*

   By what *Authority* therefore the *Oaths of Allegiance and Supremacy* are now administred by *the Archbishop,* or the *Master of the Faculties,* to those upon whom His Grace is pleased to bestow Degrees; and how these Oaths come to be administred in *a private Place,* where there is *no Assembly to witness the same,* I am at a loss to know; and, if there be a want of Power in the Archbishop *to give the Oaths,* which *all Graduates* are appointed to take, this alone seems to imply a want of Power in him to *give Degrees.*

13, 14 Car. 2.
   The same Order is made in the Rubrick before the Common-Prayer, as in 1 *Eliz.* and 2 *Ed.* 6.

17 Car. 2. c. 3.
§. 6.
   Entituled, *An Act for uniting Churches in Cities and Towns Corporate.* It is provided that every Minister of Churches and Chapels united according to this Act shall be full and lawful Incumbent thereof, so as such Minister be *a Graduate in one of the Universities* of this Kingdom.

22, 23 Car. 2.
c. 9. §. 71.
   Entituled, *An Act for laying Impositions on Proceedings in Law.* "For every Dispensation to hold two Ecclesiastical Dignities, 15s.

§. 72.
   "For every other Dispensation, which shall be passed by the Lord " *Archbishop of Canterbury,* or the Master of the Faculties, 10s.

   No Tax is here laid upon *Degrees taken in the University,* from whence, as well as from the *Title* it self of the Act, it seems very evident that it was not the Intention of this Act to tax *any Degrees* at all.

                                            Then

(23)

Then the Words *every other Diſpenſation, &c.* plainly ſhew, that all manner of Inſtruments or Writings, which are paſſed by the Maſter of the Faculties, are, in the Eye of the Law, no other than *Diſpenſations*; becauſe every *Faculty* or *Licenſe*, which paſſed under the Seal of the Archbiſhop's Faculty-Office, was taxed by this Act.

In that which is commonly called *the Stamp Act*, it is ſaid, *5 & 6 W. & M. c. 21. ſ. 3.*

" For every Piece of Parchment —— or Paper, upon which any Re-
" giſter, Entry, Teſtimonial or Certificate of a *Degree taken in either of*
" *the Univerſities*, or *Four Inns of Court*, ſhall be ingroſſed or written, 40s.

" On which any Diſpenſation to hold two Eccleſiaſtical Dignities ——
" or any other Diſpenſation or Faculty from the Archbiſhop, or the Ma-
" ſter of the Faculties, is ingroſſed or written, 40s.

Now it is plain from hence, that it was the Intention of this Act to lay a Tax upon *all Degrees* whatever; and yet that *Degrees given by the Archbiſhop* were not thought of; both becauſe *Diſpenſation* and *Faculty* are here uſed as Words of the ſame import; and becauſe no *Teſtimonial* or *Certificate* of a *Degree taken by Faculty* is taxed, as all Certificates of *other Degrees* are.

In the Journals both of *Edw. 6.* and Q. *Eliz.* we find (ſays Bp. *Gibſon*) *Gibſon's Cod.* a Bill depending in Parliament, that Adminiſtration of Laws may be *Jur. p. 1031.* made by *Graduates in the Univerſity.*

The Archbiſhop *cannot, by virtue of that Act of* 25 H. 8. *which concerns 25 H. 8. c. 21.* *Diſpenſations, do all things that* the Pope *did de facto ; but the Statute is Hobart's Rep. to be underſtood of thoſe things as the Pope was, by the erroneous Opinion of* Colt. v. Glo. *ver.* *that Time, ſuppoſed to do lawfully in mere Spirituals —— The Archbiſhop is reſtrained to thoſe things only that the Pope did* quaſi Jure, *that is, in* Spiritualibus *only* ——

And in Heads and Caſes, which were accounted ſpiritual ; *the Archbiſhop is reſtrained by the Statute —— that nothing be done againſt* the King's Prerogative, *the Laws and Statutes of the Realm in general —— And that no Diſpenſations be granted but to ſuch Perſons as* ought of a good, juſt, and reaſonable *Cauſe, to have the ſame.*

Now 'tis certain, that tho' the Pope did de facto *give Degrees*, yet he never was *ſuppoſed to do it lawfully*, in order to *qualify* Perſons for Eccleſiaſtical Preferment in *England* ; becauſe it was contrary to Decrees both of *General Councils*, and an *Engliſh Synod*, then in force, to grant Degrees for any ſuch purpoſe. Neither can giving Degrees be reckoned among the *mere Spirituals*, which were the *only* things in which *the Pope* did *lawfully* or *quaſi Jure* exerciſe his Power in this Country : neither were there any Perſons here who *ought of a good, juſt and reaſonable Cauſe* to have Degrees from *Rome*, becauſe it was *better, more reaſonable*, and *more agreeable to the Laws* of the Land, to have them from one of the *Univerſities within this Realm.* And therefore *the Archbiſhop cannot, by virtue of this Act, confer Degrees* ; nor can *the Statute be ſo underſtood*, were ſuch a Power as this conſiſtent with *the King's Prerogative* ; but this I think it is not, becauſe the Power of *erecting Univerſities*, and *enabling them to give Degrees in Learning*, was an undoubted *Prerogative of the Crown* long before this Statute was made. *13 Eliz. c. 11.*

Dodderidge the King's Serjeant, in his Pleadings for Dr. *Bonham* againſt *Brownlow & Goldſbo-* the College of Phyſicians, ſays —— " the Statutes of this Realm have *rough.* " always had great reſpect to *the Graduates of the Univerſity* ; and it is *Dr. Bonham's* " not *Caſe, A. 1609.*

(24)

"not without caufe; for *fudavit & alfit*, and hath no other Reward,
"but this Degree, which is Doctor. And for that the Statute 2 1 *H. 8.*
"prefers *Graduates*, and provides that *Doctors of Divinity* or *Batchelors*
"fhall be capable of two Benefices with Cure ——— and *fo* 1 3 *Eliz.* pro-
"vides, that none fhall be prefented to a Benefice above 3 o*l. per Ann.*
"if he be not a *Doctor* or *Batchelor of Divinity.*

From whence it is very plain, that Serjeant *Dodderidge* by *Batchelor
in Divinity* in 1 3 *Eliz.* underftood fuch as had taken their Degree in *one
of our Univerfities*, tho' it be not fo expreffed in the Act; becaufe he
underftands it in *the fame Senfe* in *this* Act *as* in 2 1 *H. 8.* where *the Univerfities* are named.

Juftice *Walmfley*, in his Argument upon the fame Cafe, fays, that
"1 4 *H. 8. c.* 4. excepts only thofe which are *Graduates of* Oxford or
"Cambridge (from being examined by the College of Phyficians) *which
"have accomplifhed all things for their Form without any Grace*; and if this
"Exception fhall be intended to extend to *others*, then *all the Univer-
"fities* fhall be excepted by it, and this Exception is too general. From
which Reafoning 'tis very evident, that this Learned Judge knew of no
other Degrees but what were taken in *fome Univerfity* or other.

As *before* 2 5 *H. 8.* it was ordered by *Popifh Councils*, that Ecclefiaftical
Dignities and Benefices fhould be given to fuch as had taken *Degrees
in fome Univerfity*, without the leaft regard fhewn in any fuch Conftitutions to *Degrees* conferred by *the Pope*; fo in *the Council of Trent*, the
laft General Council, and which is of higheft Authority in *the Romifh
Church*, the fame good Orders and Provifions were made with relation
to *Degrees* in the Difpofition of Ecclefiaftical Preferments, *viz.*

Conc. Trid.
Sef. 22. de.
Reform. c. 2.
An. 1562.

"Quicunque pofthac ad Cathedrales Ecclefias erit affumendus ———
"fcientiâ hujufmodi polleat ut muneris fibi injungendi neceffitati pof-
"fit fatisfacere; ideoque antea in *Univerfitate Studiorum Magifter* five
"*Doctor*, aut *Licentiatus* in facrâ Theologiâ, vel Jure Canonico meritò
"fit promotus;" with divers other Conftitutions of the like kind. *Vid.
Seff.* 24. *de Reform. c.* 1 2. *& Seff.* 2 5. *c.* 5.

An. 1568.

And a few Years after, Pope *Pius* V. in purfuance of thefe Decrees
——— *Decretis* Concilii Tridentini *inhærentes* ——— (as he expreffes it)
publifhed *a Bull*, wherein he *annulls* and *makes void* all *former Bulls*, granted by himfelf, or any of his Predeceffors, to any Perfon or Perfons, of
what Dignity or Order foever, which empower'd them to make *Doctors,
Licentiates* or *Mafters*; and declares thofe who were promoted to any
Degrees by virtue of fuch Bulls, *Quoad Beneficia Ecclefiaftica nullâ Gradûs
prærogativâ frui & gaudere poffe.*

Thefe Paffages are not brought to *explain* the Statute 2 5 *H. 8.* but,
being conformable to the Regulations made by Councils held *before*
that time, are evident Proofs, that in all Attempts made for Reformation, *giving Degrees of Learning*, by *Bull*, *Faculty*, or *Commiffion*, or any
other way than by the regular Methods ufed *in Univerfities*, was conftantly looked upon by *Papifts*, and often owned by *Popes* themfelves,
to be *an Abufe*, fit to *be reformed*; and that no fuch *irregular Degrees*
ought to be efteemed proper *Qualifications* for any Dignity or Benefice
in the Church. And therefore, when this Abufe has been long ago con-
demned and taken away in *the Church of Rome*, and, when Degrees given
by *Papal Bulls* or *Faculties* do *not qualify* Perfons for Preferment in any
Popifh Country, where Degrees are required in the Perfons preferred, it
is

(25)

is to be hoped, that no Degrees, built purely upon *Papal Authority*, will now be allowed to pass for *Legal Qualifications*, in this *Reformed Country*, which were not suffered to take place here even *before the Reformation*.

ADVERTISEMENTS *or* ARTICLES *agreed upon, and subscribed, by* Matthew, *Archbishop of* Canterbury, *and others, and injoined by the Queen's Letters,* An. 1564.

" The Bishop, against the Day of giving Orders appointed —— shall Sparrow's
" give notice, that none shall sue for Orders but within their own Collection, 1684. p. 116.
" Diocess, where they were born, or had their long time of dwelling, ex-
" cept such as shall be *of Degree in the Universities.*
" All Deans, Archdeacons, &c. —— Doctors, Batchelors of Divinity Pag. 127.
" and *Law,* having Ecclesiastical Living, shall wear a Side Gown with
" Sleeves in their own common Apparel abroad——and Tippets of
" Sarcenet, as is lawful for them by the Act of Parliament 24 *H.* 8.
" *All Doctors* of Physick, or of any other Faculty, having any Living
" Ecclesiastical —— shall wear *the like* Apparel. *Vid.* 24 *H.* 8. *c.* 13. before cited. By which it appears, that the *Graduates* here meant are
such as have *taken their Degrees in some University*; because, by that Act,
no *other Graduates* were allowed to wear such Apparel, as is there mentioned.

Liber quorundam CANONUM —— in quos plenè consensum est in Synodo à *Matth. Archiepisc. Cant.* & reliquis omnibus ejus Prov. Episcopis, A. 1571.

" *Decanus, Archidiaconus, &c.* —— *In ecclesiis quisque suis utentur* Pag. 227.
" *Scholastica Epomide, quæ suo cujusque* Scholastico *Gradui & Loco con-*
" *veniat.*
" *Archidiaconus non substituet sibi Officialem quenquam, nisi qui in* Acade- Pag. 229.
" *mia fuerit educatus, & Juri Civili operam dederit.*
" *Archidiaconus & Officiales* —— *in Visitationibus vocabunt Clerum ad* Ibid.
" *rationem* —— *Et, quicunque ex illo Ordine ad* Magisterium Artium *in*
" *Academiis non attigerint, illis proponet partem aliquam Novi Testamenti me-*
" *moriter ediscendam* ——
" *Quivis Cancellarius, Commissar. & Official. erit institutus in Legibus* Pag. 230.
" *Ecclesiasticis, qui in Scholis Doctrinæ nomine* Gradum *aliquem susce-*
" *perit.*
" *Cancell. &c* —— *curabunt* —— *ut Rect. Vicar, &c. sibi Libros Ordini* Pag. 231.
" *& Professioni suæ congruentes comparent, ut quicunque ad* Magisterium
" Artium *non accesserint* (Vid. supra p. 229.) *emat sibi Libros duos Novi*
" *Testamenti* —— *ut illorum quisque memoriter ediscat pensam,* &c. Vid. In-
" junct. 1547. p. 7. & 1559. p. 72.

H   ARTICULI

(26)

ARTICULA pro Clero per *Archiepiscopum*, Episcopos & Clerum —— in Synodo ftabiliti, Anno 1584.

Pag. 193.

" *Ne quis Episcopus posthac aliquem in Sacros Ordines cooptet, qui*
" *non ex suâ ipsius Diœcesi fuerit, nisi vel ex alterâ nostrarum Acade-*
" *miarum prodierit —— vel nisi Litteras Dimissorias —— attulerit*
" *ac etiam in alterâ dictarum* Academiarum Gradum *aliquem* Scholaſticum
" *fusceperit ——*

CAPITULA five CONSTITUTIONES Ecclef. per *Archiepiſc.* Epifcopos & Clerum —— in Synodo tractatæ Anno 1597. ac poftea per Regiam Majeftatem confirmatæ, & ûtriqué Provinciæ promulgatæ.

Pag. 243.

" *Ut Homines idonei ad Sacros Ordines & Beneficia admittantur,*"
the *fame Order* is made as before, *Ann. 1584.* p. 193. and in the very
fame Words ——

Now from thefe two *Constitutions* made *Ann. 1584.* and *1597.* and
from the two other *Canons* agreed upon *An. 1571.* as alfo from *the Injunctions* of K. *Edw. An. 1547.* and of Q. *Eliz. An. 1559.* it muft be concluded
that, if there were in thofe Times any *Batchelors*, or *Doctors of Divinity*, *Law*, or *Physick*, created *by Faculty*, they were ranked, both by
the Crown, and *the Synod*, in a lower Form than *Mafters of Arts*, and
even than fuch as had taken *any Degree inferior* to that in *the University*.

P. 229, 231.
Pag. 7, 72.

CONSTITUTIONES five CANONES Ecclef. per Epifcopum London. Præfidem Synodi Cantuar. tractati & conclufi, Anno, 1603.

Pag. 276.
Can. 17.

" *In omnibus ûtriufque* Academiæ *Collegiis —— Socii —— Scholares ——*
" *in Ecclefiis, & Capellis, per Dies Dominicos & Feftivos —— tempore Divi-*
" *norum fuperpelliceis utentur. Quotquot verò Gradum aliquem fufceperint*
" *Caputia fuo cujufque gradui competentia fuperpelliceis fuis fuperinducent.*"
By *Degrees* here muft neceffarily be meant Degrees taken in either of
the *Univerfities*.

Pag. 279.
Can. 25.

" *Ecclefiarum Collegiat. Decani, Magiftri, & Præfect. itemque Canonici &*
" *Præbendar. (dummodo* Graduati) *cum fuperpelliceis caputia Gradibus fuis*
" *refpectivè congrua inter Rem Divinam gerere tenebuntur.*

From the foregoing Canon, and from the Statute of *Ed. 6.* before
quoted, 'tis plain that the Degrees meant in this Canon muft be *Academical Degrees. Vid. infra Can. 58.*

Pag. 285.
Can. 33.

" *Ne quis deinceps in Sacros Ordines admittatur, nifi —— vel nifi fidem*
" *fecerit fe effe actu Socium —— vel defignatum Capellanum in aliquo Collegio*
" Cantab. *vel* Oxon. *vel etiam ad Magiftri Gradum ante Quinquennium*
" *provectum, fuis ibidem fumptibus degere, vel nifi ——*

Ibid.

" *Ne quis Epifcopus in Sacros Ordines quénquam de cætero cooptabit, qui*
" *non —— &c. ac etiam in alterâ dict.* Academ. Gradum *aliquem* Scholafti-
" cum *fufceperit*, Vid. p. 193.

" *Nemini*

(27)

" *Nemini in posterum Facultas seu Dispensatio concedetur de pluribus* —— Pag. 289.
" *Beneficiis curatis simul retinendis, nisi tali duntaxat qui pro Eruditione sua* Can. 41.
" *dignior, & ad Officium suum plenius præstandum habilis & idoneus censebi-*
" *tur; nimirum qui ad* Gradum Magisterii *ad minus in* alterâ *nostrarum*
" Academiarum *promotus fuerit.*

" *Quotquot ex Ministris* Gradum *aliquem in* Academiâ *susceperint, ii in-* Pag. 296.
" *ter sacra peragenda superpelliceis suis adjicient & Caputia singulorum Gra-* Can. 58.
" *dibus convenientia, quorum tamen usu Ministris* minimè Graduatis *sub*
" *pœnâ Suspensionis interdicimus* ——

" *Nullus in posterum ad Officium Cancellarii, Commiss. vel Official. admit-* Pag. 327.
" *tetur, nisi qui* —— *in Jure Civili & Canonico eruditus existat, sitque ad* Can. 127.
" *minimum* Magister Artium *aut in* Jure Baccal." —— *Vid. Decret.*
" *An.* 1430. *& Can.* 1571. *Vid. etiam* 37 *H.* 8. *cap.* 17. and Journals of
Parliament in *Edw.* 6. and Q. *Eliz.*'s time before cited. All which do
plainly shew, that, in the opinion both of *Parliaments,* and *Convocations,* the *Degrees* necessary to qualify Persons for the *Exercise of Ecclesiastical Jurisdiction* can be no other than such as are taken in *Schools*
or *Universities.*

From this Collection of Canons it manifestly appears, that the several
Archbishops, by whom they were approved, and by whose direction chiefly they were framed, have frequently, in divers Instances, shewn a great
respect to *Academical Degrees,* without the least regard had to Degrees
conferred *any other* way. Of which no other Account can be given, but
either, that they did not then pretend to any *Power of conferring Degrees*
themselves; or, if they did, that they did not look upon such Degrees
as proper *Qualifications,* in any of those Instances, where they judged
Degrees in Learning requisite.

That one of these Suppositions is true, seems very evident to me
from what I find in a Book written by *Archbishop Parker's Chaplain,* or
rather by the *Archbishop himself,* (who was the *first Archbishop* after the
Revivour of the Act of 25 *H.* 8. and a strenuous Asserter of the Rights
and Privileges of his See) styled, *De Antiq. Brit. Ecclef. & nominatim de
Privilegiis Ecclef. Cantuar.* &c. For in this Book, where his express Design is to reckon up and enumerate *all the Privileges and Prerogatives* then
belonging to the Seé of *Canterbury,* he not only makes no mention of
this Power of conferring Degrees; but he gives such an Account of the
Purport and Design of that Act, upon which it is now founded, as can
by no manner of Construction take in or include this Power. His Words
are these, *viz.*

Henricus 8. *Rex, Anno Domini* 1534. *exclusâ & exactâ suo regno tot* Antiq. Brit.
annis usu captâ autoritate Papali —— *multisque Papalibus ceremoniis dele-* P. 30.
*tis, Cantuar. Sedis Prærogativam, lege tàm suâ quàm populi consensu latâ,
stabilivit, totumque illud Legum rigorem mitigandi Jus, quod* Dispensare
*dicitur, quod usucapione sibi Romanus Pontifex vindicavit & usurpavit,
in* Archiepisc. Cantuar. *simili lege latâ transtulit. In quâ lege cautum est
ne præter divina, Regisque atque Regni avita Jura, Cantuar. Archiep. quic-
quam decerneret.*

Hanc igitur tam latè patentem Jurisdictionem (sc. antea descriptam) *ut
absolveret, Fora varia & Tribunalia ordinavit, quæ doctû peritisque Judicibus,
Advocatis, Procuratoribus, Scribis, Notariis & Actuariis ad Causas agendas
& Judicia reddenda paravit & instruxit.*

And

(28)

And here, having given an Account of all the other Courts belonging to the Archbishop, he writes thus:

Pag. 32. *Tandem, ejectâ prorsus Autoritate Papali, cùm Henricus Octavus, ut diximus, Juris. Ecclef. moderationem & æquitatem lege latâ in Cantuar. Archiepifc. pofuiffet, conftituta nova Curia est; cui & Judex Præfectus, qui defideria cognovit eorum, qui Juris quandoque rigidi atque stricti relaxationem petunt, & Registrarius, qui conceffas Difpenfationes in fcripta refert: Ille Magister feu Custos Facultatum, hic earum Registrarius appellatur.*

Pag. 33. *His Privilegiis, Prærogativis, Eminentiis, Immunitatibus, Tribunalibus atque Curiis Cant. Archiepifc. Dignitas tanquam fuis numeris perfecta & abfoluta conftat; quarum rerum fides ne dubia & incerta fit, fciendum est, ea partim ex Archivis Turris Londinensis, partim ex domesticis Archivis in publicâ Cantuar. Sedis custodia repofitis, defumpta fuiffe.*

Pag. 30. *In Curiâ de Arcubus*——— *Doctores Legum in celebri aliquâ Studiorum Univ. ordinantur, antequam ad hoc tam insigne Tribunal accedant.*

There is now preferved in the Archives of the Church of *Canterbury* a MS, ftyled *Registrum Facultatum à Matt. Parker Archiepifc. Cant. conceffarum*; but it cannot be concluded from any Entries in this Book (in which are contained abundance of all other kind of Faculties during the space of about fix Years) that *Archbishop Parker* did ever confer Degrees. There feems indeed to have been a Defign of *procuring a Faculty* for a Degree from that *Archbishop* a little before his Death; but there is good reafon to believe that fuch Degree was *never granted*; and, if it were, 'tis very certain, that it was granted *to no manner of purpofe*: as shall be shewn to a Demonstration, whenever fuch proof is demanded; which is now omitted, only becaufe it is too long, as well as unneceffary.

Strype's Life of Parker; p. 422. An. 1573. But that *Faculties for Degrees* were not *in ufe in Parker's time*, is very plain from his Anfwer to *Cartwright's* Book, which clamour'd against the Archbishop's Courts, and the Faculties and Difpenfations iffuing thence, where he writes thus:

Pag. 423. *As to* the Faculty-Office; *the Prince hath eftablished by Parliament the Laws Ecclefiaftical, not repugnant to the Word of God, nor contrary to the Laws of the Realm.*

The Prince hath Authority in thofe cafes, which by the Ecclefiastick Law were referved *to the Pope.*

The Execution of Law in feveral of thefe Cafes ——— *is referred, not to the Perfon of* the Prince, *but to the Perfon of the Archbishop of Canterbury, fo authorized* ——— *by Authority of the High Court of Parliament.*

Of the number of thofe Cafes referved *be thofe, which do pafs by Difpenfation in Her Highnefs's Court of Faculties, which in manner are thefe now in ufe only.*

A Commendam. "A Difpenfation for a Bishop to retain or receive any Ecclefiaftical "Living *in Commendam*. The Tax is 16*l*.

A Plurality. "A Difpenfation for thofe which are qualified either by the Prince, "by Noblemen, or by Degree of School, to receive *two Benefices with* "*Cure*. 6*l*. 10*s*. And with this Claufe: *Quòd in uno Beneficiorum tuorum pro* "*arbitrio tuo refidendo, in alio refidere minimè tenearis*. 7*l*. 13*s*. 4*d*.

A Triality. "A *Triality*, to have two Benefices with Cure, and a third to be a "Benefice, a Prebend, or Dignity, which hath no Cure. Tax 9*l*.

Quadrality. "*Quadralities*, or *Tot Quot's*, we grant none.

"For

(29)

"For him that is not born in lawful *Matrimony*, to be made *habilis* Legitimatio.
"*ad Ordines Ecclef. & recipere Beneficium.* Taxed at 4*l.*

"To take a Prebend or a Benefice without Cure, is not granted to Pro Minore.
"any *under the Age of* 18 Years. The Tax is 4*l.* 6*s.* 8*d.* Altho' by the
"Book of Taxations such Dispensations might be granted from 10
"Years of Age, and so upward to a far greater Gain.

"For such Persons as enjoy Ecclesiastical Livings, and are occupied in De non pro-
"the common Affairs of the Realm. Tax 4 *l.* movendo ad Ordines.

" *Non-residence* is not granted to any but upon just Cause ; which De non resi-
"Cause is expressed in his Dispensation (*viz.*) for Recovery of Health, dendo.
"*&c.* The greatest Tax is 53*s.* 4*d.*

"A *perinde valere* is granted in Cases of lack of Dispensation, or Perinde va-
"when the former Dispensation was insufficient, or when the Party lere.
"hath by some Act incurred the Ecclesiastical Censures, or is made
"*inhabilis* either *ad retinendum*, or *ad recipiendum. Beneficium Ecclef.*
"Tax 6*l.*

"For a Person to be admitted to receive the *Orders* of Deacon and Ad utrofque
"Priest *at one time.* Tax 13*s.* 4*d.* Ordin. simul.

" To give leave to a Clerk to *seek his Bishop* to take Orders. Tax Litt. Dimis-
"6*s.* 8*d.* soriæ.

"None may marry but in their own Parish Churches in *Times pro-* Ad matrimo-
"*hibited*, nor *without Banes* be three several Holydays proclaimed, but nium.
"by Dispensation ; either from *the Faculties* or from *the Ordinary.*
"10*s.*

" None, without offending the Laws, may *eat Flesh* upon Days for- Ad esum car-
"bidden, but by Dispensation either from *the Faculty* for ever, or from nium.
"*the Ordinary*, or *Curate*, for Time limited. Tax 40*s.*

"The *Creation of Notaries Publick.* Tax 13*s.* 4*d.* Creatio Notariorum
In all which Dispensations the Archbishop referreth himself to the Judgment Publicorum.
of the Queen's Highness and her Honourable Council.

And that this was a true and exact Account of all the Faculties and
Dispensations, which were *then granted,* or were lookt upon by the
Archbishop to be duly and *legally grantable* , is confirmed by the
like Account given of this matter, about three Years after, by *Archbishop Grindall,* in the two following Papers presented to the Lords of
the Council.

"I. *Dispensations left to the Consideration of the Lords of the* Pap. I.
"*Council.* Strype's Life
of *Abp.* Grin-
1. A *Commendam.* It is to be considered , whether this kind of dal, p. 202.
"Dispensation may have continuance, being used in this case 203.
"only, where certain of the smallest Bishopricks want Suf-
"ficiency for Maintenance of the Bishops, and therefore
"have need of some Supply.

"2. A *Plurality.* It is also to be considered, whether thi. Dispen-
"sation may have continuance ; so as only learned Men,
"being Batchelors of Divinity, or Preachers lawfully al-
"lowed, may enjoy the same ; the Distance between the
"Benefices not exceeding twenty Miles: With a Proviso
I "also,

(30)

"alfo, that the Party difpenfed withal preach at the Bene-
"fice, whereupon he commonly dwelleth not, thirteen Ser-
"mons every Year, according to the Queen's Injunctions ;
"and alfo keep Hofpitality there eight Weeks in every Year
"at the leaft.

" 3. *Legitimation.* This kind of Difpenfation, which is the onabling
"of Men bafe-born to take Ecclefiaftical Orders and Pro-
"motions, feemeth not convenient to be ufed, but where
"there is good Proof of great Towardnefs in Learning, and
"of godly Difpofition in the Party fo difpenfed withal :
"For that Baftards feldom prove profitable Members of
"God's Church which is likewife to be confidered of in
"the faid Cafe.

" 4. *Non-refidence.* To be confidered, whether this Difpenfation may
"be granted for fome fhort Time only, for Recovery of
"Health, or fuch like urgent Caufe, and not during Life,
"or for any long Time; as it hath been heretofore ufed.

" 5. *Licence to eat Flefh.* Whether this Difpenfation be to be con-
"tinued for fome Perfons.

" 6. *Creation of Notaries.* Whether this Faculty be to be retained ftill
"in *Actuaries* and *Scribes.*

" 7. *De non promovends.* Whether, in cafe of the Prince's Service,
"this Difpenfation may be granted to a Doctor of the Civil
"Law, to enjoy fome kind of Ecclefiaftical Promotion, not-
"withftanding he be not within Orders.

" II. *Difpenfations to be utterly abolifhed.*
" 1. *Trialities,* and Faculties for *more Benefices,* or for fo many as
"the Parties could get.

" 2. Difpenfations for Children, and young Men *under age,* to take
"Ecclefiaftical Promotions.

" 3. Difpenfations called by the name of *Perinde valere,* making
"Grants good, which by Law were void, and a Right grown
"to fome other Perfon.

" 4. Difpenfations to take *all Orders* of the Miniftry *at one time.*

" 5. Difpenfations to take Orders *out of their own Diocefs* at any other
"Bifhop's hands.

" 6. Licences to *marry without Banes asking,* and out of the *Parifh-Church*
"of any of the Parties.

And for the better underftanding of the State of this Faculty-Office, *and
the various* Difpenfations *granted out of it, and the refpective Fees, a Table hereof was drawn out for the Infpection and Confideration of the Privy Council. Which is here tranfcribed.*

(3·1)

The Faculty-Office. The Dispensations with their Prices. MS. Grindal.

Pap. II. Append. *to* Life of Grindal.

Dispensation and Tax.	To the Queen.	L. Chancellour.	Clark.	Archbishop.	Commissary.	Register.
Commendam 16l.	8l.	35s. 6d. q.	13s. 9d. ob. q.	3l. 11s. 1d.	17s. 9d. ob. q.	17s. 9d. ob. q.
Plurality 6l. 10s. 00.	3l.	13s. 5d. ob.	7s. 2d. ob.	28s. 10d. ob.	7s. 2d. ob. q.	7s. 2d. ob. q.
Legitimation 4l.	43s. 4d.	8s. 10d. ob.	4s. 5d. ob.	17s. 8d.	4s. 6d.	4s. 6d.
Non-residence 2l. 13s. 4d.	30s.	Nil.	3s. 4d.	8s. 10d. ob.	4s. 9d. ob.	4s. 5d. ob.
Licence to eat Flesh 40s.	———	———	3s. 4d.	6s. 8d.	3s. 4d.	3s. 4d.
Creation of Notaries 13s. 4d.	Nil.	Nil.	4s. 5d. q.	Nil.	4s. 5d. q.	4s. 5d. q.
De non promovendo; that is for a Dr. of Civil Law to enjoy some Ecclesiastical Preferment, 4l.	43s. 4d.	8s. 10d. ob.	4s. 5d.	17s. 8d.	4s. 6d.	4s. 6d.

Trialities, 9l.

As many Benefices as the Party could get. } The Tax here much greater according to the Quality of the Grant.

Dispensation for Children and young Men under Age, to take Ecclesiastical Benefices. If the Party were 18 Years of Age, or more, 4l. 16s. 8d. If under 18 Years of Age, much greater.

Perinde valere; that is, making Grants good, which by Law were void, and a Right grown to some other Person, 6l.

Dispensation to take all Orders together, 13s. 4d.

Dispensations to take Orders out of ones own Diocess, 6s. 8d.

Licenses to marry without Banns, 10s.

These Propositions of the Archbishop concerning his Faculties, together with their respective *Prices* or Fees, *were allowed and approved of by the Queen's Council;* as appears by an *authentick Entry in the Council Books,* Jan. 15. 1578. when the Lords of the Council " having perused the Original " of a certain *Order* taken and subscribed by their Lordships the 20th
" of

(32)

"of *June* in the Year of our Lord God 1576, their Lordſhips pleaſure
"was, that the ſame ſhould be regiſtred and entered into the Counſel-
"Book as followeth.

The 20th of
June 1576.

*Diſpenſations to be utterly aboliſhed as not agreeable to Chriſtian Religion
in the Opinion of the Lords of the Counſel.*

Trialities; and Faculties for moe Benefices, or ſo many as the Parties
  could get.
  The Taxe of Trialities was *ix*^l.
  The Taxe of thother much greater according to the Qualitie
    of the grannte to be devided after the rate of the others.
Diſpenſations for Children and younge Men *under Age*, to take Eccle-
  ſiaſtical Promotions.
  The Taxe whereof, the Party being *xviij*. yeres of Age and
    more was, *iiij*^l *vj*^s *viij*^d.
  The Taxe much greater, the Parties being under *xviij*. Yeres.
Diſpenſations called by the Name of *Perinde Valere* making graunts
  good which by Lawe were voide, and a Right growne to ſome
  other Perſon.
  The Taxe whereof was *vj*^l.
Diſpenſations to take *all Orders* of the Miniſtry at one time.
  The Taxe whereof was, *xiij*^s *iiij*^d.
Diſpenſations to take *Orders out of their own Dioceſſe* at any other Bi-
  ſhoppes Handes except where he was borne or where he hath been
  moſt uſually for two Yeres.
  The Taxe whereof was, *vj*^s *viij*^d.
Licenſes to *marry without Banes asking*, and *oute of the Pariſhe Churche* of
  any of the Parties.
  The Taxe whereof was, *x*^s.

*Diſpenſations left to the Conſideration of the Lords of the Counſell, and by
them allowed as they be here qualified.*

A *Commendam.* It is to be conſidered, whether this kinde of Diſpenſation may have Continuance, being uſed in this caſe only, where
  certaine of the ſmalleſt Biſhoprickes wante Sufficiencye for Maintenance of the Biſhoppes, and therefore have nede of ſome Supply.
  The Taxe whereof is *xvj*^l to be devided thus, *viz.*
    To the Quene, *viij*^l.
    To the Lord Chauncellor, *xxxv*^s *vj*^d *q.*
    To the Clerke, *xiv*^s *ix*^d *ob. q.*
    To the Archebiſhop, *iij*^l *xi*^s *j*^d.
    To the Commiſſary, *xvij*^s *ix*^d *ob. q.*
    To the Regiſter, *xvij*^s *ix*^d *ob. q.*
A *Dualitie.* It is to be conſidered, whether this Diſpenſation may have
  Continuance, ſo as only lernid Men, being Bachelers of Divinitie,
  or Preachers lawfully allowed by the Biſhop, where the ſeconde
  Benefice is, may enjoie the ſame, the diſtaunce betwene the Benefices not exceeding 20^ti Miles; with a Proviſo alſo, that the Partie
  diſpenſed withall, preache at the Benefice whereupon he dwelleth
  not, *xiiij*. Sermons every Yere, upon Sondayes and Hollidaies, according to the Quenes Injunctions, and alſo kepe hoſpitalitie there
  8. wekes in every yere at the leaſt.
                                                             The

(33)

The Tax whereof is *vj*. *x*. to be divided thus, *viz*.

To the Quene, *iij*.
To the Lord Chancelor, *xiiij*. *v*. *ob*.
To the Clerk, *vij*. *ij*. *ob*.
To the Archebifhop, *xxviij*. *x*. *ob*.
To the Commiffarie, *vij*. *ii*. *ob*. *q*.
To the Regifter, *vij*. *ij*. *ob*. *q*.

A Legitimation. This kinde of Difpenfation, which is the enabling of men bafe borne to take eccliaftical Orders and Promotions, femeth not convenient to be ufed but where is good proofe of grete towardnes in Lerning and of godlie Difpofition in the Partie fo difpenfed withall ; for that baftardes feldome prove profitable members of Gods Church; which is likewife to be confiderid of in the faid cafe. The Taxe whereof is *iv*. to be divided

To the Quene, *xliiij*. *iv*.
To the Lord Chancelor, *viij*. *x*. *ob*.
To the Clerck, *iv*. *v*. *ob*.
To the Archebifhop, *xvij*. *viij*.
To the Commiffarie, *iv*. *vj*.
To the Regifter, *iv*. *vj*.

Non-Refidence. To be confiderid, whither this Difpenfation may be graunted for fome fhorte tyme only, for recoverie of helth, or fuch like Urgent caufe, and not during life, or for any longe time, not exceding one yere, as it hath ben heretofore ufed. The Taxe whereof is *liij*. *iv*. to be devided

To the Quene *xxx*.
To the Lord Chauncelor, *nihil*.
To the Clerk, *iij*. *iv*.
To the Archebifhop, *viij*. *x*. *ob*.
To the Commiffarie, *iv*. *v*. *ob*.
To the Regifter, *iv*. *v*. *ob*.

Licenfe to eate Flefhe. Whither this Difpenfation be to be continued for fome Perfons. The Taxe whereof is *xl*. to be devided

To the Quene, *nihil*.
To the Lord Chauncelor, *nihil*.
To the Clerck, *iij*. *iv*.
To the Archebifhop, *vj*. *viij*.
To the Commiffarie, *iij*. *iv*.
To the Regifter, *iij*. *iv*.

Creation of Notaries. Whether this Facultie be to be retained in Actuaries and Scribes ftill. The Taxe whereof is *xiij*. *iv*. to be devided

To the Quene, *nihil*.
To the Lord Chauncelor, *nihil*.
To the Clerck, *iv*. *v*. *q*.
To the Archebifhop, *nihil*.
To the Commiffarie, *iv*. *s*. *q*.
To the Regifter, *iv*. *v*. *q*.

De non promovendo. Whether, in cafe of the Princes Service, this Difpenfation may be graunted to a Doctor of the Civil Lawe, to enjoye fome kinde of Eccliaftical Promotion, notwithftanding he be not within Orders.

K   The

(34)

Though note that the ecclesiastical Premunire be ministred such as hath no special Care of Souls.

The Taxe whereof is *iv*^{l.} to be devided .
    To the Quene *liij*^{s.} *iv*^{d.}
    To the Lord Chauncelor, *viij*^{s.} *x*^{d.} *ob*.
    To the Clerck, *iv*^{s.} *v*^{d.} *ob*.
    To the Archebifshop, *xvij*^{s.} *viij*^{d.}
    To the Commiffarie, *iv*^{s.} *vj*^{d.}
    To the Regifter, *iv*^{s.} *vj*^{d.}

Bacon C. S.	*W. Burghley.*	*E. Lincoln.*	*T. Suffex.*
Arundel.	*F. Bedford.*	*R. Leycefter.*	
	F. Knollys.	*Jamys Croft.*	
	W. Myldmay.		

I have feen another Copy of this Original Order of the 20th of *June*, 1576. (from whence I have added the Names of the fubfcribing Lords) that was found among Archbifhop *Whitgift*'s Papers ; which by the bye is a Proof, that this was the Rule for granting Difpenfations in *his* time, as well as his Predeceffor's.

And that *this Order* was intended by the Lords of the Councel for a *ftanding Rule* to be obferved in all times to come, by the Officers concerned in granting *Faculties*, is plain from another Minute in the Councel-Books, of the fame Date with what is before tranfcribed from thence, *viz.* "A Letter to Mr. Doctor *Lewis*, Mafter of the *Faculties*, that "He may, without ferving any fpecial Warrant from their Lordfhips, "exercife the Faculties : provided that the fame be in fuch points as "heretofore hath been allowed by their Lordfhips *former Order*, accord-"ing to a Minute remaining in the Cheft." By which *former Order*, muft needs be underftood, that of *June* 20, 1576; which it was their Lordfhips Pleafure fhould then be regiftred, and which follows immediately after this Minute.

Now, from the Accounts before given of *Faculties* and Difpenfations *then in ufe*, we are naturally led to make the following Obfervations : *viz.* That the 25 H. 8. having been *repealed* by Queen *Mary*, the Tax-books drawn in purfuance of that Act (if any fuch there were) fell together with the Statute ; but when the Act was revived by Q. *Eliz.* the *Authority* of the old *Tax-Books* was not revived with it, but a *Direction* only to make *new* ones. And, confidering the great Change that was made in Religion in her Reign from what it was in the 25 *H.* 8. there was a neceffity of putting the *Faculty-Office* upon a different foot, and confequently of making *new Tax-Books* ; as plainly appears by comparing *the old Book* now kept in the Office with *Grindal's MS.* and *the Order of Councel* made in his time. For in the former the number of Heads upon which Faculties were granted were 225, and in the latter but 13. And therefore it cannot be fuppofed that a Book where 225 feveral kinds of Faculties were taxed, fhould be look'd upon as an *authentick* Standard for granting Faculties, at a time when but 13 only were judged grantable, which were no way diftinguifhed from the other in the *old* Book.

Vid. Life of Parker. p. 298, 300. Grindal. p. 202, 219.

Both *Parker*, and *Grindal*, had endeavoured to reform the Abufes complained of in the *Court of Faculties* ; and both of them had publickly expreffed their Willingnefs to have this *Offenfive Court* (as one of them calls it) fuppreffed. But, notwithftanding the diligent Endeavours of thefe Archbifhops, and their Succeffors, it is very obfervable, that many *illegal* Difpenfations have all along been granted : as *Quadralities*
                             and

(35)

and *Totquots*, which the two Archbiſhops acknowledge *ought not to be granted*; Diſpenſations of *Perinde valere*, which are owned before to be intended for making Grants good, which by Law are void, which 'tis certain they *cannot do*; *Trialities* with Cure of Souls, which have been adjudged void in Law; and particularly in the Caſe of *Cox*, who was Chaplain to one of theſe very Archbiſhops; as may be ſeen in *Dyer's Reports*, 18 *Eliz.* and of late Years (as I am informed) *Pluralities* to Perſons not qualified by *Academical*, but only by *Faculty Degrees*, contrary to the expreſs Words of *Statute*. And divers other Inſtances, I believe, upon a ſtrict Search, might be produced, of *irregular* and *illegal Faculties*, which have paſſed, and have been taken to be *good* and *effectual*, only becauſe they were never queſtioned: All which I take to have been founded upon the *ſuppoſed Authority of the old Tax-Book*, which never was *confirmed by Parliament*, and never was *pleaded* upon any occaſion, where any Doubt was made in Law concerning the *Legality* of a Diſpenſation; as it would, and ought to have been, had it really been *authentick*; and particularly in the Caſe of *Cox*, and in the Caſe of *Colt* and *Glover* beforementioned. For the ſame reaſon therefore, and upon the ſame foot, may *Degrees* have been granted by *Faculty*, and yet not *legally* granted, tho' no Queſtion till now was ſtarted concerning them, becauſe no Occaſion was before given to conſider them as carrying any *legal Effects*.

It is farther to be obſerved in this place, that the Power of granting Faculties and Diſpenſations has never been duly ſettled and limited to this day; as appears plainly from *the Archbiſhop's* doing the ſame things, ſometimes by his *ordinary Power*, and ſometimes by his *Faculty-Office*; particularly, as to *Diſpenſations for Non-reſidence*, *Licences to marry without Banns*, *Licences to eat Fleſh in Lent*, and *Letters Dimiſſory*; which are four of the thirteen Diſpenſations, to which the great Number in the old *Tax-Book* was reduced by *the Reformation.* —There are likewiſe other Faculties, not in *Grindal's* Liſt, which belong to the Archbiſhop's *ordinary Juriſdiction*, and yet are often diſpatch'd in his *Faculty-Court*; as, *Licences to practiſe Surgery*, &c. From whence I infer, that there never was any regular *Book of Taxations* made according to the *Direction of the Act of Parliament*; otherwiſe common *Diſpenſations*, uſually granted by *the Archbiſhop* (and indeed by every other *Biſhop*) *before the Act*, would not have been promiſcuouſly mixt with other *extraordinary Faculties*, which *the Act alone* empowered *the Archbiſhop* to grant.

There is another Paper printed in the *Appendix to* Grindal's *Life*, from Cleop. F. 2. a MS. in *the Cotton Library*, which gives ſome further Light into the Meaning of the Stat. 25 *H.*8. with this Title to it, *viz. Arguments to be conſidered, whether a ſeveral Commiſſion be expedient for paſſing Faculties within the Realm of*, Ireland, *and no longer to be granted from the Archbiſhop of* Canterbury. The Paſſages I ſhall take notice of are theſe:

"I. At ſuch time as the Authority of the *Biſhop of Rome* was utterly "aboliſhed within Her Majeſty's Dominions for granting the ſaid Facul-"ties, *from whom only within Chriſtendom* they paſſed before that time ——

"III. Foraſmuch as *Faculties and Diſpenſations againſt the Common Law* "*Ecclef.* are of their own nature odious, and ſparingly to be granted; "therefore the Parliament thought it not convenient to have them paſs "from divers Mens hands.

There

(36)

An. 1576.
Harley-Library. 33. c. 3.
p. 253.
28 H. 8. c 19.

There is no Date to this Paper, but it was, very probably, drawn about the 19th Year of Q. *Eliz.* because, in that Year I find a *Commiffion* granted for holding *Ecclefiaft. Jurifdiction within the Realm of* Ireland, purfuant to a Claufe in an Act paffed in *Ireland* in *H.* 8's time, entituled, *An Act of Faculties*; whereby the Perfons appointed Commiffioners by the Queen (which were two private Gentlemen) were impowered to *exercife the fame Jurifdiction, and grant the fame Faculties,* &c. *as* Archbifhops *of* Canterbury *in* England *did* —— *for fuch Matters, Caufes, and Fees, as in the faid Act of Faculties is limited and taxed* —— *to caufe all Clergymen to exhibit their Orders and Faculties, by which they held any Benefice or Dignity, and to void all fuch as were not regularly held; with leave to make Deputies in their abfence.*

Now it does not appear likely, either from the Nature and Tenour of this Commiffion, or the Condition of the Perfons appointed to exercife it, that *the Power of conferring Degrees* was contained in it. Nor have any of the *Primates of Armagh*, who have, ever fince the Beginning of K. *James's* Reign, been entrufted with the like Commiffion, laid any *Claim* to fuch a Power as this; tho' by the *Act of Faculties* paffed in *Ireland*, they had as good a Pretence to it as *the Archbifhops of Canterbury* have by *the Statute of Difpenfations* paffed here in *England.* Nor is there any one *Inftance* to be found of a *Degree* given by *Faculty* in *Ireland*; as I have been well affured from a very good Hand, after a diligent Enquiry made into all Books and Papers relating to the *Power of granting Faculties* in that Kingdom.

Cott. Libr.
Julius F. X.
16.

In the firft Year of King *James* I. there happened a Difpute, between the *Serjeants at Common Law,* and *the Doctors of Civil Law,* about *Precedency.* The Serjeants alledged, that theirs was a *publick Degree of the Commonwealth*, and that of the Doctors only a *private Degree of the Univerfities* or *Schools;* that Serjeants receive their Degree immediately from *the King,* Doctors only by Grants of *the Congregation* or *Convocation in the Univerfities:* &c. To which the Doctors replied, that a Degree taken in *the Inns of Court* is neither *more publick,* nor *more proper to the Commonwealth,* than one taken in *the Univerfities;* that Serjeants take their Degree from *the Lord Chancellor, authoriz'd by the King,* but Doctors from the *Univerfities, authorized* thereto by *Grants of Letters Patents from the Crown;* that Serjeants are only called *fub pede Sigilli,* but Doctors are virtually made by *Letters Patents under the Great Seal* &c. The Serjeants urged farther, that they were *more felected,* fparingly chofen, few in Number; but Doctors were infinite, without Limitation: To which the Doctors anfwered, that they are *as much felected,* being never admitted till they have *kept many Acts,* and be prefented *upon Oath for their Sufficiency,* which cutteth off all corrupt Working either by Favour, or Fee, &c.

From all which, and a great deal more that is faid on both Sides, it is very plain, that *the Lawyers* of that Time had no Notion of any *other* Degrees but what were taken in *the Univerfities,* or *Inns of Court;* and that, if there had been then any *Faculty Doctors,* they would not have prefumed to conteft the Point of *Precedency* with *Serjeants:* and, fhould thofe now in being have any Difpute of this Nature with any other Perfon whatever, *the Heralds* would be very much puzzled to know where to place them.

Statutes

(37)

Statutes of *Hereford* Cathedral, drawn up by *Whitgift*, when *Bishop of* <small>Strype's Life</small>
Worcester, by Order of *Queen Eliz.* and afterwards revised and corrected, <small>of Whitgift.</small>
with several Additions, by *Archbishop Laud* : every Page of which is <small>p. 106.</small>
signed *W. Cant.* and confirmed by *K. Charles* I. under his Privy Seal in
the 12th Year of his Reign.

Cap. 1. *Qualitates in futuris Præbend. & Canonicis.*

" *Nullum posthac Præbendarium sive Canonicum* —— *Sinimus,* —— *prius-* <small>Stat. Eccles.</small>
" quam Gradu *aliquo* Academico *in Theolog. vel saltem Magisterii in Artibus,* <small>Heref.</small>
" *aut Baccalaureatûs in Legibus, insigniatur, eundemque Scholasticis exercitiis*
" *(prout alterius Academiæ Statuta postulant,) præstitis, consecutus fuerit.)* ——

Cap. 9. *De Prælectione Sacrâ.*

" *Quemlibet ex Canonicis aut Præbendariis huic muneri Judicamus impa-*
" *rem, nisi* —— *fit vel in* Theolog. Graduatus, *vel ad minimum* Artium
" Magister, *aut in Legibus Baccal. Justis & temporum spatiis, & exercitiis, in*
" *alterâ nostrate Academiâ exantlatis creatus.* ——

These Statutes, which are the same for Substance in the *Old* Draught
of Q. *Eliz.*'s Time, and in *the New*, are a plain Proof both of *Whitgift's*
and *Laud's* Opinion, that *no other Degrees* but such as were taken *re-*
gularly, and according to due Form, *in the Universities*, were *proper*
Qualifications for such as were admitted *Canons in any Cathedral.* From
whence we may also fairly conclude, that this was the *general Opinion*
of those Times: and consequently, that the *two Charters of Manche-*
ster-College, the one in Q. *Eliz.*'s, and the other in K. *Charles's* Reign,
bearing very near the same Date with *the old* and *new Statutes of Here-*
ford, the Degrees there required must be understood to be *University-*
Degrees, tho' it be not so particularly expressed : Especially when it is
consider'd, that *a higher Degree of Learning* is made necessary to *qualify*
a Man to be *Warden of Manchester,* than what is required for a *Canon of*
Hereford, or of *any other Church.*

Besides, *the Difference of Degrees* required in these Charters for *the*
Warden, the Fellows, and *the Chaplains,* agreeable to the *different Dig-*
nity of their Places; *and the different Professions* or *Kinds of Learning* in
which those Degrees were to be taken, is a certain Argument that
University-Degrees were intended; because there is *no certain Age,* or
Time of Study; no particular Exercises or Performances in *any sort of Learn-*
ing; no certain Degrees or *Proofs of Proficiency in any Profession*; and in
short *no manner of Gradation* at all requisite for the Attainment of a
Faculty for any Degree whatever.

Articles *of* Enquiry *at the Visitations of Arch-*
bishops, Bishops, Archdeacons, &c.

Visitation of *Chichester* Diocese by Authority of *Archbishop Whitgift,* <small>Strype's Life</small>
Sede vacante. " Of what Age and *Degree of School is* He ? [your Mi- <small>of Whitgift</small>
" nister ?] <small>Append. F.</small>
<small>106,</small>

Archbishop Bancroft in his Metrop. Visitation An. 1606.

" Whether doth your Minister wear the Surplice whilst he is saying <small>Printed Art.</small>
" the publike Prayers and ministring the Sacraments ? And, if he be *any*
" *Graduat,* whether then doth he also weare upon his Surplyce, during
" the times aforesaide, such a whood as by the *orders of his University* is
" agreeable to his *Degree* ?

I.   *Tho.*

(38)

Tho. Bilson Bishop of Winchester Anno 1606.

"Whether the Parson, Vicar, or Minister —— saying the publick "Prayers, or ministring the Sacraments —— hath neglected to wear "a Surplice? And whether such of them as are *Graduates* have omitted "to wear upon their Surplices, at such times, such Hoods as by *the Or-* "*ders of the Universities* are agreeable to their *Degrees?*

Henry Cotton Bishop of Salisbury Anno 1614.

" —— And he be *a Graduate*, (your Minister) whether then doth he "wear upon his Surplice —— such a Hood as by the *Orders of his Uni-* "*versity* is agreeable to his *Degree?*

The same Enquiry by *W. Bishop of Landaff* Anno 1640.

Archdeacon of Norfolk 1625.

"Doth your Minister, in time of Divine Service —— wear a Surplice? "And, if he be a *Graduate*, a Hood suitable to his *Degree in the Univer-* "*sity.*

" ——suitable to *his Degree*, B. *Duppa Bishop of Winchester* Anno 1638.

Commissary of Essex and Hertford An. 16—— printed *An.* 1625.

Same Enquiry as before *Anno* 1614. with this Addition —— "Ac-"cording to the 58th Canon.

S. Harsnet Bishop of Norwich Anno 1627.

"Whether is your Minister, Parson, Vicar, or Curate, *a Graduate in* "*either of the Universities*, or no? if yea, then of *what Degree?*

"What Physician, or Chirurgeon is in your Parish unlicensed, and, "being not a *Doctor of Physick, in either of the Universities*, doth practise "Physick?

" ——not being *a Doctor of Physick*, or otherwise sufficiently licen-"sed *in either of these Universities*". M. *Wren Bishop of Norwich*, Anno 1636. and when *Bishop of Ely*, Anno 1662.

R. Mountague Bishop of Chichester Anno 1628.

"Whether is your Minister a Preacher or not? of *what Degree* is he "*in the University?*

The same Enquiry by the same Bishop, *Anno* 1637.

J. Williams Bishop of Lincoln, 1630.

"Whether are there in your Parish any, not *known Doctors* of that "Profession, that practise Physick?

R. Neil Archbishop of York Metrop. Vis. Anno 1633.

"Whether doth your Minister wear a Surplice? and, being a *Graduate*, "doth he always wear therewith a Hood by *the Order of the University* "agreeable to his *Degree?*

The same Enquiry by *Archdeacon of York* Anno 16——

By *Archdeacon of Surry* Anno 1638.

By *G. Ironside Bishop of Bristol* Anno 1662.

By *William Goulston Bishop of Bristol* Anno 168——

William Laud Archbishop of Canterbury, Metrop. Vis. An. 163.——

"Are your Ecclesiastical Judges, and their Substitutes, *Masters of Art*, "or *Batchelors of the Laws* at least.

The same Enquiry by *J. Williams Bishop of Lincoln* An. 1641.

Matthew Wren Bishop of Norwich, Anno 1636.

"Is your Minister, Parson, Vicar, or Curate *a Graduate in either of* "*the Universities?* And, if he be a Graduate, of *what Degree* is he? "And what kind of Hood doth he use to wear in the Church?

The

(39)

The same Enquiry by *Dr. Pearson Archdeacon of Suffolk* Anno 1638.

W. Juxon Bishop of London Anno 1640.

"Do the Chancell. Commiss. &c. —— or any of them Substitute
"any in their absence to keep Court for them that is not, either a grave
"Minister, and a *Graduate*, or *a Batchelor of Law*, or *Master of Arts* at
"the least.

William Bishop of Landaff Anno 1640.

"Hath your Minister, without License from *the Court of Faculties*, or
"from the Archbishop, or —— solemnized Marriage?

Degrees by Faculty might as properly have been mentioned in Articles of Visitation, as *Marriage Licenses*, if they had been of the same
Authority.

Hen. King Bishop of Chichester Anno 1662.

"Doth your Minister wear the Surplice, together with such other
"*Scholastical Habit* as is suitable to his *Degree*?

The same Enquiry by *B. Laney Bishop of Peterborough* An. 1662.

And when *Bishop of Lincoln* Anno 1663.

By *G. Morley Bishop of Winchester* Anno 1662.

By *R. Saunderson Bishop of Lincoln* Anno 1662.

By *W. Fuller Bishop of Lincoln* Anno 1671.

And by *M. Honeywood Dean of Lincoln* Anno 1672.

Matthew Wren Bishop of Ely Anno 1662.

"Is your Minister, Parson, Vicar, or Curate reputed to be *a Graduate*
"*in either of the Universities*? And, if he be a Graduate, then of *what*
"*Degree* is he?

"Doth he preach with his Surplice, and Hood also, if he be a *Gra-*
"*duate*?

"Hath any, being no Priest, or Deacon, presumed at any time (under
"Pretence of being *Graduate*, or a Scholar *of the University*) to read
"Common Prayer in the Church?

W. Juxon Archbishop of Canterbury Anno 1663.

"Doth your Parson, Vicar, or Curate —— wear a Surplice, with a
"Hood (if he be a *Graduate*) agreeable to his *Degree in the University*?

P. Gunning Bishop of Ely Anno 1682.

"Doth your Minister —— at the reading or celebrating any Divine Can. 58.
"Office, constantly wear the Surplice, and other *Scholastical* Habit ac-
"cording to his *Degree*, if he be a *Graduate*; and without a Hood, (only
"instead thereof a Tippet of black Stuff, not Silk, being permitted
"him) if he be *no Graduate*.

N. Stratford Bishop of Chester upon visiting his Cathedral An. 1692. Reg. Cestr.

Art. 8. "Is every one of the Prebendaries at least a *Master of Arts*,
"or *Batchelor of Law* according to the tenth Statute?

Answer in writing. "Each Prebendary is reputed to be *a Master of*
"*Arts* at the least, and we presume that each will upon demand give
"Evidence of his *University Degrees*.

Upon a view of these *Articles* relating to *Degrees*, publish'd by a great
number of *Bishops, Archbishops,* and other *Ordinaries,* at several times
during the space of a hundred Years, it cannot but appear very strange,
that, if *Degrees by Faculty* had been *commonly* granted, and had been
always look'd upon as *good in Law,* no mention should be made of them
in

(40)

in any Article of Enquiry upon this Subject: And that no Care should
be taken all this time that *the Archbishops Graduates* should be provided
with *proper Habits*, so as not to be liable to *Suspension* (as they now
plainly are by Can. 58.) for wearing such Habits as are *suitable to the
Degrees bestow'd upon them by Faculty*, because they are *not agreeable to any
Degrees which they have taken in the University.*

But what account can be given of *Archbishop Juxon's* making this Enquiry in his Visitation *Anno* 1663. *viz.* Whether every Minister wore
a *Hood* upon his Surplice (if he were *a Graduate*) agreeable to *his Degree
in the University?* 'Tis certain that he gave his Chaplain Mr. *Brabourn*,
a Faculty for the Degree of Doctor in Divinity; and yet (had *Brabourn* been
a Minister in his Diocese when he visited, and had worn a *Doctor's
Hood*) he might have been *presented, and suspended*, for not wearing his
Master of Arts Hood, which was the highest *Degree* he had taken *in the
University.* The least that I can conclude from hence is, that *Faculty-
Degrees* are *mere Titles of Honour*; and, as they are conferred without
Investiture, so they give no Right to any *Habit* at all.

HONORARY DEGREES *given by* the University.

Reg. Univ. L.
Wood's *An-
tiq.* p. 224.
Anno 1593.
Sir *John Mason*, Chancellor of the University, had a Dispensation from
the Congregation of Regents to wear the *Habit of a Doctor*, tho' he was
only *Master of Arts.*

I Mariz.
Wood's Fasti,
p. 714. An.
1556.
John Feckenham, Batchelor of Divinity, (who was then either Dean of
St. *Paul's*, or Abbot of *Westminster*) had the *Degree of Doctor of Divinity*
conferred upon him when absent ———— with leave for three Doctors
of Divinity, named by the University, to carry him the Ensigns or
Badges of his Doctorship.

P. 715. A.D.
1558. 5 & 6
Mar.
T. Boxall, Batchelor of Divinity, Secretary of State to Queen *Mary*,
Dean of *Windsor*, &c. was, tho' absent, created *Doctor of Divinity*; The
Ensigns of his Degree being delivered to him by the Abbot of *West-
minster*, and two Doctors in Divinity, who were likewise employed to
give him the Oath for observing the Privileges of the University: Which
Favour he acknowledged in a very kind Letter of Thanks to the Vice-
Chancellor and Masters.

Reg. Univ. L.
An. 1561.
W. Alley, Bishop of *Exeter*, supplicated for the Degree of *Batchelor
of Divinity*; which being given him, he afterwards desired to be admitted
to his *Doctors Degree*; which was likewise granted him, provided
he preach'd once in the University before he took that Degree upon
him. Then a Dispensation passed for all Exercises required for both Degrees, one reason of which assigned was, *quia non receptum est ut Episcopus
conditionibus vulgaribus subjiciatur.* And this was granted upon Condition
he took the Oath to observe the Statutes and Privileges of the University, and paid the Fees due to the Officers.

Ibid.
An. 1562.
W. Dunham, M. A. Bishop of *Chester*, had both Degrees in Divinity
given him in the same manner, only the latter was granted upon this
Condition, *viz. modò incipiat proximis Comitiis.*

Strype's *Life
of* Parker, p.
183. An. 1564.
Grindal Bishop of *London*, and *Scambler* Bishop of *Peterborough*, went out
Doctors of Divinity *per Gratiam* at *Cambridge.*

Life of Grin-
dal, p. 9.
Bishop *Grindal* in his Supplication for his Degree set forth, that
he had studied twelve Years after his Degree of Batchelor, *and had
preached*

(41)

preached two Sermons, one ad Clerum, *and the other at St.* Paul's Cross, *within a Year after his Admiffion, and praying that it might fuffice for him to be an Inceptour in Sacred Theology*——

The Inftrument whereby he was admitted is enter'd in the Bifhops Regiftry: and his Admiffion is thus enter'd in the Univerfity Regifter; (*viz.*) *Rev. in Chrifto Pater Edmondus London Epifcopus, admiffus S. T. D. in palatio fuo London, per Doct.* Coverdale *Apr.* 15. *An.* 1564. *à Domino Pro-Cancellario fubftitutum. Item Concionatus eft ad Clerum* 4 *Julii die Comitiorum per mag.* Johan. Young *Capellanum fuum.*

The fame Year *Tho. Young, Archbifhop of York,* was created *Doctor of* ^{Reg. Univ.} *Laws* at *Oxford*, by Commiffion from that Univerfity——He having ^{K. K.} fupplicated the Congregation under this Form——*Quatenus ftudium viginti annorum in jure civili pofuerit.*

Jewel, Bifhop of Salisbury, and *Cheney, Bifhop of Gloucefter,* created Doctors of Divinity by the like Commiffion. ^{Wood's Fafti, p. 724. An. 1565.}

The Bifhops of *Norwich, Chefter, Litchfield* and *Coventry, St. David,* and *Carlifle,* were created *Doctors* in the fame manner at *London*, in the Prefence of *W. Standifh,* Publick Notary, and Regifter of the Univerfity, and feveral others. ^{p. 728. An. 1566. Univ. Reg. K. K.}

H. Cotton, Bifhop of Salisbury, was created *Doctor of Divinity* at *Salisbury,* by the Vice-Chancellor, King's Profeffor of Divinity, both the Proctors, with the fuperior Beadle attending them by Virtue of a Commiffion. ^{P. 981. An. 1599.}

H. Rowlands, Bifhop of Bangor, and *J. Bridgett, Bifhop of Oxon,* were created *Doctors of Divinity* at a time, when feveral Noblemen and Gentlemen had Degrees conferred upon them, the King being then at *Oxford.* ^{P. 795. An. 1605.}

Sir *John Dodderidge,* Juftice of the *King's Bench,* was created *Mafter of Arts* in his Chambers at *Serjeants-Inn,* in the Prefence of the Vice-Chancellor, the two Proctors, and five other Members of the Univerfity——*propter operam Academiæ in caufis ejufdem agendis & defendendis navatam.* v. Wood's *Antiq.* p. 433. ^{P. 817. An. 1613.}

R. Skinner, Chaplain in Ordinary to his Majefty, and *Bifhop elect of Briftol,* was created *Doctor of Divinity,* by *Diploma* under the Seal of the Univerfity. ^{P. 886. An. 1636.}

Sir *J. Banks,* Lord Chief Juftice of the *Common Pleas,* (who, being Attorney General in the Year 1636, very probably drew up *the Charter of Manchefter College*) was, together with feveral other Judges, created *Doctor of Laws.* ^{Part 2. p. 709. An. 1642.}

H. Carpenter, Chaplain to the Houfe of Commons, was declared *Doctor of Divinity* by *Diploma,* upon the earneft requeft of *the Speaker,* Sir *Edward Turner,* to the Chancellor of the Univerfity. ^{P. 825. An. 1662.}

Thefe Inftances (being a very few out of a great number) of Perfons who had Degrees conferred upon them out of regard to their eminent *Merit,* or *Station,* or upon Application made by *the King, the Chancellor,* or *other* Great Men, are produced to fhew, that *Honorary Degrees,* and fuch as are called *by Grace,* when given by *the Univerfity,* have been ever fince the 25 *H.* 8. till after the Reftauration, efteemed fo highly, as to leave no room to fuppofe, that the *like Honours* could be conferred any *other* way.

And, fince that time, when *Faculties for Degrees* have been frequently granted, the prefent *Bifhop of London,* and the prefent *Bifhop of Salisbury,* (when *Bifhop of Oxford*) had the Degree of Doctor of Divinity

M   conferred

(42)

conferred upon them by *Diploma* under the Seal of *the University of Oxford*, without any mention, either in the Chancellor's Letters, or in the University Instruments, of their being Doctors by *the Archbishops Faculty*, tho' they had been so styled, and entituled, some time before.

There is another Way of conferring Degrees in the University, and that is by *Incorporation*; which, in the very Nature of it, excludes all Degrees granted by *Faculty*, as will plainly appear by what follows.

Wood's Ant. p. 293. An. 1576.

Controversia oriebatur (in Convoc.) de Incorporatione Cantabrigiensium, *eorundemque in finum Univ. receptione, ita ut eodem apud nos sint loco & numero quo apud suos (i. e.)* Cantabrigienses *fuerunt.* It was carried that they should.

Deinde mota est Controversia de bis qui in aliis Academiis *promoti, an, obtentâ apud nos Incorporatione, eisdem censeri debeant Loco & Statu quibus in aliis* Univ. *gaudebant. Placuit Convocationi favorabiliter decernere——* "*Ut quilibet nactus Incorporationis Beneficium eisdem habeatur Loco & Statu* " *quibus in aliquâ* forinsecâ Univ. *gaudebat.*

And by the present *Statutes of the University of Oxford*, drawn up by the Appointment of *Archbishop Laud*, and revised by him, and confirmed by *Charles* I. *Anno* 1636. The Matter stands thus:

"*Statutum est, quod quilibet Incorporationis Beneficium nactus, eodem ha-* "*beatur Loco & Statu, quibus in aliquâ aliâ* Universitate *gaudebat.*

Every Person incorporated, before his Admission, has this Oath administred to him by the Vice-Chancellor, (*viz.*)

"*Tu dabis fidem ad observandum Statuta, Privilegia, Consuetudines & Li-* "*bertates istius Univ. quatenus Statut. & Privileg. Consuetud. & Libertat.* Uni- "versit. (A. B. C.) *non repugnant.*

Afterwards he is admitted by the Vice-Chancellor under this Form; " *——— Ego admitto te ad eundem Statum, Gradum & Dignitatem hic apud* "nos Oxonienses *quibus ornatus es apud* Tuos (A. B. C.)

The like Form of Admission is, as I am told, used at *Cambridge*.

Which way then can a Person who has taken a Degree in *no University* be *incorporated* into *ours*? If there are any Instances of such Incorporations; (and some few I believe there are) they are manifestly *irregular* and *improper*; and they must be supposed to amount to *Creations*, in order to convey any real Effects.

The STATUTES of the College of Physicians.

De Candidatis.

Cap. 11.

"*Volumus, ut nemo admittatur in illorum Ordinem, qui non sit* in Me- "dicinâ Doctor *& natione Britannus, & Medicinam exercuerit per Qua-* "driennium.

"*Quòd si Doctoratûs gradum* in exterâ aliquâ Academiâ *adeptus fuerit,* " *volumus ut antequam admittatur ad examen, Diploma sive Litteras testimo-* "niales veras & Authenticas illius Academiae proferat & ostendat Collegio, & "*praeterea ab* alterutrâ nostrarum Academiarum *Incorporationis suae Testi-* "monium habeat & adducat.

A short

(43)

A short Account of the Institution and Nature of the College of Physicians, published 1688.

"*Candidates* must be *Doctors in Physick*, admitted to that Degree in
"one of our *own Universities*, must not be Foreigners———

"*Honorary Fellows* are such Doctors in Physick, as by reason of their
"being Foreigners, or having taken their Degree in *some University be-*
"*yond the Seas*, are not incorporated into either of ours; or for some
"other Reason (having not been Candidates) are not of the number of
"those, who have Votes in the Affairs of the College.

"*Licentiates* are such other Persons skilled in Physick, who by rea-
"son of their being Foreigners, or their not being admitted Doctors
in one of our Universities——— or such like Causes, are not capable to be
elected into the number of the Candidates.

The Publisher of these Statutes, and the short Account together in
1693, makes great Complaints of the frequent Admission of Persons
into the College, contrary to the Institution and Nature of that Society
(*viz.*) such as had *no Degree* at all, or had taken *Degrees in some Foreign
University* only, where the Statutes required they should be admitted,
or at least *incorporated* in one of our *own Universities*. But there was
then no Complaint, because no Apprehension, of any Persons pretend-
ing to be qualified for *Candidates* by the *Archbishop's Degree*.

And, as 'tis manifest from the foregoing Account, that a Person is
not *qualified by the Archbishop's Degree to be admitted into the College of
Physicians*; so is it plain from 14 *Hen.* VIII. before cited, that *no Degree in Physick conferred by the Archbishop* does of it self *qualify* the Person upon whom it is conferred *to practise Physick any where in England*;
and, if such Degree does not give a Physician *Liberty to Practise*, it
can give him *no other Privilege* but that of styling himself what the
Archbishop's Instrument styles him. Since therefore *Degrees in Physick* are granted by *Faculty*, when 'tis known that they can be no more
than *Honorary*, or *Titular*; This seems a very strong Proof, that *all
other Degrees*, which pass the same way, are to be, and are, so esteemed also.

What Orders or Constitutions have been made with regard to the
Qualifications of Persons admitted into *Doctors-Commons*, I cannot tell:
But Custom has so far prevailed to have none other but *Doctors of Civil
Law in one of our own Universities* admitted into the number of *Advocates*
in that Society, that, tho' all of them come in by the Favour of *the
Archbishop*, and are in a peculiar manner dependent upon him, yet when
a Person had a Title given him to be of their Number by a *Faculty for a
Doctor's Degree* from *Archbishop Sancroft*, 'tis very well known how that
Matter was resented, tho he had also before taken the same Degree
in a *Foreign University*. But this is a Matter so fresh in Memory, that I
shall make no particular Observations upon it.

From what hath been hitherto said upon this Subject, it seems pretty
evident to me, that there is nothing at all to be met with in any of our
Laws,

(44)

Laws, Canons, or *Histories,* or indeed in any *MS.* or *printed Book* whatever, (before *Bishop Gibson* publish'd his *Codex*) that *proves, favours,* or so much as barely *mentions,* the *Archbishop's Power of conferring Degrees.*

I shall now shew from the *Form of the Faculty* it self, that the founding this Power upon 25 *Hen.* VIII. Cap. 21. seems to be ill warranted.

For in the first place, (not to mention a very extraordinary *Preamble,* where *the Custom of giving Degrees in Schools* is alledged as a Pretence for giving Degrees *out of Schools,* that is, without any regard had to *Standing,* or *Exercise*) when it is said —— *Antecessorum nostrorum exempla imitati,* it is obvious to remark, that this part of the Form must have been contrived long after the said Act was made; because the *two first Archbishops* that lived after the Act, had this been the *sole* ground of their Power, could not with any Propriety of Speech have used this Expression in their Faculties. And, should any such Faculty for a Degree be found during all the time that *Cranmer* and *Parker* continued in the See of *Canterbury,* we must conclude, that the Power, by which it was granted, was built upon some other Foundation than this Act. (I take no notice of *Cardinal Poole,* who came between them, because all the while he was *Archbishop* the Act stood repealed.) Neither can I see of what Service it could be to any of the *succeeding Archbishops* to cite *the Example of their Predecessors* in their Faculties, when the Practice of former Archbishops in this Case can be no Proof, or Corroboration, of their Power who claim under *an Act of Parliament.* Nor can any tolerable Reason be given why they should use this Expression in their *Faculties for Degrees,* which is not to be found in any *other Faculties* or *Dispensations* granted by any Archbishop *by Virtue of the same Act.*

The next thing I shall observe in the *present Form* of the Archbishop's Faculty is, that, after it is said that the Archbishops of *Canterbury,* (*publicâ Legum Authoritate muniti*) do enjoy, and have long enjoyed this Power of conferring Degrees; to make good what is affirmed in this Parenthesis, it is added in another (*prout ex Libro Authentico de Taxandis Facultatibus Parliamenti autoritate confirmato plenius apparet.*) But, if the Power here claim'd were certainly derived from 25 *Hen.* VIII. what need would there be of inserting this Clause to prove it; which (as was just before observed with relation to another Clause) was never made use of by the Archbishop in any *other Faculty* that this Statute empowers him to grant? The best account that can be given of this is, that it was added some time after the Act, when *the Right* of giving Degrees was *questioned,* or at least thought *disputable:* But it does not seem to be properly inserted at all; for, had 25 *H.* VIII. been here particularly meant, it should rather have been expressed thus (*viz.*) *prout ex Statuto* 25 *Hen.* VIII. *& Libro Taxationis per dictum Statutum confirmato plenius apparet.* However, not to insist upon this, it may be farther enquired, why the Words *plenius apparet* should be referred to a *Tax-Book,* which is said to be *authentick,* and *confirmed by the Authority of Parliament;* when the Book now extant, and manifestly intended in the Faculty carries no appearance of such Authority with it, as I have shewn before at large? And why all this reasoning and arguing in an *Instrument,* when *the Authority* upon which it is granted ought to be *plain* and *positive,* according to the usual Style of all *legal Grants* whatever?

Another thing very fit to be observed upon this Subject is, that (as far as we can judge by the Entry in 1544.) *the present Form* is entirely
ly

(45)

ly of a different Caſt from that which was *then* uſed. For, beſides that *this* is drawn up in the Style of a *Creation*, and not a *Diſpenſation*, as *the other* was, that whole Clauſe concerning *Privileges*, *Preeminences*, *and Prerogatives*, which is found in the *old Form*, is left out in all the *later* ones: From whence it may be fairly concluded, that thoſe Archbiſhops, who have *ſince the Reformation* beſtowed Degrees by Faculty, intended to give only *Titles of Honour*, and not *Qualifications for Preferment*; for *capacitating a Man for a Benefice*, is a *ſpecial Favour*, and ſuch as (if it could be granted by the Archbiſhop) is not to be *underſtood*, unleſs it be *expreſſed*, (as it always was in every Inſtrument granted to ſuch purpoſe, by *the Pope*, or *thoſe commiſſioned by him*) and therefore, when all Expreſſions tending to *qualify*, or *capacitate* a Man for any *Benefice*, or *Office*, were left out in the *Proteſtant* Faculties, it could be done for no other Reaſon but to prevent any Umbrage that might be taken by *the Univerſities* upon that account, as if *the Archbiſhop's Graduates* were entituled to the ſame Rank, and to all the ſame Privileges, as *Univerſity Graduates* are.

From theſe Remarks upon *the Form* in which *the Archbiſhop's Faculty* for Degrees is drawn, I am naturally led to make this *General* Obſervation; (*viz.*) that the great Liberty which hath been taken by *Archbiſhops* in changing the Form ſhews, that the Foundation of their Power is weak and uncertain; and that therefore old Clauſes have been left out, and *new* ones ſometimes added in their Inſtruments, to ſupport it. The juſtneſs of which Concluſion is evidently confirmed by *the ſuperaddition* made by *the preſent Archbiſhop* in Mr. Peplo's *Faculty*; (viz.) *Cumque proviſum ſit per ejuſdem Collegii Statuta——— ut Guardianus ſit ad minus* gradu Baccalaureatûs *in Sacrâ Theologiâ vel Jurium inſignitus———* For *the Archbiſhop's Degrees* were, till *very lately*, looked upon as only *Honorary Titles*, and not *legal Qualifications*; but an opportunity now offering to raiſe the value of them, a new Clauſe was put in, in order to give them a *legal Effect*. And, if the Diſpute which hath happened thereupon doth not prevent it, this Clauſe will in all probability be conſtantly inſerted, upon the like Occaſions for the future, and ſo will come in time to be accounted as neceſſary a part of the Form as any of the other now uſed; ſome of which muſt be allow'd to have a much later Original than that Act of Parliament which is the ſuppoſed Foundation of the whole.

There is one Obſervation more which I think proper to be added in this place, *viz.* That as the Archbiſhops have *varied* their *Forms*, and built their *Power of giving Degrees* upon *different Foundations*; ſo have they been always ſhy of *claiming* ſuch a Power in any *publick* manner, or of *exerciſing* it where there might be the leaſt likelyhood of a *Diſpute*.

Now, if we ſuppoſe the *Cuſtom of giving Degrees by Faculty* to have conſtantly obtained ever ſince 25 *Hen.* VIII. this Obſervation will hold of *all the Archbiſhops before the Reſtauration*; becauſe no notice at all is taken of the *Archbiſhops Degrees* in any *Canons*, *Articles of Viſitation*, *Injunctions to the Clergy*, *Orders about the increaſe of Learning*, and *Preferment of Learned Men*, *Letters requiring an Account of the Character*, *Degree*, *and Condition of Preachers*, &c. in all which there was frequent occaſion to mention *Degrees*. Nor has that diligent Writer of the *Lives of Archbiſhops*, Mr. *Strype*, found any thing among their

N

Papers

(46)

Papers that gave him the least intimation of their *Claim to confer De-grees.*

But ever *since the Restauration,* when it is known that *every Archbishop has given Degrees by Faculty,* not one of them hath taken the least no-tice of his *Right* so to do any *other* way than by his *Instruments.*

Juxon had a fair occasion offered him to drop somewhat in Favour of his *Faculties* in his *Articles of Visitation;* but in his enquiry concerning *Degrees,* he hath regard only to those taken *in the University.*

Sheldon, in his Letter to *the Archbishop* of Guesna in Poland, gives an Account of *all the Privileges and Prerogatives* belonging to the See of *Canterbury;* but says nothing of his *Power of conferring Degrees,* which *that Archbishop* would have been pleased to know as well as the other, since it was in his *Grant* to enjoy all that the *See of Canterbury* ever did.

When *Sancroft,* about half a Year after King *James* came to the Crown, perceived what Measures were taking, he never ventured *to give a Degree* during the rest of that Reign; and, had a *Degree conferred by his Faculty before,* been pleaded, as a *Qualification* for *the Wardenship of Manchester* at that time, I don't doubt but *the Archbishop* would have disclaim'd it, and *a Bishop of Chester* would certainly have been justify'd *in Law* for not admitting it. In which Opinion I am very much con-firmed by what past the latter end of that Reign, with relation to Mr. *Lowth,* who (as I have been credibly informed) applied to *Sancroft* for *a Doctor's Degree* in order to qualify him for the *Deanry of Rochester;* but was refused. Whether the Fact were exactly so or not, I cannot be positive; but what the Archbishop thought of this Matter, will plainly appear from the following Letter to Dr. *Covell Vice-Chancellor* of *Cambridge,* the Original of which I have by me.

Mr. Vice-Chancellor,

Mr. Simon Lowth *Master of Arts in* Clare-Hall, *of 28 Years stand-ing, is appointed by his Majesty, Dean of the Cathedral Church of* Rochester, *but the Statutes of the said Church, require him to be either Doctor of Divinity, Batchelor of Divinity, or a Doctor of Laws, wherefore I desire you (it being also the Desire of his Diocesan) that you would grant to him the Degree of Do-ctor of Laws, that he may be* qualified *to enjoy this his Majesty's Favour, and you will hereby oblige*

Nov. 17. 1685.   *Your affectionate Friend*
Lambhith-House.

                                                            W. Cant.

Had the Archbishop been truly persuaded that *his Degree was a legal Qualification,* he would readily have granted it to Mr. *Lowth,* for whom he had a particular Friendship. And it would have been a singular Kindness to him at that Juncture; because, by the delay of taking it at *Cambridge* (where he went out Doctor of Divinity, *Jan.* 18.) he lost the Deanry in-tended him. But there was no such Doctrine stirring at that time.

The late Archbishop *Tennison,* upon great importunity, (which he often complained of) gave *many Degrees by Faculty;* but when he was pres-sed in some Instances to grant them, where they might be made use of as *Qualifications,* he utterly refused; because (as he said upon this Occasion)

it

(47)

it would make a Noise. Nay, I am well affured that, upon a certain Occafion, where he was asked to give a Degree, and was very well difpofed
towards the Perfon for whom that Favour was defired, he was pleafed,
after fome time of Confideration, to exprefs himfelf to this effect, *viz.*
" That the more he thought of it, the more he was confirmed in his
" Opinion of the *Invalidity* of *his* Degree as to its being any *Qualifica-*
" *tion* ; that, if it were made ufe of in that cafe, it would be difputed
" by the *Univerfity*, and might come to be queftioned at Common-
" Law, and decided againft as an infignificant thing, and fo be made
" contemptible for the future ; which was a Confequence that he would
" avoid.

All that now remains for compleating the Argument concerning Degrees granted by the Archbifhop is, to confider two Cafes, in which it
is *lately* pretended that the Archbifhop's Degrees have been admitted as
legal Qualifications ; (viz.) where certain Degrees are required *for holding
Dignities in Cathedrals,* by *Local Statutes* ; and *for exercifing Ecclefiaftical
Jurifdiction,* by *the Canons of the Church.*

As to the *firft* Cafe ; I know of no *Cathedrals,* where Perfons are fuppofed to hold their Dignities by virtue of *the Archbifhop's Degrees,* but
fuch as were erected by *Hen.* VIII. and it is generally acknowledged,
that none of *the Statutes* given to thefe Churches are *in force.*

But, however that be, this is certain, that in moft, if not every one,
of them, feveral have enjoyed their Dignities without having *thofe
Degrees,* which *the Statutes of their Church* required they fhould have,
either from the *Univerfity,* or *by Faculty* : And therefore, if a Man may
be *a Dean,* or *a Prebendary* of one of thefe Churches, where the Statutes fay, he ought to be *a Batchelor of Divinity* at the leaft, when he
is only *a Mafter of Arts,* (as many fuch there have been, and as feveral
there now are) it makes nothing at all for *the Archbifhop's Degrees,* that
fome of thefe Dignitaries have been created *Doctors,* or *Batchelors of
Divinity* by *Faculty,* when, by all that yet appears, they had been as
well qualified to hold their Preferments *without* thefe Titles, as they are
with them.

It may be obferved farther upon this Head ; that no *Faculty* was ever
granted to any of thefe *Dignitaries* with any Claufe inferted in it to render it a *Qualification* ; that moft, if not all *the Archbifhop's Graduates,*
who have been preferred in thefe Churches, had their Degrees given
them fome time *before* they were preferred, and without any *defign of qua-
lifying* them thereby for fuch Preferment ; and that the Perfons by whom
they were admitted into their Dignities feldom *knew,* or *confidered,* how
they came by their Degrees ; and, if they did, they might think they had
no reafon to take notice of it, nor any concern to refufe them, as not
looking upon *any Degrees* to be neceffary to their *Admiffion,* however
the *Perfons admitted* might be liable to the Cenfures of their *Vifitors* afterwards for not complying with the Statutes of their Founder.

But in the prefent Difpute about *Manchefter College,* I take the Matter in queftion to be of a very different Nature. For *the Warden* of
the College is required to be a *Batchelor of Divinity at leaft* ; not by
any *Statute fubfequent to the Foundation,* but by the *Charter of Foundation* itfelf, and by the firft *incorporating Claufe* in it, which conftitutes
the

(48)

the Body, in such a manner, that neither *the Warden*, nor *Fellows*, can have any Title to their Places, unless they have the Degrees there specified *before they are admitted*: And there is no manner of doubt concerning *the Validity* of this Charter. Then the Person nominated to be Warden tenders *the Bishop* (by whom the Charter directs that he should be *instituted*) *a Faculty from the Archbishop* for the Degree of Batchelor of Divinity, together with his *Majesty's Patent* for the Wardenship: And this Faculty is granted with an *express design to qualify* him for this Preferment; (as the Words here added to the old Form plainly import) so that the Bishop could not help taking notice of this Faculty; and he could not institute upon it, without allowing a Degree given by *the Archbishop* to be of *the same Force and Validity* with the like Degree taken in *the University*; and without owning that the former comes as truly within *the meaning of the Charter* as the latter; neither of which he could possibly grant without being false to his own Judgment, as well as to *the Privileges of the University*, which he hath sworn to maintain.

To the other Case which concerns *Ecclesiastical Officers*, who are required by a *Canon* made *Anno* 1603. to be at least *Masters of Art*, or *Batchelors of Law*, several Answers may be given, all of them, I think, sufficient to shew, that Degrees conferred upon such Persons by the Archbishop are no *legal Qualifications*.

In the first place then I say; 'tis very plain from *other Canons* made *at the same time*, where Degrees are mention'd, that *University Degrees* are either *expressly named*, or *evidently meant*; and therefore it must be supposed that *University Degrees* are *intended here* also, tho' not particularly expressed.

It does likewise appear from *Canons* established by *former Convocations*, (from whence these are mostly transcribed) from *a Statute* made 37 *Hen.* VIII. and from *Bills depending in Parliament* in the Reigns of *Edw.* VI. and Queen *Eliz* (all of them before-cited) that it was the *constant Meaning* and Design both of *Parliament* and *Convocation*, that the Persons chiefly concerned *in the Administration of Ecclesiastical Laws* should be *Graduates in the University*: In Conformity to which the *Canons of* 1603 ought to be interpreted.

If *the Decree of the Synod* convened under *Archbishop Chichley* An. 1430, which is mentioned in *A. B. Parker's Antiquities*, (*v. supra* p. 14.) be allowed to be a *regular Act*, (as there is good Reason to affirm it is) then is it certainly unlawful for any Person, at this time, to exercise Ecclesiastical Jurisdiction, unless he hath taken *some Degree*, either *at Oxford, or Cambridge*; because by 25 *Hen.* VIII. Cap. 19. *All Canons, Constitutions, and Ordinances of Provincial Synods, made before this Act, and not repugnant to the Laws of the Realm, or the King's Prerogative, are confirmed by this Act*. But, whether any *Canons*, made *since* this Act, and not confirmed by any other, will be allowed to affect *Property*, so as to take away any *Right, Title*, or *Interest*, which a Man was duely qualified by *the Laws of the Realm* to enjoy *before* such *Canons* were made, I will not pretend to determine.

This however I am sure of, that, if the *want of such a Degree* in an Ecclesiastical Officer as *the Canons* require, be not any *legal Ground to*
void

(49)

void his Patent, then an *Archbishop's Degree* can never be reckoned a *Qualification* for holding an Office, where the Poſſeſſion might
be as well ſecured *without any Degree* at all. But ſhould the Patent
be adjudged void at *Common Law* upon this Account, It would, I am
confident, be at the ſame time adjudged, that the Degrees mentioned
in the Canon muſt be underſtood to be *Univerſity Degrees*, there being
no other *legal* Notion of Degrees when thoſe Canons were made, and
no Inſtance I believe to be produc'd ſince, till *after the Reſtauration*, (I may ſay till *after the Revolution*) of any Eccleſiaſtical Officer,
who was not a *Graduate of ſome Univerſity*, if he had *any Degree* at
all.

There is another general Anſwer that may be given to all the Inſtances that can be brought under both the forementioned Heads, which
is this; that no *Judgment* having yet been given in favour *of the
Archbiſhop's Degrees*, no expreſs *Allowance* of them upon any Diſpute,
nor indeed any *Diſpute* raiſed about them, theſe may have been true
Blots, though never yet hit; as ſome Perſons have enjoyed, and ſome
Perſons may at preſent enjoy *Pluralities*, without any other Qualification than *the Archbiſhop's Degree*, tho' the Statute 21 *Hen*. VIII. directly, and in plain Terms, ſays, that no other Degree ſhall qualify for
a Diſpenſation in that Caſe, but what is taken *in the Univerſity, and
without Grace*. Which Statute hath been very ſtrictly and worthily obſerved by *the preſent Archbiſhop*.

To conclude this Argument; whatever *the Ground*, or *the Anti-
quity*, of *the Archbiſhop's Claim* to a Power of conferring Degrees may
be, no pretence to *qualify* Perſons for any Preferment by ſuch Degrees was ever, that I can hear of, ſet up *before the Revolution*; at
which time there was hardly a *Lawyer* in the Kingdom, and but very
few of *the Clergy* that had ever heard of this extraordinary Prerogative of the Archbiſhop. And, though Degrees have been diſtributed
ſince very frequently, little Notice hath been taken of them, and little Regard hath been ſhewn to them, by any others, but what were
concerned in the beſtowing, or receiving them. Of thoſe few, who
have made any Enquiries about them, ſome have been of Opinion,
that it was part of the ancient Ceremony at the *Inſtallation of an Archbiſhop*, for his Grace at that time to create *a Doctor* or *Maſter* in each
Faculty: Others, taking the Archbiſhop to have ſome *Papal*, or *Legantine* Prerogatives ſtill belonging to him, have ſuppoſed, that he had
a Power of giving Degrees to his *Domeſticks* and *Dependents*, ſuch as
are, in the Canon Law, ſtyled *Familiares*. But a *general unlimited
Power*, derived from *Act of Parliament*, to confer Degrees of *all kinds*,
at *all times*, to *any Perſon* whatever, was never heard or thought of,
even by thoſe who attended upon Archbiſhops in their Families, before *Biſhop Gibſon* publiſhed his *Codex*: and, if the Plea will hold in
the manner there urged, then may the Archbiſhop make *Serjeants* and
Barriſters as well as *Doctors* and *Maſters*: For thoſe are called *Degrees in Learning* in many Acts of Parliament as well as the other; And
the *Creatio aliorum Graduatorum in quacunque Facultate* mentioned in
the Tax Book, is equally applicable to all manner of Degrees beſides
Doctors, whether they are taken in *the Inns of Court*, or *in the Schools*.
And then, by adding *Exempla Anteceſſorum* to the Authority of Parlia-

O   ment,

(50)

ment, he may make *Knights* also, as *Archbishop Lanfrank* did, and other Archbishops, both before, and after him, probably might; and as *the Pope hath long used and accustomed to do.*

Burnet Hist.
Reg. part 2.
App. p. 272.
And, that this is no extravagant Supposition, will appear from *the Bull* which constitutes *Cardinal Beaton Legate à Latere* in *Scotland*, An. 1543. whereby he is empowered to make *Knights*, *Counts Palatine*, and *Poets Laureat*, as well as *Doctors*, and *other Graduates*. And *there*
Part 2. B. 2.
p. 292.
is no doubt (says *Bishop Burnet*) but *Cardinal Pool's Bull was in the same Form*; it being very reasonable to suppose, that the same Powers were granted to *every Legate*, *viz*. all that belonged to *the Pope himself* whose *Vicar* he was.

Upon the whole then it were to be wished, that the following Questions were, upon a due and careful Examination, resolv'd, (*viz.*)

1. Whether *the Statute* of 25 *Hen*. VIII. Cap. 21. has given *the Archbishop of Canterbury* for the time being *a Power of conferring Degrees of all kinds*?

2. Whether the *Tax-Books*, directed by that Statute to be drawn up, if they had been made according to the Direction there given, would have been *good and effectual in Law*, without any express Declaration in the said Act, that they should be so taken and accounted; and without any subsequent Act to confirm them?

3. If it be supposed that these Tax-Books, when made as the Act directs, would have been of the same Authority as the Act it self; whether, when no such Tax-Books can be produced, and no legal Proof can be given that any such Books were ever made, it may not fairly be pleaded, *Nul tiel Record*?

4. If any *authentick Tax-Book* be now extant; whether every Faculty for a Degree granted by the Archbishop which is there rated at 4*l.* ought not to be *confirmed under the Broad Seal*, and inrolled in Chancery?

5. Whether, if the Archbishop had constantly exercised this Power of conferring Degrees ever since the Date of the said Act, such Degrees would be esteemed *due Qualifications in Law*, where Degrees were required to qualify Persons for any Dignity, Benefice, or Preferment, by *Act of Parliament*, *Canon of the Synod*, *Royal Charter*, or *Local Statute*?

6. Whether it can be made to appear, by *the Judgment of any Court*, *Opinion of any Lawyer*, or *History of the Fact*, that the Framers of any *Act*, *Canon*, *Charter*, or other legal Instrument whatever, when they mention *Degrees*, did, or could, mean any *other* Degrees, but what were taken in *some University*?

7. Whether *any Instance* can be shewn, where an Archbishop did confer a Degree by Faculty, from *the Revivour of the Act* before mentioned to the time when *the Charter of Manchester-College* was granted?

8. Supposing Degrees were conferred during that time, whether any Archbishop, by whom they were conferred, did look upon them as *legal Qualifications*, and made use of his Power to that special End and Purpose.

9. Whether

(51)

9. Whether any *Custom* that has *lately* obtained, and of which no certain Footsteps are to be found for near a hundred Years together, since the making of the Act, can be sufficient to establish a Claim, which hath no *other* Foundation but a *Tax-Book*, said, without any Proof, to be confirmed by Authority of Parliament?

As to *the Pope's power of conferring Degrees*, from whence *the Archbishop's* is derived; it is the Opinion of some eminent Canonists, that this Power extended no farther than *the Patrimony of St. Peter*.

Then it is certain, that several *Decrees* and Orders have been made by *Popes*, and *Councils* call'd by *Popes*, in favour of *University Degrees*, and never any, (that I have heard of) which put the Degrees given by *the Pope's Authority alone* upon the same Foot with those that were taken in *some University*.

But, whatever the *Pope's* Power in this respect was, it was never *submitted to*, or acknowledged, or (as far as I can learn) ever *exercised*, or pretended to, here in *England*; much less called in to support any Pretensions to Ecclesiastical Preferment before 25 *Hen.*VIII. On the contrary, what was decreed in Parliament in *Hen.* IV's time concerning the University of *Oxford*, viz. " That *the Pope's Bull* should not impeach, " or alter *the Right*, or *Custom*, of any thing concerning *that University*; this I take to have been *always* the Law with relation to *both Universities*. ^{Rot. Parl.13. Hen. IV. n. 15, 16, 17. Cook's Inst. Part 4. p. 228.}

The only Questions then, which arise from hence, relating to the Case before us, are,

1. Whether a *Faculty for a Degree* be one of those Faculties or Dispensations, which were *wont and accustomed to be had at the See of Rome*, or by Authority thereof, *before* the making of the aforesaid Statute?

2. Whether a Degree given by *the Pope*, or by any *Authority of the See of Rome*, was taken and reputed here in *England*, as a *good and effectual Qualification in Law* for any Ecclesiastical Dignity or Benefice, which *Graduates only* were capable of, *before the Reformation* took place?

Which way all these Questions ought to be determined, I will not take upon me to say: But, from what has been offered upon the whole Subject, I may venture to conclude; that *Degrees conferred by* the Archbishop of Canterbury, (whatever respect they may claim upon account of his Grace's favour in granting them) *cannot be accepted and admitted to be good and effectual in Law, and as beneficial to the Persons obtaining the same, as the like Degrees would be, if taken in one of our* Universities.

For these Things may now be affirmed with some Assurance: *viz.* That *many Extraordinary Privileges and Favours* have been granted by *Popes*, *Princes*, and *General Councils abroad*, and by *Kings*, *Parliaments*, and *Convocations in England*, to *University-Graduates, exclusive* of all other. E. G. *Pluralities*, *Unions*, all manner of *Ecclesiastical Dignities and Benefices*, *exercise of Ecclesiastical Jurisdiction*, *admission to Orders*, *liberty to practise Physick*, *distinction of Apparel*, both in *the Performance of Divine Service*, and in *common Habit*; &c.

That

(52)

That thefe peculiar Favours have been granted by a *great number*, and *variety* of *publick Acts*, made at *different times*, during the Space of three hundred Years; without the leaft *faving*, or *mention*, in any of them, of any *other Degrees* but fuch as were taken in *fome Univerfity*;

And that there never was any *publick Act*, *Decree*, *Order*, or *Rule* made, by *the Authority* either of *Church*, or *State*, in any *Kingdom, Popifh*, or *Proteftant*, which gave the leaft *Favour*, or *Countenance*, to *Degrees* conferred *any other way* than by *Univerfities*.

It is therefore humbly *hoped*, that an *old Popifh abufe*, long fince exploded, and banifh'd from *other Parts of Europe*, will not now be adjudged a *convenient and neceffary practice* here in *England*, *warranted by the Laws of this Realm*, and *a part of our Reformed Conftitution*.

F I N I S.

3 Principal manuscript holdings relating to Lambeth degrees in British archives

William Gibson

Lambeth Palace Library, Archbishops of Canterbury Archives, Archbishops' Papers

Faculty papers

Lambeth MS.1133 gives the names of two clergy granted degrees by the Pope in 1492 and 1497.
Ref: FVI.

Register of Lambeth degrees 01 March 1883–31 January 1905.
Ref: FVI/1/1.

Registers of Lambeth degrees
These are small volumes in which are entered the names of the sponsors of the grantee, the work for which the degree was given. 1883–1874
Ref: FVI/1.

Register of Lambeth degrees 1905–1931.
Ref: FVI/1/2.

Register of Lambeth degrees 01 December 1931–30 September 1951.
Ref: FVI/1/3.

Register of Lambeth degrees 1953–1974.
Ref: FVI/1/4.

Printed form of service for the conferment of Lambeth degrees.
Ref: FVI/2/9.

Letters found in the 'Folly'. Letters, re: Lambeth degrees.
Ref: AA/F/6/3/1.

Precedent Book II.
Papers relating to the procedure and forms to be adopted in the application for,... Contains papers relating to dispensations to hold in plurality (pp.541–731), Lambeth degrees (pp.735–775), commendams (pp.78–791), public notaries (pp.797–1093), chaplains (pp.1119–1125), commissions.
Ref: FVII/1/2.

Papers relating to the procedure and forms to be adopted in the application for, ...Consisting of (a) forms of commissions for various degrees: 3 items, (b) form of oath for taking a degree and form of affirmation for a Quaker, (c) forms of faculties for the degrees of M.A., D.D.
Ref: FVII/1/7.

Lambeth degrees. Miscellaneous papers. List of degrees, 1870–1883.
Ref: FVI/2/7.

Lambeth degrees. Miscellaneous papers. List of degrees 1783–1793.
Ref: FVI/2/5.

Lambeth degrees. Miscellaneous papers. List of degrees, 1869–1882.
Ref: FVI/2/6.

Lambeth degrees. Correspondence concerning degrees, filed in the Faculty Office. Correspondence.
Ref: AA/F/6/4/1.

Lambeth degrees. Miscellaneous papers. Photocopy of typescript list of degrees, 1947–1970.
Ref: FVI/2/7a.

Question papers for Lambeth M.A.s
Incomplete series. 1885–1902.
Ref: FVI/2/8.

Act Books. Pluralities, and Lambeth degrees licences for non-residence until 1677, royal and special marriage licences until 1750, bishops' appointments and commendams, and *sede vacante* instruments.
Ref: AA/V/B/1.

Lambeth degrees. Miscellaneous papers.
Ref: FVI/2.

Lambeth degrees. Papers relating to contested or abandoned applications. 1832–1862.
Ref: FVI/5.

Summary of sources and information for the early history of the degrees drawn up for Archbishop Benson by S. W. Kershaw in 1883.
1844.
Ref: FVI/2/2.

Stubbs' article with manuscript lists of degrees, 1539–1635 and 1869–78, and M.D.s granted, 1663–1880.
Ref: FVI/2/4.

Correspondence concerning Lambeth degrees. These letters relate to procedure rather than academic qualifications.
Ref: FVI/4.

Pamphlet by Bishop Stubbs on the early history of the degrees, with a list of degrees granted, 1539–1848, from the Gentleman's Magazine (May and June 1844), and a MS. list of degrees 1848–71.
Ref: FVI/2/1.

Details of the procedure for issuing the faculty after the oath of allegiance has been taken.
Ref: FVI/2/3.

Papers relating to an application for fees to be reduced for a Lambeth degree granted in the colonies. 1841.
Ref: FVII/3/7.

Lambeth degrees. Papers relating to contested or abandoned applications. Contested/abandoned applications: general papers, 1832–1862.
Ref: AA/F/6/5/1-7.

Letters found in the 'Folly'.
Lambeth degrees. Letters relating to applications for Lambeth degrees, mainly M.A.s, some addressed to Dr. Henry Wace, Principal of King's College London, and probably Archbishop's examining chaplain.
Ref: FVI/3.

Miscellaneous Papers of Henry Wace, Professor of Ecclesiastical History, King's College, London (later Dean of Canterbury), concerning Lambeth degrees. It includes correspondence with Archbishop Benson, 1888–99.
Ref: MS 3120 (ff. 136–65).

Miscellaneous letters and papers
Manuscripts. GIBSON PAPERS. List of Lambeth degrees given by the Archbishop.
Ref: MS 1742.

FIATS

Warrants for Lambeth degrees while the Faculty Office draws up and seals the grant. The largest group of fiats not signed by the Archbishop are those for licences for public notaries.
Ref: FII.

CORRESPONDENCE REGARDING LAMBETH DEGREES FOR COLONIAL CLERGY

Correspondence and papers on degrees for colonial clergy, 1882.
Ref: Tait 281 ff. 40–1.

Correspondence and papers on degrees for colonial clergy, 1874.
Ref: Tait 196 ff. 275–9, 463–4.

Correspondence and papers on degrees for colonial clergy, 1876.
Ref: Tait 226 ff. 89–92, 141–4.

Correspondence and papers on degrees for colonial clergy, 1879.
Ref: Tait 246 ff. 363–70.

Recommended for a Lambeth degree
BRETT (William Henry), Rector of Holy Trinity, British Guiana, by AUSTIN (William Piercy), Bishop of British Guiana; WYATT (Francis James), Archdeacon of Demerara, British Guiana 1878.
Ref: Tait 237 ff. 259–60.

Lambeth degrees – Correspondence and papers on degrees for colonial clergy CHALMERS (William), Bishop of Goulburn (1892) – Correspondence and papers on his application for a Lambeth degree. 1877.
Ref: Tait 228 ff. 290–6.

Letters on a Lambeth degree for LIGHTFOOT (Thomas Fothergill), S.P.G. missionary, South Africa, 1879.
Ref: Tait 249 ff. 234–7.

QUAKER (Rev. James), Principal of Freetown Graimar School, Sierra Leone Recommended for a Lambeth degree; correspondence on Lambeth degrees for colonial clergy, 1881.
Ref: Tait 273 ff. 35–8.

BLUNDUN (Rev. Thomas), Principal of the Collegiate School, Victoria, British Columbia
Application for a Lambeth degree; correspondence on Lambeth degrees for colonial clergy, 1876.
Ref: Tait 225 ff. 59–60.

TEMPLE (Robert), S.P.G. missionary, Newfoundland
Application for a Lambeth degree; correspondence on Lambeth degrees for colonial clergy, 1880.
Ref: Tait 263 ff. 300–1.

KIRKBY (William West), Archdeacon of York, Manitoba
Recommended for a Lambeth degree; correspondence on Lambeth degrees for colonial clergy 1877.
Ref: Tait 234 ff. 292–3.

GRISDALE (John), Bishop of Qu'Appelle (1896)
Recommended for a Lambeth degree; correspondence on Lambeth degrees for colonial clergy 1875.
Ref: Tait 208 f. 168.

GRISDALE (John), Bishop of Qu'Appelle (1896)
Recommended for a Lambeth degree; correspondence and papers on Lambeth degrees for colonial clergy, 1875.
Ref: Tait 214 ff. 368–9, 395–6.

SMITH (George), S.P.G. missionary, Natal
Recommended for a Lambeth degree; correspondence and papers on Lambeth degrees for colonial clergy, 1879.
Ref: Tait 253 ff. 245–6.

COWIE (William Garden), Bishop of Auckland
Correspondence on applicants for Lambeth degrees and a visit to the diocese by missionaries from MELANE-SIA, 1876.
Ref: Tait 225 ff. 24–7.

ANDERSON (David), Bishop of Rupert's Land
Letter from on KIRKBY (William West), Archdeacon of York, Manitoba, recommended for a Lambeth degree, 1876.
Ref: Tait 226 ff. 141–4.

GELL (Frederick), Bishop of Madras
Letters from on clergy in his diocese; correspondence on Lambeth degrees for colonial clergy; correspondence on a Lambeth degree for BOWER (Henry), S.P.G. missionary, Madras. 1872.
Ref: Tait 92 ff. 133–4.

PUXLEY (Edward Lavallin), former C.M.S. missionary, India
Letters on providing him with a Lambeth degree; correspondence on Lambeth degrees for colonial clergy, 1875.
Ref: Tait 210 ff. 379–82.

TUCKER (Henry William), Secretary of the SOCIETY FOR THE PROPAGATION OF THE GOSPEL IN FOREIGN…
Recommendation of S.P.G. missionaries for Lambeth degrees; correspondence on individual missionaries; recommendation of KELLY (William Frederick), former chaplain in Ceylon, for a Lambeth degree, 1880.
Ref: Tait 261 f. 1.

TUCKER (Henry William), Secretary of the SOCIETY FOR THE PROPAGATION OF THE GOSPEL IN FOREIGN…
Recommendation of S.P.G. missionaries for Lambeth degrees; correspondence on individual missionaries; recommendation of MARKS (John Ebenezer), S.P.G. missionary, Burma, for a Lambeth degree, 1879.
Ref: Tait 250 ff. 111–12.

COURTENAY (Reginald), Bishop of Kingston, Jamaica
Correspondence on the Church of England in Jamaica; recommendation of CROSKERY (Hugh), Curate of Clarendon, Jamaica, for a Lambeth degree; correspondence on Lambeth degrees for colonial clergy, 1873.
Ref: Tait 195 ff. 39–40.

COWIE (William Garden), Bishop of Auckland
Recommendation of KINDER (Rev. John), Master of St. John's College, Auckland, New Zealand, for a Lambeth degree; correspondence and papers on Lambeth degrees for colonial clergy, 1872.
Ref: Tait 185 ff. 255–259.

CHURCH MISSIONARY SOCIETY: Canada
Letters from on C.M.S. missionaries in Canada and their work among the Indians; correspondence and

papers on Lambeth degrees for colonial clergy [including TOMLINSON (Robert), C.M.S. missionary, 1880.
Ref: Tait 264 ff. 66–7.

FRERE (Sir Henry Bartle Edward), 1st Bart.
15. Recommendation of the Rev. G. P. Badger for a Lambeth degree, 1873.
Ref: Tait 187 ff. 88–90.

MARTIN (Sir William), former Chief Justice of New Zealand
Recommendation of the Rev. J. Kinder for a Lambeth degree, 1872.
Ref: Tait 185 ff. 258–9.

GENERAL CORRESPONDENCE

Correspondence and papers on applicants for medical degrees, 1879.
Ref: Tait 248 ff. 97–102.

Letters on applicants for music degrees, 1879.
Ref: Tait 248 ff. 113–20.

Correspondence and papers on applicants for medical degrees, 1881.
Ref: Tait 271 ff. 184–90.

Papers relating to Lambeth degrees (1861).
Ref: Tait 126 ff 211–18.

Correspondence between Archbishop Temple and the Rev. Louis John Baggott, Vicar of Great Yarmouth, regarding the possibility of his receiving a Lambeth D.D. and the suggestion that he instead apply 30 June 1943 – 05 July 1943.
Ref: W.Temple 32, ff. 106–9.

Correspondence on awarding degrees to Nonconformists and members of the Roman Catholic Church, 1881–2.
Ref: Tait 272 ff. 299–301.

Correspondence regarding an offer of a Lambeth D.D. to Frank Russell Barry, Bishop of Southwell 11 December 1942–03 August 1944.
Ref: W.Temple 32, ff. 89–96.

Correspondence on the awarding of a Lambeth D.D. to Anthony Charles Deane, Canon of Windsor 19 November 1943–20 December 1943.
Ref: W.Temple 32, ff. 97–105.

Letters on the conferment of Lambeth degrees, 1876.
Ref: Tait 219 ff. 59–62.

Correspondence and papers on examinations for Lambeth degrees. 1871.
Ref: Tait 174 ff. 249–73.

Correspondence and papers on examinations for Lambeth degrees.
Ref: Tait 273 ff. 214–38.

Correspondence and papers on examinations for Lambeth degrees, 1876.
Ref: Tait 218 ff. 415–29.

Correspondence and papers on examinations for Lambeth degrees, 1874.
Rcf: Tait 198 ff. 335–61.

Correspondence and papers on examinations for Lambeth degrees, 1872.
Ref: Tait 182 ff. 36a–ff.

Letter and paper on a medical Lambeth degree for ROGERS (James), surgeon, 1880.
Ref: Tait 263 ff. 266–8.

Letters and paper on a Lambeth degree for HILL (Joel Hawkins), Vicar of All Souls, Grosvenor Park, Surrey, 1878.
Ref: Tait 237 ff. 220–34 .

LETT (Francis Neville), chaplain at Rosario, Argentina
Recommended for a Lambeth degree, 1882.
Ref: Tait 290 ff. 446–62.

TAIT (James Hill), assistant chaplain at Pau, France
Application for a Lambeth degree, 1879.
Ref: Tait 254 ff. 35–52.

PLUMPTRE (Edward Hayes), Dean of Wells
Letters from on examinations for Lambeth degrees, 1874.
Ref: Tait 198 ff. 346, 356–7.

BENEDICT (Sir Julius), musician
Letters from on applicants for Lambeth degrees. 1873.
Ref: Tait 191 ff. 136–137.

IRVIN (Thomas), Vicar of Ormesby, Yorks.
Recommended for a Lambeth degree, 1874.
Ref: Tait 198 ff. 283–4.

PLUMPTRE (Edward Hayes), Dean of Wells
Letters from on examinations for Lambeth degrees, 1871.
Ref: Tait 174 ff. 271–3.

LONGHURST (William Henry), organist
Recommended for a Lambeth degree, 1875.
Ref: Tait 209 ff. 196–9.

PIGGOTT (Robert Turtle), Secretary of the Poor Clergy Relief Corporation
Recommended for a Lambeth degree, 1874.
Ref: Tait 199 ff. 275–6.

WATSON (Sir Thomas), 1st Bart.
Letters from on applicants for Lambeth degrees, 1878.
Ref: Tait 237 ff. 30–1.

WATSON (Sir Thomas), 1st Bart.
Letter from on applicants for Lambeth degrees, 1881.
Ref: Tait 271 f. 186.

PURTON (Walter), Rector of Kingston, Kent
Application for a Lambeth degree, 1881.
Ref: Tait 273 ff. 29–34.

LIGHTFOOT (Joseph Barber), Bishop of Durham
Letter from on Lambeth degrees, 1871.
Ref: Tait 174 ff. 249–51.

SPOONER (Rev. William Archibald), Warden of New College, Oxford (1903)
Reports on examinees for Lambeth degrees, 1872.
Ref: Tait 182 ff. 36t, 36aa–bb.

SPOONER (Rev. William Archibald), Warden of New College, Oxford (1903)
Report on examinees for Lambeth degrees, 1874.
Ref: Tait 198 f. 352.

WYSE (John), Curate-in-charge of St. John, March, Cambs.
Application for a Lambeth degree, 1872.
Ref: Tait 184 ff. 374–9.

BOWEN (Croasdaile), incumbent of Riccarton, New Zealand
Recommended for a Lambeth degree, 1874.
Ref: Tait 196 ff. 275–279.

BROWNE (Edward Harold), Bishop of Ely, and (1873) of Winchester
Testimonials for candidates for Lambeth degrees, 1876.
Ref: Tait 218 ff. 418.

BROWNE (Edward Harold), Bishop of Ely, and (1873) of Winchester
Testimonials for candidates for Lambeth degrees, 1872.
Ref: Tait 182 f. 36p.

PLUMPTRE (Edward Hayes), Dean of Wells
Letters from on examinations for Lambeth degrees, 1876.
Ref: Tait 218 ff. 424–5.

LETT (Francis Neville), chaplain at Rosario, Argentina
Recommended for a Lambeth degree, 1882.
Ref: Tait 281 ff. 282–7.

CAUDWELL (Francis), Vicar of St. Matthias, Stoke Newington, Middx.
Application for a Lambeth degree, 1880.
Ref: Tait 259 ff. 30–39.

GOSS (Sir John), composer
Recommends musicians for Lambeth degrees, 1875.
Ref: Tait 209 ff. 196–7.

PAYNE (Joseph Francis), Fellow of Magdalen College, Oxford
Letters from on examinations for Lambeth degrees, 1874.
Ref: Tait 198 ff. 348–51, 358–9.

PAYNE (Joseph Francis), Fellow of Magdalen College, Oxford
Letters from on examinations for Lambeth degrees, 1876.
Ref: Tait 218 ff. 426–7.

BURT (Frederick), chaplain in Ontario
Application for a Lambeth degree, 1874.
Ref: Tait 196 ff. 463–4.

DEANE (James Parker), Vicar-General of the Archbishop of Canterbury; Kt. (1885)
Letter from on Lambeth degrees, 1876.
Ref: Tait 219 ff. 61–62.

BROOKES (William), chaplain at Hyeres, France
Letter from on his Lambeth degree, 1880.
Ref: Tait 258 ff. 257–262.

JONA (Rev. Henry), Secretary of the Friends of the Clergy Corporation
Application for a Lambeth degree, 1879.
Ref: Tait 249 ff. 58–9.

VERRINDER (Charles Garland), composer and organist
Letters from on his receiving a Lambeth degree; correspondence on applicants for Lambeth degrees in music, 1873.
Ref: Tait 193 ff. 287–92.

DRUITT (Robert), M.D.
Application for a Lambeth degree; correspondence and papers on applicants for medical Lambeth degrees, 1878.
Ref: Tait 237 ff. 26–33.

MACFARLANE (Duncan), Principal of Glasgow University
Letter from on medical degrees. 1833.
Ref: Tait 76 ff. 82–3.

EALES (Samuel John), Principal of St. Boniface Missionary College, Warminster, Wilts.
Letters from and on his applications for a Lambeth degree, 1871.
Ref: Tait 174 ff. 249–251, 254–255, 258.

EALES (Samuel John), Principal of St. Boniface Missionary College, Warminster, Wilts.
Letters from and on his applications for a Lambeth degree, 1881.
Ref: Tait 270 ff. 151–165.

MOORE (George), merchant and philanthropist
Recommendation of SIMPSON (James), Vicar of Kirkby Stephen, Westminster, for a Lambeth degree, 1872.
Ref: Tait 183 ff. 243–8.

BENEDICT (Sir Julius), musician, ELVEY (Sir George Job), composer, and GOSS (Sir John), composer
Letters to C.G. Verrinder on his application for a Lambeth degree (copies), 1873.
Ref: Tait 193 f. 289.

COPELAND (George Dale), Vicar of St. Stephen, Walworth Common, Surrey
Letter on his application for a Lambeth degree, 1876.
Ref: Tait 216 ff. 379–80.

CHRISTIE (James), minister of Turriff, Aberdeens.
Letters from and on his application for a Lambeth degree, 1875.
Ref: Tait 207 ff. 140–149.

SPOONER (Henry Maxwell), Vicar of Boughton under Blean, Kent; nephew of Mrs. A.C. Tait
Letters and papers from on examinations for Lambeth degrees, 1881.
Ref: Tait 273 ff. 230–1.

SPOONER (Henry Maxwell), Vicar of Boughton under Blean, Kent; nephew of Mrs. A.C. Tait
Letters and papers from on examinations for Lambeth degrees, 1873.
Ref: Tait 191 ff. 92–6.

MALET (William Wyndham), Vicar of Ardeley, Herts.
Letters from and on his application for a Lambeth degree, 1879.
Ref: Tait 250 ff. 45–8.

MALET (William Wyndham), Vicar of Ardeley, Herts.
excluding 162. Letters from and on his application for a Lambeth degree, 1878.
Ref: Tait 238 ff. 203–12.

VAUGHAN (Charles John), Dean of Llandaff
Recommendation of HOPKINS (Edward John), organist, for a Lambeth Degree; correspondence on applicants for Lambeth degrees in music, 1882.
Ref: Tait 281 ff. 128–33.

CRAWLEY (Samuel), Headmaster of Masham Grammar School, Yorks.
Letters and papers on his examination for a Lambeth degree, 1872.
Ref: Tait 182 ff. 36a–36j, 36aa–36bb, 36ee–36ff.

PAPILLON (Rev. Thomas Leslie), Fellow of New College, Oxford
Letter from on examining candidates for Lambeth degrees, 1872.
Ref: Tait 182 ff. 36cc–dd.

WHITWELL (John), M.P.
Recommendation of the Rev. J. Simpson for a Lambeth degree, 1872.
Ref: Tait 183 ff. 245–8.

SIMPSON (James), Vicar of Kirkby Stephen, Westm.
Letters from and on his receiving a Lambeth degree.
Ref: Tait 90 ff. 123–4.

HOBBS (C.P.), curate of St. Luke, Chelsea, Middlesex
Papers relating to Lambeth degrees (printed) (not registered in Letter Register: Tait 294). 1860.
Ref: Tait 118 ff 15–16.

SUMNER (John Bird), Archbishop of Canterbury
Letter from on the status of Lambeth degrees, 1861.
Ref: Tait 79 ff. 239–40.

JACKSON (John), Bishop of Lincoln, and (1869) of London
Letter from on the conferment of Lambeth degrees, 1870.
Ref: Tait 88 ff. 55–6.

HAYNES (John Frederick), Curate of St. Jude, Southwark, Surrey
Letters from and on his application for a Lambeth degree, 1876.
Ref: Tait 218 ff. 161–6.

JACKSON (Joseph Edward), Headmaster of Sheffield Grammar School, Yorks.
Letters and papers from and on his application for a Lambeth degree, 1873.
Ref: Tait 191 ff. 37–60.

HARPER (Henry John Chitty), Bishop of Christchurch; Primate of New Zealand
Recommendation of the Rev. C. Bowen for a Lambeth degree, 1874.
Ref: Tait 196 ff. 275–6.

LEMARE (William), organist
Letters from and on his application for a Lambeth degree, 1873.
Ref: Tait 191 ff. 118–37.

CLARK (Samuel), Rector of Chaffcombe, Somt.
Letter and papers on his examination for a Lambeth degree, 1876.
Ref: Tait 218 ff. 415, 424–425, 428.

BELL (John Dickenson), Chaplain to the Earl of Strafford
Letters and papers on his examination for a Lambeth degree; correspondence on the examination of
THOMSON (Robert), Curate of Mere, Wiltshire, for a Lambeth degree, 1874.
Ref: Tait 198 ff. 352, 355.

KLAMBOROWSKI (Leonard), Vicar of Denston, Suffolk
Letters and papers on his examination for a Lambeth degree, 1874.
Ref: Tait 198 ff. 340-7, 352, 355.

PHILLIPS (Rev. R.)
Letters and papers on his examination for a Lambeth degree, 1874.
Ref: Tait 198 ff. 348-52, 355, 258-9.

WILBERFORCE (Samuel), Bishop of Oxford, and (1869) of Winchester
Recommendation of the Rev. F.B. Proctor for a Lambeth degree, 1872.
Ref: Tait 182 ff. 36y–z.

BADGER (Rev. George Percy), Arabic scholar
Letters from and on his application for a Lambeth degree, 1873.
Ref: Tait 187 ff. 85-91.

BULLOCK (Charles), Rector of St. Nicholas, Worcester
Letters from and on his application for a Lambeth degree, 1875.
Ref: Tait 206 ff. 327-340.

HORE (Samuel Coode), S.P.G. missionary in British Guiana
Letters from and on his application for a Lambeth degree, 1878.
Ref: Tait 237 ff. 253-62.

NICHOLSON (Rev. John), of Carlisle, Cumb.
Letters from and on his application for a Lambeth degree, 1881.
Ref: Tait 272 ff. 287-98.

PARKER (Matthew), Vicar of St. Saviour, Birmingham, Warwickshire.
Letters from and on his application for a Lambeth degree, 1882.
Ref: Tait 282 ff. 251-7.

JONES (William), Lecturer at St. Katharine Cree, London
Letters and papers from and on his examination for a Lambeth degree, 1876.
Ref: Tait 218 ff. 415-28.

OUSELEY (Rev. Sir Frederick Arthur Gore), 2nd Bart.; Professor of Music, Oxford
Recommendation of W.H. Longhurst for a Lambeth degree, 1875.
Ref: Tait 209 ff. 198-9.

WILBERFORCE (Samuel), Bishop of Oxford, and (1869) of Winchester
Correspondence with the Rev. J. Wyse on his application for a Lambeth degree, 1872.
Ref: Tait 184 ff. 377-9.

COTTERILL (Henry), Bishop of Grahamstown, and (1872) of Edinburgh
Recommendation of the Rev. J. Overend for a Lambeth degree, 1874.
Ref: Tait 198 ff. 335-6.

OVEREND (Rev. James), Headmaster of Colonel Scott's Endowed School, Edinburgh
Papers on his examination for a Lambeth degree, 1874.
Ref: Tait 198 ff. 335–9, 346, 350–2, 355, 358–9.

HORDEN (John), Bishop of Moosonee
Recommendation of Archdeacon W.W. Kirkby for a Lambeth degree 1876.
Ref: Tait 226 ff. 143–4.

BICKERSTETH (Robert), Bishop of Ripon
Recommendation of S. Crawley for a Lambeth degree, 1872.
Ref: Tait 182 ff. 36g.

PERRY (Frederick), Vicar of St. Saviour, St. Pancras, Middx.
Letters and papers from and on his examination for a Lambeth degree, 1871.
Ref: Tait 174 ff. 249–53, 258.

GOVETT (Thomas Romaine), Vicar of All Saints, Newmarket, Cambs.
Letters from and on his examination for a Lambeth degree, 1872.
Ref: Tait 182 ff. 36k–r, 36cc–dd .

PROCTOR (Francis Bartlett), Curate of Camden Chapel, Camberwell, Surrey
Letters and papers on his examination for a Lambeth degree, 1872.
Ref: Tait 182 ff. 36s–z, 36aa–bb, ee–ff.

PHELPS (Philip Edmund), Perpetual Curate of St. James' chapel, Kennington, Surrey
Letters and papers from and on his examination for a Lambeth degree, 1871.
Ref: Tait 174 ff. 259–66, 271–3.

BENHAM (William), Vicar of Margate, and (1880) of Marden, Kent
Letters to the Rev. H.M. Spooner on Lambeth degrees, including letters and papers of John Dickenson BELL, Chaplain to the Earl of Strafford, on his examination for a Lambeth degree, 1873.
Ref: Tait 191 ff. 92–5.

PRESTON, Lancs.
Letter on the curacy of St. Luke's church; correspondence on examinations for Lambeth degrees; correspondence on the examination of THOMSON (Robert), Curate of Mere, Wiltshire, for a Lambeth degree, 1874.
Ref: Tait 200 ff. 228–9.

RYLE (John Charles), Bishop of Liverpool
Letter from on POSTANCE (Henry), Vicar of Holy Trinity, Toxteth Park, Lancashire; recommendation of Postance for a Lambeth degree, 1882.
Ref: Tait 282 ff. 284–8.

THOMSON (William), Archbishop of York
Correspondence with Archbishop Thomson. Correspondence on JACKSON (Joseph Edward), Headmaster of Sheffield Grammar School, Yorkshire, and his application for a Lambeth degree.
Ref: Tait 101 ff. 180–1.

STIRLING (Waite Hockin), Bishop of the Falkland Islands
Correspondence on Anglican chaplaincies in South America; recommendation of HOSKIN (Thomas Raffles), chaplain at Montevideo, Uruguay, for a Lambeth degree, 1876.
Ref: Tait 225 ff. 242–3.

STIRLING (Waite Hockin), Bishop of the Falkland Islands
Correspondence on Anglican chaplaincies in South America; recommendation of HOSKIN (Thomas Raffles), chaplain at Montevideo, Uruguay, for a Lambeth degree, 1877.
Ref: Tait 234 ff. 173-6.

SPOONER (Henry Maxwell), Vicar of Boughton under Blean, Kent; nephew of Mrs. A.C. Tait
Letters and papers from on examinations for Lambeth degrees; correspondence on the examinations of MAITLAND (Adam Gray), Curate of Woodford, Essex, and SLADE (Robert Trim), Curate of Dronfield, 1879.
Ref: Tait 249 ff. 202-4.

The National Archives: Chancery, the Wardrobe, Royal Household, Exchequer and various commissions

Chancery: Dispensation Rolls. Faculties included the degrees of master of arts, thought necessary for a clergyman, doctor or bachelor of divinity, and doctor or bachelor of laws, the so-called Lambeth degrees; 1595–1747.
Ref: C 58.

The National Archives: Lord Chancellor's Office

Grants of various Lambeth Degrees
Lord Chancellor's Office and Lord Chancellor's Department: Registered Files. Crown Office in Chancery. Warrants and patents. Grants of various Lambeth Degrees. 1919–1921.
Ref: LCO 2/2254.

Lord Chancellor's Office and Lord Chancellor's Department: Registered Files. Crown Office in Chancery. Warrants and patents. Grants of various Lambeth degrees. 1922–1924.
Ref: LCO 2/2398.

Lord Chancellor's Office and Lord Chancellor's Department.
Lambeth Degrees: question whether the Archbishop of Canterbury has power to confer the degree of a Doctor of Divinity on a person who is not a British subject: correspondence. 1931–1968.
Ref: LCO 2/8507.

WARRANTS AND PATENTS. Lambeth Degree. Edgar T. Cook, B.Music. 1934.
Ref: LCO 6/1340.

WARRANTS AND PATENTS. Lambeth Degree. H. Grace. 1930.
Ref: LCO 6/1330.

WARRANTS AND PATENTS. Lambeth Degree. The Rev. C. D. Symons MC, MA. 1939.
Ref: LCO 6/1364.

WARRANTS AND PATENTS. Lambeth Degree. H. W. Hunt; W. Ellis. 1929.
Ref: LCO 6/1323.

WARRANTS AND PATENTS. Lambeth Degree. S. H. Nicholson MVO, MA, B.Music. 1928.
Ref: LCO 6/1318.

WARRANTS AND PATENTS. Lambeth Degree. The Rt. Rev. D. H. Crick. 1940.
Ref: LCO 6/1643.

WARRANTS AND PATENTS. Lambeth Degree. R. B. Henderson MA 1934.
Ref: LCO 6/1342.

WARRANTS AND PATENTS. Lambeth Degree. Rt. Rev. H. V. Stuart MA 1924.
Ref: LCO 6/1303.

WARRANTS AND PATENTS. Lambeth Degree. The Rt. Worshipful Sir P. W. Baker-Wilbraham Bt. 1936.
Ref: LCO 6/1348.

WARRANTS AND PATENTS. Lambeth Degree. Nelson Wellesley, Bishop of Damaraland. 1925.
Ref: LCO 6/1305.

WARRANTS AND PATENTS. Lambeth Degree. The Rev. E. H. Lea. 1927.
Ref: LCO 6/1312.

WARRANTS AND PATENTS. Lambeth Degree. The Rev. H. L. C. V. de Candole MA; The Rev. L. B. G. J. Ford MA, 1926.
Ref: LCO 6/1309.

WARRANTS AND PATENTS. Lambeth Degree. The Rev. Canon F. Underhill MA, 1932.
Ref: LCO 6/1337.

WARRANTS AND PATENTS. Lambeth Degree. The Rev. G. F. G. Brown MA, OBE, 1932.
Ref: LCO 6/1336.

WARRANTS AND PATENTS. Lambeth Degree. Rt. Rev. G. R. Woodward. 1924.
Ref: LCO 6/1302.

WARRANTS AND PATENTS. Lambeth Degree. The Rt. Rev. E. S. Woods; The Very Rev. F. S. M. Bennett. 1937.
Ref: LCO 6/1354.

WARRANTS AND PATENTS. Lambeth Degree. The Rt. Rev. C. Salisbury Bishop of Bristol. 1933.
Ref: LCO 6/1339.

WARRANTS AND PATENTS. Lambeth Degree. C. Brown, FRCO. 1940.
Ref: LCO 6/1644.

WARRANTS AND PATENTS. Lambeth Degree. The Rt. Rev. M. C. James, Bishop of St. Arnaud. 1927.
Ref: LCO 6/1313.

WARRANTS AND PATENTS. Lambeth Degree. The Rev. A. C. Martin OBE, 1938.
Ref: LCO 6/1355.

WARRANTS AND PATENTS. Lambeth Degree. The Rev. E. H. Thorold MA, 1931.
Ref: LCO 6/1332.

WARRANTS AND PATENTS. Lambeth Degree. The Rt. Rev. B. S. Batty MA, OBE, 1939.
Ref: LCO 6/1367.

WARRANTS AND PATENTS. Lambeth Degree. G. T. Thalben-Ball FRCO. 1935.
Ref: LCO 6/1346.

WARRANTS AND PATENTS. Lambeth Degree. A. B. N. Johnson BA, 1928.
Ref: LCO 6/1319.

WARRANTS AND PATENTS. Lambeth Degree. The Rt. Rev. H. Lord, Bishop of Southwell. 1928.
Ref: LCO 6/1320.

WARRANTS AND PATENTS. Lambeth Degree. J. Soar, B.Music. 1934.
Ref: LCO 6/1341.

WARRANTS AND PATENTS. Lambeth Degree. R. Wassell, FRCO, 1939.
Ref: LCO 6/1366.

WARRANTS AND PATENTS. Lambeth Degree. The Rt. Rev. C. E. Curzon. 1936.
Ref: LCO 6/1352.

WARRANTS AND PATENTS. Lambeth Degree. The Rt. Rev. G. C. Lester; The Rt. Rev. F. Partridge. 1936.
Ref: LCO 6/1351.

WARRANTS AND PATENTS. Lambeth Degree. The Rt. Rev. R. Thomas, Bishop of Willochra. 1928.
Ref: LCO 6/1317.

WARRANTS AND PATENTS. Lambeth Degree. C. L. Lee Williams; The Rt. Rev. G. C. Hubback. 1929.
Ref: LCO 6/1324.

WARRANTS AND PATENTS. Lambeth Degree. The Rev. E. L. Macassey MA, BD, 1935.
Ref: LCO 6/1347.

WARRANTS AND PATENTS. Lambeth Degree. H. B. Vaisey KC, 1939.
Ref: LCO 6/1360.

WARRANTS AND PATENTS. Lambeth Degree. C. L. Lee Williams; The Rt. Rev. G. C. Hubback. 1929.
Ref: LCO 6/1324.

WARRANTS AND PATENTS. Lambeth Degree. The Most Revd. H. Frewen, Archbishop of Perth, Primate of Australia. 1936.
Ref: LCO 6/1349.

WARRANTS AND PATENTS. Lambeth Degree. The Rev. M. G. Haigh MA, 1931.
Ref: LCO 6/1329.

WARRANTS AND PATENTS. Lambeth Degree. The Ven. S. W. Lavis. 1925.
Ref: LCO 6/1308.

WARRANTS AND PATENTS. Lambeth Degree. The Rev. M. Williams. 1928.
Ref: LCO 6/1322.

WARRANTS AND PATENTS. Lambeth Degree. W. H. Reed MVO, 1939.
Ref: LCO 6/1361.

WARRANTS AND PATENTS. Lambeth Degree. The Rt. Rev. W. G. George Bishop of Jamaica. 1932.
Ref: LCO 6/1338.

WARRANTS AND PATENTS. Lambeth Degree. The Ven. & Hon. K. Gibbs MA, 1935.
Ref: LCO 6/1325.

WARRANTS AND PATENTS. Lambeth Degree. Rt. Rev. J. B. Simpson MA; Rt. Rev. T. H. Burley MA, 1925.
Ref: LCO 6/1307.

WARRANTS AND PATENTS. Lambeth Degree. The Rt. Rev. R. S. M. O'Ferrall MA, 1926.
Ref: LCO 6/1310.

WARRANTS AND PATENTS. Lambeth Degree. The Very Rev. F. W. Dwelry MA, 1931.
Ref: LCO 6/1333.

WARRANTS AND PATENTS. Lambeth Degree. Rt. Rev. N. B. Hudson; Rt. Rev. W. L. Anderson, DSC, MA; Rt. Rev. H. A. Skelton, MA; The Rev. N. V. Gorton, MA; The Most Rev. Joseph, Lord Archbishop of Melbourne. 1941–5.
Ref: LCO 6/1900.

WARRANTS AND PATENTS. Lambeth Degree. G. Shaw, B.Music; M. E. F. Shaw. 1934.
Ref: LCO 6/1334.

WARRANTS AND PATENTS. Lambeth Degree. G. H. Moreton, B.Music, FRCO. 1932.
Ref: LCO 6/1335.

WARRANTS AND PATENTS. Lambeth Degree. A. Hamer. 1937.
Ref: LCO 6/1353.

WARRANTS AND PATENTS. Lambeth Degree. T. T. Noble ARCM. 1931.
Ref: LCO 6/1331.

WARRANTS AND PATENTS. Lambeth Degree. The Rt. Rev. David Lewis Bishop of St. Davids; G. B. J. Aitken. 1930.
Ref: LCO 6/1328.

WARRANTS AND PATENTS. Lambeth Degree. The Rt. Rev. W. G. George Bishop of Jamaica. 1932.
Ref: LCO 6/1338.

WARRANTS AND PATENTS. Lambeth Degree. The Ven. & Hon. K. Gibbs MA, 1929.
Ref: LCO 6/1325.

WARRANTS AND PATENTS. Lambeth Degree. The Rt. Rev. W. Thomas Bishop of St.Asaph; The Rev. F. P. Harton. 1934.
Ref: LCO 6/1344.

WARRANTS AND PATENTS. Lambeth Degree. The Ven. E. N. Lovett CBE, MA, 1927.
Ref: LCO 6/1314.

WARRANTS AND PATENTS. Lambeth Degree. The Rev. G. A. Chambers MA, B.Econ. 1927.
Ref: LCO 6/1315.

WARRANTS AND PATENTS. Lambeth Degree. The Rev. E. F. Brown MA, 1930.
Ref: LCO 6/1327.

WARRANTS AND PATENTS. Lambeth Degree. Rt. Rev. A. E. C. Jarvis BD, 1925.
Ref: LCO 6/1306.

WARRANTS AND PATENTS. Lambeth Degree. The Rt. Rev. M. Williams, Bishop of Dover. 1928.
Ref: LCO 6/1321.

WARRANTS AND PATENTS. Lambeth Degree. The Rt. Rev. M. R. Carpenter-Garnier M.A., Bishop of Colombo. 1924.
Ref: LCO 6/1304.

WARRANTS AND PATENTS. Lambeth Degree. The Rt. Rev. C. R. Hone. 1938.
Ref: LCO 6/1359.

WARRANTS AND PATENTS. Lambeth Degree. C. M. Spurling. 1936.
Ref: LCO 6/1350.

WARRANTS AND PATENTS. Lambeth Degree. The Rev. E. W. Williamson MA, 1939.
Ref: LCO 6/1365.

WARRANTS AND PATENTS. CONFIRMATION OF Lambeth degrees: DOCTOR OF MUSIC; DOCTOR IN DIVINITY. Gwilym Owen Williams, Bishop Elect of Bangor; Lewis Mervyn, Bishop of Worcester; Kenneth, Bishop of Lincoln; Robert Wright, Bishop of Peterborough; Angus Campbell McInnes, Archbishop.1945–71.
Ref: LCO 6/3675.

WARRANTS AND PATENTS. CONFIRMATION OF Lambeth degrees: DOCTOR OF MUSIC; DOCTOR IN DIVINITY. Cecil John Grimes Archdeacon of Northampton; John Henry Arnold; John McLeod Campbell, Hon Cannon of Canterbury Cathedral; Harold William Bradfield; Herbert Whitton Sumsion; Frank Russell.1945–71.
Ref: LCO 6/3674.

The National Archives: HM Treasury

Taxation Stamp Duty: Abolition of stamp duty on Lambeth degrees 10 March 1938 – 29 July 1938.
Ref: T 160/768/16.

Bedfordshire Archives and Record Service

JOHN GREEN OF WOBURN AND FAMILY. Personal records. Bundle of correspondence regarding the grant of a Lambeth M.A. degree to John Green so as to enable him to become Commissary and Official of the Archdeaconry of Bedford, 1867–1868.
Ref: Z 742/15.

Royal College of Physicians of London

Robert William Innes Smith (1872-1933): Papers, early 20th century. Chronological list of Lambeth medical degrees, 1663–1841
Ref: MS-SMITR/MS.875.

West Sussex County Record Office, Chichester

The Druitt papers
The Druitt papers, documents relating to a nineteenth century London physician and surgeon and his family The collection contains a great deal of material relating…
Admin history: 1856, a Fellowship of the Pathological Society of Montreal in 1856, honorary membership of the Society of Physico-Medica of Erlangen (Germany) in 1858 and in 1874 he was awarded the Lambeth degree, 1689–1945.
Ref: DRUITT MSS.

Receipt for cheque for Lambeth Degree
The Druitt papers. DOCTOR ROBERT DRUITT. ACCOUNTS. GENERAL. Receipt for cheque for Lambeth Degree. 1878.
DRUITT MSS/35.

Wiltshire and Swindon History Centre

TROWBRIDGE: St. James with St. Stephen. INCUMBENT. Deed conferring Lambeth Degree of Bachelor of Laws on George Crabbe, Rector and poet. 1789.
Ref: PR/Trowbridge: St. James with St. Stephen/608/75H.

4 Chronological list of Lambeth degrees

Melanie Barber[1]

The list below gives Lambeth degrees arranged chronologically. See also lists arranged by name and type of degree. The list covers the period 1539–1995, but note that there are gaps in the early records. The dates given are the dates of the faculties.

The central series of records documenting Lambeth degrees are those of the Faculty Office. See the following archive records:

- Faculty Office registers (ref: F I)
  Ostensibly indexed to 1835 (see electronic archives catalogue), but there may be gaps in indexing. However, the volumes also have their own internal indexes.
- Faculty Office fiats (ref: F II)
  From 1660. These are only intermittently entered in the archives catalogue. Having found an F I entry, you should be able to locate the associated F II documents (if they survive) by date.
- Vicar General Act Books (ref: VB 1)
  Degrees recorded here 1663–1859 are entered in the archives database.

These formal records do not generally give extensive detail on why degrees were granted, although the F II documents can be informative in the late 17th century. Note that there is some correspondence on Lambeth degrees (and in some instances degrees refused) in the Archbishops' Papers (see the archives catalogue), but principally only from the late 19th century. It is often difficult to discern the precise reason for the conferment of degrees. There are further lists held in the Library arranged by date:

- MS 1715 (list covering 1539–1948)
  There are possibly omissions in this list: for instance, Peter Sandiford does not appear, yet is recorded as DD in the records.
- F VI/1 (registers covering 1883–1997)

Lambeth degrees in Australia, New Zealand and Melanesia are listed on pp. 349–50 of Anglicans in the Antipodes: an indexed calendar of the papers and correspondence of the Archbishops of Canterbury, 1788–1961, relating to Australia, New Zealand, and the Pacific (ed. R. & L. Frappell, R. Withycombe, and R. Nobbs, 1999). Note that Lambeth diplomas are not the same as Lambeth degrees. These were founded in 1905. For some records see the archives catalogue ref: LD, including LD/3 (record book of graduates, 1906–1953). See also printed books catalogue: *List of those who hold the Lambeth Diploma in Theology and some information as to their work …* [1925–86] [ref: PB2385.L2].

Degrees and diplomas are administered from Lambeth Palace to whom queries on current practice or recent degrees should be directed.

---

[1]Reproduced by permission of Lambeth Palace Library

Date	Surname	First name(s)	Degree
17 Feb 1539	Ferrers	Eligius	DD
6 Dec 1544	Broke	George	BA
1559–75	Blage		BD

Date	Surname	First name(s)	Degree
14 March 1615	Purchas	Samuel	BD
20 Nov 1617	Hillyard	John	BD
28 June 1619	Neile	William	MA
9 Dec 1635	Layfield	Edward	BD
24 Nov 1660	Sudbury	John	DD
24 Dec 1660	Braborne	William	DD
24 Sep 1661	Sanderson	Robert	LLB
23 Feb 1662	Berkenhead	Peter	MA
11 May 1663	Fyffe	William	MD
12 May 1663	Freeman alias King	Edmund	MB
9 Sep 1663	Dakyn	Policarp	MD
17 Sep 1663	Cheeke	Alexander	LLB
21 Sep 1663	Clements	John	LLB
22 Sep 1663	Exton	Everard	LLB
24 Sep 1663	Thompson	Robert	LLB
30 Sep 1663	Randolph	John	DD
31 Oct 1663	Pell	John	DD
4 Feb 1664	Selleck	John	DD
4 Feb 1664	Thoroton	Robert	MD
2 May 1664	Hawkins	William	DD
25 Oct 1664	Pritchett	John	DD
15 March 1664	Cary	George	DD
17 June 1668	Dryden	John	MA
3 Jan 1671	Seddon	Laurence	DD
22 Oct 1672	Saunders	Anthony	DD
19 Aug 1674	Woodford	Samuel	DD
8 Nov 1675	Harrison	William	DD
7 Dec 1675	Eachard	John	BD
9 April 1675	Rosewell	William	MD
21 Nov 1677	Taylor	Robert	MA
10 Dec 1677	Blow	John	DMus
11 Dec 1677	Clifford	James	MA
1 Feb 1678	Towerson	Gabriel	DD
5 Feb 1678	Shippen	William	DD
6 Feb 1678	Barnard	Francis	MD
9 Feb 1678	Newell	John	MA
13 May 1678	Bishop	Samuel	DD
13 May 1678	Thorpe	George	DD
4 June 1678	Speed	George	MA
28 June 1678	Comber	Thomas	DD

Date	Surname	First name(s)	Degree
9 March 1678	Dent	Peter	MB
29 Sep 1680	Burnet	Gilbert	DD
1 Nov 1680	Batty	William	DD
1 Nov 1685	Stanley	William	DD
6 Dec 1685	Marshall	John	LLB
13 Aug 1691	Patrick	John	DD
19 Nov 1691	Barker	James	MA
19 Nov 1691	Barker	Ralph	DD
7 Dec 1691	Hooke	Robert	MD
21 Dec 1691	Manningham	Thomas	DD
2 July 1691	Hobbs	Thomas	MD
8 June 1691	Talbot	William	DD
25 June 1691	Walmsley	William	LLB
3 March 1692	Coatsworth	Caleb	MD
27 March 1693	Blagrave	Jonathan	DD
18 Jan 1695	Green	Thomas	DD
18 Jan 1695	Knighton	John	DD
4 Feb 1695	Woodward	John	MD
8 Feb 1695	Gee	Edward	DD
16 April 1695	Geddes	Michael	LLD
6 June 1695	Bragge	Francis	BD
27 March 1695	Willis	Richard	DD
22 Sep 1696	Robinson	John	DD
3 March 1697	Tenison	Edward	LLB
10 Jan 1698	Wilson	Thomas	LLD
16 May 1698	Vernon	Edward	MA
5 March 1699	Jones	Owen	MA (revoked)

Date	Surname	First name(s)	Degree
26 Jan 1700	Newell	George	LLB
1 Sep 1701	Waite	Thomas	LLB
26 Nov 1701	Crompton	John	MD
13 May 1702	Moore	John	LLB
22 July 1702	Knipe	Richard	MA
18 June 1702	Gibson	Edmund	DD
1 Feb 1704	Hayley	Thomas	MA
29 Nov 1705	Lloyd	William	DD
10 July 1706	Harris	John	DD
18 Feb 1707	Bembrigg	John	MD
18 Feb 1707	Smith	Posthumus	LLB
13 April 1708	West	Richard	DD
6 July 1708	Barton	Joseph	MA
9 March 1708	Wotton	William	DD
5 June 1711	Parkhurst	Dormer	LLB
17 May 1712	Jones	James	MA

Date	Surname	First name(s)	Degree
17 May 1712	Pearson	William	LLD
1 Oct 1714	Goodwin	Timothy	DD
23 April 1714	Tenison	Edward	DD
26 April 1714	Talbot	Charles	LLB
4 Aug 1715	Rider	Richard	LLB
26 Jan 1716	Hoadley	Benjamin	DD
28 Jan 1716	Blackburn	Lancelot	DD
27 Nov 1716	Tullie	Thomas	LLD
3 July 1716	Cranmer	Thomas	MD
3 July 1716	Ibbetson	Richard	DD
23 July 1716	Whitfield	William	DD
26 June 1716	Bowers	Thomas	DD
28 June 1716	Trimmell	David	DD
14 Jan 1717	Downes	Henry	DD
10 March 1718	Peploe	Samuel	BD
28 Sep 1720	Birch	William	DD
28 April 1720	Cobb	Charles	DD
28 June 1720	Bradshaw	William	DD
19 March 1720	Hill	Daniel	DD
16 Jan 1721	Lisle	Samuel	DD
27 March 1721	Ott	John Henry	MA
10 Aug 1722	Lambe	Charles	DD
24 June 1723	Chicheley	Richard	LLB
8 Jan 1724	Gilbert	John	LLD
6 Oct 1724	Wake	Edward	DD
1 June 1724	Pearche	Zachary	DD
5 March 1724	Naylor	Charles	LLD
12 March 1724	Horner	James	MA
13 Feb 1725	Payne	Dennis	MA
26 May 1725	Lardner	Richard	LLB
20 Nov 1725	Walker	John	BD
22 Oct 1726	Stillingfleet	James	DD
10 March 1727	Fleming	George	LLD
2 Feb 1728	Heber	John	MA
13 Feb 1728	Newey	John	DD
5 June 1728	Ayerst	William	DD
14 March 1729	Sleeth	Stephen	MA
27 Feb 1731	Cary	Mordecai	DD
9 Sep 1731	Howell	John	MD
11 Nov 1731	Pownall	William	LLB
10 May 1732	Bundy	Richard	DD
12 Feb 1733	Lancaster	Nathanael	DD
7 Nov 1733	Maurice	Peter	DD
15 Jan 1734	Bolton	Robert	LLD
20 May 1735	Abbott	John	MA
26 July 1736	Metcalfe	John	LLD

Date	Surname	First name(s)	Degree
17 Aug 1737	Billingsley	John	MA
21 Jan 1738	Chandler	Richard	MA
10 April 1738	Eyton	Robert	DD
3 April 1739	England	George	MA
2 May 1741	Shuckford	Samuel	DD
15 March 1742	Jones	John	MA
4 Jan 1743	Hoadley	John	LLD
8 Oct 1747	Potter	Thomas	LLD
3 June 1747	Cawthorn	James	MA
14 Jan 1749	Cresset	Edward	DD
6 Feb 1749	Comberbach	Roger	LLB
2 June 1749	Head	John	DD
7 Sep 1750	Aylmer	John	MA
18 April 1750	Brereton	Robert	LLB
May 1751	Foote	Francis Hender	LLB
4 Oct 1751	Gyll	Thomas	MA
4 Nov 1751	Lewis	Thomas	MA
6 Nov 1751	Johnson	Peter	MA
11 April 1751	Hughes	Hugh	DD
22 April 1751	Herring	William	DD
22 April 1751	Hill	John Samuel	DD
1 July 1751	Thomas	John	DD
19 July 1751	Salter	Samuel	DD
14 May 1753	Le Moine	Abraham	DD
9 March 1753	Birch	Thomas	DD
10 Jan 1754	Coulter	John	MA
10 Jan 1754	Warburton	William	DD
4 Sep 1754	Jubb	George	DD
5 March 1754	Warner	Ferdinando	LLD
8 Jan 1755	Hildesley	Mark	DD
8 Jan 1755	Jekyll	Richard Blackett	MA
29 May 1755	Dayrell	Richard	DD
27 Aug 1755	Wilson	William Worcester	MA
1 Sep 1755	Jortin	John	DD
31 Oct 1755	Pery	John	DD
19 May 1756	Langhorne	William	MA
4 Sep 1756	Osborne	John	MA
29 Nov 1756	Barton	Cutts	DD
29 Nov 1756	Holme	Thomas	LLB
4 Dec 1756	Hawkesworth	John	LLD
14 April 1756	Payne	Joseph	MA
14 July 1756	Pettingal	John	DD
1 Jan 1757	Seaman	Lionel	DD
8 Sep 1757	Gilbert	Robert	DD
2 Aug 1758	Davis	John	DD
2 Aug 1758	Tattan	William	DD

Date	Surname	First name(s)	Degree
3 Aug 1758	Adkin	Robert	MA
26 May 1759	Pitcairn	James	LLB
30 June 1760	Murray	William	DD
18 May 1761	Cumberland	Denison	DD
1 June 1762	Secker	George	DD
6 May 1763	Ballard	Reeve	DD
21 Aug 1764	Halhead	Nicolas	LLB
18 Sep 1764	Ford	James	MD
16 May 1766	Dering	Heneage	DD
13 Sep 1766	Burrough	Henry	LLD
4 June 1766	Sutton	Richard	DD
12 June 1766	Bunting	Tomlinson	LLB
15 June 1767	Knowles	Thomas	DD
23 Dec 1768	Crookhall	John	MA
28 April 1768	Place	Lionel	LLB
6 Sep 1769	Majendie	John James	DD
21 Feb 1770	Matthew	Joseph	MA
6 Sep 1770	Benson	John	DD
6 Sep 1770	Palmer	Richard	DD
6 Sep 1770	Storer	Bennett	DD
24 Dec 1770	Arnold	John	DD
21 Feb 1771	Wollaston	Frederick	LLD
9 Nov 1771	Robinson	Richard George	DD
12 June 1771	Lloyd	Peirson	DD
13 Aug 1772	Banks	Joseph	LLB
27 Nov 1772	Pinnell	Peter	DD
27 July 1772	Foster	Mark	MA
12 May 1773	Corsellis	Nicholas	MA
10 Aug 1773	Burton	Edmund	MA
7 June 1773	Berdmore	Samuel	DD
28 June 1774	Jekyll	John	LLB
23 May 1775	Cadogan	William Bromley	MA
30 May 1775	Stoup	Richard	LLB
22 July 1775	Wakeham	Nicolas	DD
27 Oct 1776	Monson	John (?Lord)	LLD
11 Dec 1776	Hayter	George	MA
3 July 1777	Farish	James	LLB
26 July 1777	Lucas	Richard	DD
5 Jan 1778	Langford	William	DD
18 Feb 1778	Apthorpe	East	DD
1 Sep 1778	Walker	Charles	MA
16 Feb 1779	Ramsden	William	DD
20 May 1779	Thompson	Matthew	MA
19 Feb 1780	Jones	John	MA
26 Nov 1780	Broughton	Sir Thomas	LLD
27 April 1780	Exon	Thomas	MA

Date	Surname	First name(s)	Degree
1 March 1780	Bowlby	Peter	LLD
30 Jan 1781	Morice	William	DD
16 Feb 1781	Carwardine	Thomas	MA
9 May 1781	Smith	James	MA
1 Dec 1781	Ramsay	James	MA
11 Dec 1781	Spooner	Joseph	MA
17 Dec 1781	Hodgson	John	MA
23 April 1781	Snowe	Richard	MA
12 Aug 1782	Fairfax	Denny Martin	DD
29 Aug 1782	Hastings	Robert	MA
12 April 1782	Hudson	Joseph	DD
24 July 1782	Beauvoir	Osmund	DD
24 July 1782	Vyner	Thomas	LLD
8 June 1782	Bayford	David	MD
24 Jan 1783	Hallifax	Robert	MD
11 Feb 1783	Hoole	Samuel	MA
3 July 1783	Bromwich	Brian L'Anson	MA
16 May 1784	Thomas	John	LLB
28 Oct 1784	Stockdale	Percival	MA
14 May 1785	Sinclair	Robert	MA
30 May 1785	Vaughan	Edward	DD
2 Aug 1785	Knollis	Francis	MA
29 May 1786	Robert	William	LLB
13 Oct 1786	Evans	Daniel	LLB
23 May 1787	Buckner	John	LLD
22 Dec 1787	Becher	Michael Thomas	MA
13 July 1787	Cheston	Richard Brown	MD
15 March 1787	Brown	William	MA
7 March 1788	Coates	Charles	LLB
8 March 1788	Ford	John	MD
9 Jan 1789	Myers	Thomas	LLB
10 Jan 1789	Crabbe	George	LLB
1 Sep 1790	Vere	Nicolas	MA
8 April 1790	Llloyd	Thomas	MA
20 April 1791	Heath	George	DD
29 April 1791	Vardill	John	LLB
19 July 1791	Hey	Thomas	DD
23 Jan 1792	Montgomery	John	MA
5 Dec 1792	Rutton	Matthias	MA
26 April 1792	Jefferson	Joseph	MA
9 Jan 1793	Cornewall	Ffolliott Herbert Walker	DD
29 Jan 1793	Cooper	William Henry	MA
July 1793	Ireland	John	MA
10 Jan 1795	Warburton	Charles Morgan	MA
20 Feb 1795	Jackson	William	MA
11 May 1795	Randolph	Francis	DD

Date	Surname	First name(s)	Degree
29 May 1795	Goodwin	John	MA
11 Dec 1795	Sproule	John Rowland	BCL
17 July 1795	Pretyman	John	DD
30 June 1795	Cole	William	DD
30 June 1795	Luxmoore	John	DD
11 March 1795	Gale	Samuel	MA
27 Feb 1796	Hawkins	John	MA
19 Dec 1796	Ingles	Henry	DD
28 April 1796	Baker	Philip	MA
3 Aug 1797	Watts	Robert	MA
24 April 1797	Moore	John	LLB
31 Oct 1798	Williams	William	MA
3 Dec 1798	de Guiffardiere	Charles	MA
15 Dec 1798	Weston	Samuel Ryder	DD
10 Jan 1799	Tait	William	LLB
27 May 1799	Horlock	Isaac William Webb	MA
8 March 1799	Robinson	Nicolas Waite	MA

Date	Surname	First name(s)	Degree
24 May 1800	Gomm	William	MA
9 Oct 1800	Jenkins	Henry	MA
23 Feb 1801	Bernard	Thomas	MA
9 Nov 1801	Cracroft	Bernard	MA
3 June 1801	Inglis	John	MA
21 Jan 1803	Waddilove	Robert Darley	DD
27 Jan 1803	Pelham	George (Hon)	DD
3 May 1803	Martin	George	MA
1 April 1803	Barnard	Edward	MA
27 June 1803	Ekins	Charles	MA
4 March 1803	Pope	Robert	MD
30 March 1803	Ireland	John	DD
8 Oct 1804	Jordan	John Nesbit	DD
8 Oct 1804	Mountain	Jehosophat	DD
5 Dec 1804	Fisher	Philip	DD
18 March 1805	Goddard	Henry	MA
14 Jan 1806	Henley	Samuel	DD
3 Feb 1806	Boyd	Hannyngton Elgee	MA
13 Aug 1806	Gardiner	Frederick	MA
25 Aug 1806	Day	Thomas	MD
10 Dec 1806	Stanser	Robert	DD
6 March 1806	Lefroy	John Henry George	MA
7 April 1807	Hughes	Thomas	DD
30 June 1807	Inglis	John	DD
5 July 1808	Plumptre	John	DD
14 June 1810	Heslop	Luke	DD

Date	Surname	First name(s)	Degree
8 March 1810	Wellesley	Gerald Valerian	DD
19 March 1810	Layard	Brownlow Villiers	MA
4 Jan 1811	Gabell	Henry Dison	DD
21 Aug 1811	Hudson	Samuel	LLB
27 Aug 1811	Burney	Charles	DD
14 June 1811	Bell	Andrew	LLD
20 Aug 1812	Dakins	William Whitfield	DD
19 Sep 1812	Preston	William	MA
27 April 1812	Goddard	Charles	MA
3 July 1812	Proctor	William	MA
29 July 1812	Barry	Edward	DD
26 April 1813	Saunders	Stephen	MD
25 Sep 1815	Jones	Robert	DD
16 Aug 1816	Booth	Livingstone	MA
13 June 1817	Sandiford	Peter	DD
7 Feb 1818	Day	John	MD
14 June 1819	Fardell	Henry	MA
11 March 1819	Lucas	Carr Ellison	MD
22 July 1820	Hodgson	Christopher	MA
20 June 1820	Mountain	George Jehosophat	DD
18 Feb 1822	Smith	Richard	MA
7 Nov 1822	Locke	William Oliver	MD
22 April 1823	Barker	William Alleyne	MA
31 July 1824	Rumsey	James	MD
13 Aug 1825	Trenow	Frederick Joseph Cox	MA
31 Aug 1825	Jarvis	Daniel	MD
10 Jan 1826	Willis	Robert	DD
13 Feb 1826	Barnes	William	MA
29 May 1826	Grimstone	Edward	MD
13 April 1826	Thomas	William	DD
30 Aug 1827	Bagot	Richard	DD
3 Oct 1827	Chandler	William	MD
7 Oct 1827	Kelly alias Holdsworth	George	MA
21 Dec 1827	Clarke	Charles Mansfield	MD
12 June 1827	Wharton	Thomas	MA
27 Feb 1828	Roy	William	DD
28 May 1828	Oke	William Samways	MD
30 Dec 1828	Mill	William Hodge	DD
25 March 1828	Dallas	Alexander Robert Charles	MA
25 May 1829	Snowden	William	BD
12 Aug 1829	Morgan	John	MA
19 Aug 1829	Harris	Joseph Hemington	DD
24 Aug 1829	Wrangham	George Walter	MA
21 Oct 1829	Stockwell	Joseph Samuel	MA
4 May 1830	Bamford	Robert Walker	BD
22 May 1832	Pickthall	Thomas	MA

Date	Surname	First name(s)	Degree
12 Sep 1832	Carr	Thomas	DD
29 Dec 1832	Wallace	George	MA
13 April 1832	Stephens	Archibald John	MA
3 July 1832	Mayne	James	MA
25 Nov 1833	Newby	George	MA
29 July 1833	Walker	William	MA
12 June 1833	Robinson	John	MA
4 Aug 1834	Maddock	Samuel	BD
20 Oct 1834	Hodgson	Richard	MA
20 Oct 1834	Merest	John William Drage	MA
15 April 1834	Heap	Henry	MA
30 July 1834	Macpherson	Allan	BD
24 Feb 1835	Jennings	John	MA
25 July 1835	Oliver	George	DD
30 March 1835	Heathcote	George	MA
14 Jan 1836	Wenham	John	DD
19 May 1836	Griesbach	William Robert	MA
8 Sep 1836	Otter	William	DD
12 Oct 1836	Davies	David	MD
11 Jan 1837	Knightley	Valentine	MA
3 Feb 1837	Ditcher	Joseph	MA
23 Feb 1837	Wardle	Joseph	MA
19 Jan 1838	Taylor	Robert	MA
1 Feb 1838	Major	John Richardson	DD
10 Feb 1838	Marsden	William Buxton	MA
11 Sep 1838	Jameson	Joseph	BD
11 Oct 1838	Morgan	Morgan	MA
21 Nov 1838	Meek	Robert	MA
6 June 1838	Llewellyn	Richard Penderel	MA
17 March 1838	Fletcher	Charles	MA
28 Jan 1839	Shittler	Robert	DD
18 Feb 1839	Blanshard	William	MA
4 Oct 1839	Simpson	William West	MA
5 Dec 1839	Clark	John	MA
8 July 1839	Spencer	Aubrey George	DD
14 Feb 1840	Jessop	Thomas	DD
12 Sep 1840	Vernon	William	MA
10 Oct 1840	Hull	Robert	MD
31 Oct 1840	Tucker	Richard Thomas	DD
26 Dec 1840	Grylls	John Couch	MA
15 April 1840	Garnier	Thomas	DCL
30 July 1840	Thirlwall	Connop	DD
10 June 1840	Walton	William	MA
17 Aug 1841	Burt	John	MA
17 Aug 1841	Winter	John	MA
10 Nov 1841	Alexander	Michael Solomon	DD

Date	Surname	First name(s)	Degree
21 April 1841	Murray	James Greig	BD
22 June 1841	Pearson	William Hyde (Sir)	MD
16 May 1842	Yorke	Grantham Manton (Hon)	MA
27 July 1842	Gelling	John James	MA
21 Jan 1843	Gauntlett	Henry John	DMus
25 Jan 1843	Cowper	William	DD
27 Jan 1843	Bedford	William	DD
27 Jan 1843	Forrest	Robert	MA
27 Jan 1843	Hassall	Thomas	MA
27 Jan 1843	Sharpe	Thomas	MA
27 Jan 1843	Stiles	Henry Tarlton	MA
27 Jan 1843	Walsh	William Horatio	MA
27 May 1843	Lyne	Charles	MA
2 Aug 1843	Wallis	Thomas Samuel	DMus
13 Dec 1843	Hayes	William	MA
22 April 1843	Williams	Thomas Pierce	DD
7 July 1843	Brathwaite	Francis Robert	MA
7 July 1843	Trew	John McCammon	DD
14 June 1843	Campbell	Duncan	MA
17 June 1843	Garrard	William	MA
29 March 1843	Strachan	William	DD
10 Jan 1844	Fothergill	John	MA
22 Feb 1844	Rushton	John	DD
21 May 1844	Blackman	Charles	MA
10 July 1844	Musson	Samuel Paynter	DD
16 July 1844	Panton	Richard	DD
31 Jan 1845	Raines	Francis Robert	MA
11 Aug 1845	Trevannion	Frederick William	MA
29 Nov 1845	Broadley	William	MA
2 Dec 1845	Lyall	William Rowe	DD
8 April 1845	Campion	John	MA
18 March 1845	Lovekin	Alfred Peter	MA
6 Feb 1846	Dealtry	Thomas	DD
6 Feb 1846	Withers	George Undy	DD
9 May 1846	Cheere	Edward	MA
28 Aug 1846	Redwar	Thomas Rochford	MA
21 Oct 1846	Johnes	Thomas William	MA
22 Oct 1846	Poole	Thomas Eyre	DD
20 Nov 1846	Grant	Francis Bell	MA
11 Dec 1846	Shapley	John Congdon	MA
30 June 1846	Gobat	Samuel	DD
31 March 1846	Johnson	Samuel	MA
13 Jan 1847	Bailey	Benjamin	DD
31 Aug 1847	Baldwin	William	MA
17 Sep 1847	Short	Hugh Martin	MA
26 Oct 1847	Maclaverty	Colin	MA

Date	Surname	First name(s)	Degree
15 Nov 1847	Boardman	Thomas James	DMus
24 Nov 1847	Stone	John Campbell	MA
2 July 1847	Jackson	Edward	MA
21 July 1847	Mackie	George	DD
28 July 1847	Newham	Daniel	MA
23 March 1847	Bardsley	James	MA
6 Jan 1848	Watts	Thomas	MA
22 Jan 1848	Lee	James Prince	DD
1 Feb 1848	Maitland	Samuel Roffey	DD
19 Feb 1848	Stewart	Thomas	DD
18 May 1848	Clarke	George	MA
22 May 1848	Welby	Thomas Earle	MA
27 Dec 1848	Short	Henry	MA
5 May 1849	Kirwood	Joseph Henry	MA
9 Aug 1849	Hemming	John	MA
22 Nov 1849	Park	George	MA
29 Nov 1849	Glenie	Samuel Owen	MA
12 Dec 1849	Marriott	George Wakefield	DD
21 July 1849	Haddon	James	MA
30 June 1849	Burns	William	MA
2 March 1849	Laurie	Joseph	MA
22 May 1850	Elliott	Gilbert	DD
24 May 1850	Fletcher	Henry Thomas	MA
15 Oct 1850	Bayes	William	MD
31 Oct 1850	Bull	Edward	MA
16 Nov 1850	Isaacs	Robert MacIntosh	LLD
5 July 1850	James	David	MA
11 July 1850	Marshall	Charles	MA
7 June 1850	Warr	George Winter	MA
3 May 1851	Tuckerman	Samuel Parkman	DMus
5 May 1851	Cross	William	MA
23 Aug 1851	Webber	Richard Legge	MA
23 Sep 1851	Simpson	Samuel	MA
15 Oct 1851	Bishop	John Green	MD
18 Oct 1851	Paterson	William Thomas	MA
30 Dec 1851	Jackson	William Walrond	MA
9 July 1851	Perowne	John	MA
22 July 1851	Farr	Edmund Lacon	MA
7 June 1851	Hampton	Henry	MA
26 June 1851	Julius	Frederick Gilder	MD
6 March 1851	Johnson	Edmund Charles	MD
21 May 1852	Clarke	William Henry	LLD
28 Feb 1853	Hellmuth	Isaac	DD
20 Sep 1853	Reynolds	Joseph William	MA
10 Oct 1853	Earle	William	MA
14 Oct 1853	Peck	James	DMus

Date	Surname	First name(s)	Degree
25 Oct 1853	Reibey	Thomas	MA
30 Nov 1853	Tuckwell	Henry	MA
7 Dec 1853	Lensdale	William	DD
12 July 1853	Buck	Zechariah (or Zachariah)	DMus
19 July 1853	Davidson	Frederick Augustus	MA
21 Oct 1854	Kane	Henry Plow	MA
15 Nov 1854	Hunter	James	MA
27 Dec 1854	Canney	George	MD
27 Dec 1854	Morgan	William Leigh	MA
6 April 1854	Jenkins	Evan	MA
20 April 1854	Jones	William	MA
7 Feb 1855	Huntington	George	MA
3 May 1855	Green	Edward Dyer	MA
3 May 1855	Weeks	John Wills	DD
29 May 1855	Camidge	John	DMus
25 Aug 1855	Davies	Jekin	MA
30 Aug 1855	Smith	Thomas	MA
10 Oct 1855	Evans	Thomas	MA
19 Oct 1855	Smith	Francis	MD
4 Dec 1855	Darby	William Arthur	MA
27 April 1855	Grindrod	Ralph Barnes	MD
26 March 1855	Ramsbotham	John Hodgson	MD
4 Feb 1856	Sharpe	William Leggatt	MA
20 Feb 1856	Fidler	Daniel	MA
8 Sep 1856	Campbell	Duncan Houston	MA
4 Nov 1856	Vernon	Henry George	MA
21 Nov 1856	Pfander	Charles Gottlieb	DD
10 Dec 1856	Close	Francis	DD
10 Dec 1856	Phillips	Edmund	MD
5 July 1856	Sharpe	William	MD
24 July 1856	Seddon	David	MA
28 June 1856	Rogers	Robert Vashion	MA
28 March 1856	Courtenay	Daniel	DD
21 Aug 1857	Manning	William Montagu (Hon)	DCL
16 Nov 1857	Williams	David Archand	MA
24 Nov 1857	Selle	William Christian	DMus
28 April 1857	Woodward	Matthew	MA
4 March 1857	Brain	Thomas Henry	DD
9 Jan 1858	Shortt	Jonathan	DD
9 Feb 1858	Linstedt	Frederick William	DD
9 Aug 1858	Smith	Edmund	MD
13 Sep 1858	Cronin	Edward	MD
24 Sep 1858	Baker	William	MD
8 Oct 1858	Clere	Henry	MA
2 Dec 1858	East	Rowland Baldwin	MA
17 July 1858	Hobson	John	MA

Date	Surname	First name(s)	Degree
22 Sep 1859	Chalmers	John	MA
7 Oct 1859	Cartman	William	DD
10 Oct 1859	Bull	Charles	MA
13 Oct 1859	Bucke	Henry Walter	MA
29 Dec 1859	Beckles	Edward Hyndman	DD
11 July 1859	Stevenson	John	MA
20 June 1859	Mitford	George Newnham	MA
27 June 1859	Richardson	William	MA
4 March 1859	Armistead	Charles John	MA
4 March 1859	Mackreth	Thomas	DD
26 Jan 1860	Sandys	William Francis	DD
15 Feb 1860	Rowbotton	Frederick	MA
5 May 1860	Brendon	William Edward	MA
25 May 1860	Stevens	Henry	MA
23? May 1860	Hobbs	Charles Parson	MA
16 Aug 1860	Kettlewell	Samuel	MA
11 Dec 1860	Earnshaw	John	MA
19 Dec 1860	Jones	Thomas Robert	MA
30 April 1860	Jackson	William Walrond	DD
26 July 1860	Redford	Francis	MA
17 Jan 1861	Westall	Edward	MD
25 Feb 1861	Skrine	Clarmont	MA
25 May 1861	Hall	Thomas	MA
14 Aug 1861	Raynes	John	MD
19 Oct 1861	Carver	Alfred James	DD
14 Nov 1861	Starey	James Richard	MA
18 Nov 1861	Beach	William Roberts	MA
29 April 1861	Gibson	Timothy	DD
10 July 1861	Davis	Frederick Whylock	MA
11 July 1861	Read	Thomas Bolton	DD
12 Feb 1862	Birch	Henry Mildred	BD
21 Feb 1862	Battersby	William	MA
27 Feb 1862	Welby	Thomas Earle	DD
20 May 1862	Fisher	Frederick	MA
20 May 1862	Sherwin	William	MD
May 1862	O'Neill	James	BD
22 Aug 1862	Bowles	George Cranley	MA
25 Aug 1862	Glover	Richard	MA
30 Dec 1862	Allen	Richard Collyns	MA
28 April 1862	Daymond	Charles	MA
31 July 1862	Richards	Samuel La Rogue Bruce	MA
26 June 1862	Macdonald	Thomas Hope	MA
26 June 1862	Rogers	John	MA
25 March 1862	Ellison	John	MA
21 Jan 1863	Wright	Barrington Stafford	MA
4 Feb 1863	Tatlock	William	MA

Date	Surname	First name(s)	Degree
8 May 1863	Mitton	Welbury	MD
8 Aug 1863	Dixon	Thomas	MA
12 Aug 1863	Evans	Alfred Bowen	DD
27 Aug 1863	Wilmot	John James Tall	MA
17 Sep 1863	Harte	Edward John	MA
17 Nov 1863	Purdy	Thomas Augustus	MA
20 Nov 1863	Andrew	Samuel	MA
24 Nov 1863	Tucker	Joseph Kidger	DD
30 Nov 1863	Tarlton	Thomas Henry	MA
30 April 1863	Aldis	Charles Meeking	MA
8 July 1863	Jackson	Joseph Edward	MA
9 July 1863	Ross	John	MA
30 July 1863	Lane	Francis Charles de Lona	MA
20 June 1863	Dent	Thomas Robinson	MA
5 March 1863	Jaques	Joseph	MA
19 March 1863	Cowan	James Galloway	MA
28 March 1863	Stephenson	Robert	MA
11 Feb 1864	Fish	Ishmael	MA
11 Feb 1864	Shepperd	James Philip	MA
9 Sep 1864	Foote	John Andrewes	MA
8 Oct 1864	Forster	John Frederick	DMus
9 Dec 1864	Blunt	Richard Frederick	MA
9 Dec 1864	Grieve	William Thomas	MA
24 Dec 1864	Raven	Thomas Melville	MA
21 July 1864	Pope	George Uglow	DD
21 June 1864	Ewing	Thomas James	DD
10 March 1864	Fookes	Samuel Berjew	MA
10 Feb 1865	Woodman	Ebenezer Flood	MA
19 Aug 1865	Stephenson	John	MA
23 Oct 1865	Hitchins	Alfred	MA
28 April 1865	Hewlett	Ebenezer	MA
8 Jan 1866	Harvey	Frederick Burn	MA
18 Jan 1866	Edwards	John	MA
1 Feb 1866	Rowe	John George	MA
18 May 1866	Huxtable	Henry Constantine	MA
21 Sep 1866	Robins	Arthur	MA
19 April 1866	Elliott	William Foster	MA
4 July 1866	Maine	Lewin	MA
25 June 1866	De Boinville	William Chastel	MA
3 Jan 1867	Graham	Henry John	MA
31 Dec 1867	Esquire	John Green	MA
11 April 1867	Brooks	George Bygrave	MA
29 April 1867	Olivier	Alfred	MA
19 March 1867	Courtenay	John Polkinghorne	MA
26 Feb 1868	Jarbo	Peter John	MA
29 May 1868	Carss	Thomas	MA

Date	Surname	First name(s)	Degree
26 Sep 1868	Percival	Samuel	MA
25 July 1868	Goodman	Gabriel	DD
8 June 1869	Griffiths	John	DD
25 June 1869	Chambers	Walter	DD
13 March 1869	Woodford	James Russell	DD
11 Nov 1870	Hood	Samuel	DD
11 April 1870	Hughes	Joshua	DD
3 June 1870	Morris	Richard	LLD
3 June 1870	Perry	Frederick	MA
17 June 1870	Eales	Samuel John	MA
26 July 1871	Oakeley	Herbert Stanley	DMus
19 Jan 1872	Phelps	Philip Edward	MA
26 Jan 1872	Bower	Henry	DD
18 Nov 1872	Edwald	Frederick Christopher	BD
3 Dec 1872	Horden	John	DD
13 Dec 1872	Abbott	Edmund	DD
23 July 1872	Benham	William	BD
12 June 1872	Simpson	James	LLD
23 Jan 1873	Crawley	Samuel	MA
28 Jan 1873	Proctor	Francis Bartlett	MA
31 Jan 1873	Bacon	James	BD
4 Feb 1873	Jackson	Joseph Edward	DCL
22 Feb 1873	Simpson	William Sparrow	DD
1 Nov 1873	Badger	George Percy	DCL
31 Dec 1873	Burdon	John Shaw	DD
29 April 1873	Verrinder	Charles Garland	DMus
6 June 1873	Kinder	John	DD
21 Jan 1874	Sargent	Edward	DD
25 Sep 1874	Bowen	Croasdale	BD
17 Dec 1874	Piggott	Robert Turtle	DCL
31 Dec 1874	Overend	James	MA
17 April 1874	Bompas	William Carpenter	DD
2 Feb 1875	Longhurst	William Henry	DMus
6 Feb 1875	Klamborowski	Leonard	MA
20 May 1875	Puxley	Edward Lewellin	BD
18 Aug 1875	Puddicombe	Alfred Teed	BD
11 Nov 1875	Grisdale	John	BD
13 April 1875	Bullock	Charles	BD
28 July 1875	Pownall	William Henry	BD
21 Jan 1876	Townsend	George Tyler	DCL
4 Aug 1876	Hunter	James	DD
17 Aug 1876	Greatorex	Daniel	BD
21 Dec 1876	Copeland	George Dale	BD
4 Jan 1877	Wolff	Gustavus	DMus
13 Jan 1877	Evans	Daniel	DD
7 Feb 1877	Cowley	Abraham	BD

Date	Surname	First name(s)	Degree
7 Feb 1877	Mackenzie	Donald	BD
9 May 1877	Coe	John William	DD
14 Nov 1877	Ross	Alexander Johnston	BD
15 Nov 1877	Gomes	William Henry	BD
17 July 1877	Cawston	John	BD
9 June 1877	Griffiths	John	BD
9 June 1877	Jones	Alfred	BD
6 March 1877	Moran	Francis John Clay	BD
27 Feb 1878	Good	Thomas	BD
30 May 1878	Pilot	William	BD
9 Aug 1878	Brett	William Henry	BD
9 Aug 1878	Wyatt	Francis James	BD
12 Aug 1878	Druitt	Robert	MD
21 Aug 1878	Moule	Arthur Evans	BD
22 Aug 1878	Dyson	Samuel	BD
3 Oct 1878	Russell	Alexander	BD
3 Dec 1878	Hughes	Thomas Patrick	BD
29 March 1878	Howell	David	BD
2 Aug 1879	Marks	John Ebenezer	DD
22 Aug 1879	Nuttall	Enos	BD
15 April 1879	Storrs	William Townsend	BD
31 July 1879	How	William Walsham	DD
18 June 1879	Ridley	William	DD
21 June 1879	Wendt	Ernst Emil	LLD
27 June 1879	Gardiner	Joseph Phelps	DD
4 March 1879	Lightfoot	Thomas Fothergill	BD
4 March 1879	Smith	William Frederick Haynes	LLD
16 Jan 1880	Roger	James	MD
24 Sep 1880	Nuttall	Enos	DD
1 Nov 1880	Evans	Robert William	DD
22 Nov 1880	Mason	William	DD
13 Dec 1880	Baylis	James Gilbert	BD
9 June 1880	Edmonds	Walter John	BD
28 June 1880	Kennet	Charles Egbert	DD
12 March 1880	Pinkham	William Cyprian	BD
14 Jan 1881	Hussey	James McConnell	DD
3 Feb 1881	Brooks	William	BD
10 Feb 1881	Gritton	John	DD
10 Feb 1881	Pinsent	Robert John	DCL
2 Sep 1881	Bullinger	Ethelbert William	DD
22 Sep 1881	Farrar	Thomas	BD
5 April 1881	Maddox	Ralph Henry	BD
30 April 1881	Sell	Edward	BD
14 July 1881	Bardsley	Joseph	DD
23 July 1881	Stern	Henry Aaron	DD
30 June 1881	Blunt	Richard Frederick Lefevre	DD

Date	Surname	First name(s)	Degree
2 March 1881	Coleman	John James	MA
2 March 1881	Powell	George John	MA
2 March 1881	Woode	Enoch	MA
22 March 1881	Gray	John Henry	DD
17 Feb 1882	Slater	Samuel	DD
13 May 1882	Clarke	Edward Bloomfield	BD
23 Aug 1882	Hopkins	Edward John	DMus
27 April 1882	Bree	Herbert	DD
17 June 1882	Lansdell	Henry	DD
5 Oct 1883	Key	Brunsby Lewis (Lancelot)	DD
8 Dec 1883	Colborne	Langdon	DMus
3 April 1883	Troutbeck	John	DD
21 June 1883	Chiswell	Alfred	BD
21 June 1883	Martin	George Clement	DMus
2 May 1884	Brown	James Francis	BD
24 Oct 1884	Padfield	Joseph Edwin	BD
24 Oct 1884	Samuel	Daniel	BD
24 Oct 1884	Satthianadhan	William Thomas	BD
26 April 1884	Deen	Imad	DD
24 July 1884	Charles	Arthur	MA
13 Jan 1885	Sheppard	Joseph Brigstocke	LLD
26 Feb 1885	Edghill	John Cox	DD
26 Feb 1885	Harrison	Alexander James	BD
26 Feb 1885	Miller	John Aaron	BD
28 Oct 1885	Norris	George Michael	LLB
26 March 1885	Cox	John Charles	LLD
9 Dec 1886	William	William	MA
16 April 1886	Ainslie	Alexander Colvin	LLD
16 April 1886	Jordon	Charles Warwick	DMus
3 July 1886	Crisp	William	BD
3 July 1886	Harvey	Bache Wright	DD
15 March 1886	David	William	MA
15 March 1886	Doveton	Edward	MA
15 March 1886	Hewitt	Oscar	MA
17 May 1887	Nagel	Charles Nicholas	MA
26 Jan 1888	Hole	Samuel Reynolds	DD
7 May 1888	Lemare	William	DMus
31 July 1888	Wade	Thomas Russell	BD
7 Jan 1889	Douet	Charles Frederick	DD
11 May 1889	Tansley	George	MA
28 Nov 1889	Turpin	Edmund Hart	DMus
25 July 1889	Henniker	Henry Faulkner	DMus
7 March 1889	Mann	Frederic	MA
19 March 1890	Summers	Joseph	DMus
29 Oct 1891	Barlow	Christopher George	DD
21 Nov 1891	Ford	Henry Edmund	DMus

Date	Surname	First name(s)	Degree
2 Dec 1891	Koshi	Koshi	DD
20 March 1891	Agutter	Benjamin	DMus
7 Jan 1892	Palmer	John	BD
7 Jan 1892	Pilot	William	DD
27 July 1892	Kettlewell	Samuel	DD
31 March 1892	Hayes	James Thomas	DD
2 Feb 1893	Gray	Albert	MA
27 July 1893	Copinger	Walter Arthur	LLD
8 Feb 1894	Harrison	Alexander James	MA
8 Feb 1894	Julian	John	DD
24 May 1894	Davis	John Roland	MA
24 May 1894	Done	William	DMus
11 June 1894	Hall	Alfred James	BD
21 Feb 1895	Unmack	Edward Carl	MA
28 Nov 1895	Anderson	Ernest August	DD
28 Nov 1895	Joseph	Henry Mason	MA
28 July 1896	Mcnaught	William Gray	DMus
28 July 1896	Wood	Daniel Joseph	DMus
4 June 1897	Smith	John Taylor	DD
29 April 1898	Fraser	Edward Henry	DCL
1898	Smith	Alfred	MA
25 Aug 1899	Richards	William Joseph	DD
24 July 1899	Sinclair	George Robertson	DMus

Date	Surname	First name(s)	Degree
17 May 1900	Coles	James Oakley	BD
17 May 1900	Hamper	Ernest William	MA
15 Sep 1900	Barker	Joseph	DD
10 July 1900	Pyne	James Kendrick	DMus
13 Feb 1901	Higgs	James	DMus
7 Oct 1901	Knowles	James Hinton	BD
26 Nov 1901	Peel	William George	DD
5 July 1901	Green	James	DD
17 July 1901	Morley	Samuel	DD
7 Aug 1902	Lindsay	Robert Corbet Allan	MA
25 March 1903	Furneaux	William Mordaunt	DD
10 March 1904	Williams	Isaac James	MA
18 Jan 1905	Everingham	William	BD
18 Jan 1905	Hoyte	William Stevenson	DMus
20 Jan 1905	Darby	Alfred	MA
20 May 1905	Brewer	Alfred Herbert	DMus
25 May 1905	Harriss	Charles Albert Edwin	DMus
17 Oct 1905	Maccarthy	Welbore	DD
6 March 1906	Weitbrecht	Herbert Udney	DD
24 Nov 1907	Banister	William	DD

Date	Surname	First name(s)	Degree
16 July 1907	Douse	John	DD
25 May 1908	Twitchell	Thomas Clayton	DD
9 Oct 1908	Gwynne	LLewellyn Henry	DD
11 Dec 1908	Bankes	John Eldon	MA
18 March 1908	Barker	William	DD
17 Sep 1909	Wakefield	Henry Russell	DD
24 Nov 1909	Batchelor	John	DD
24 Nov 1909	Lea	Arthur	DD
12 July 1909	Samson	Edward Marlay	MA
16 March 1909	Mounsey	William Robert	DD
15 Aug 1910	Brown	William Henry	DD
15 Nov 1910	Denham	John Richard	BD
22 June 1910	Wigram	William Ainger	DD
22 Feb 1911	Edwards	Alfred Harold	MA
26 May 1911	Holmes	Ernest Edward	BD
29 May 1911	Slater	Ernest	DMus
11 Dec 1911	Sidwell	Henry Brindley	DD
31 July 1911	Faulkner	Edgar Thomas	DMus
22 Feb 1912	Moule	Arthur Evans	BD
26 Feb 1912	Long	George Merrick	DD
11 July 1912	Illsley	Percival John	DMus
25 Feb 1913	Thorne	Edward Henry	DMus
18 Aug 1913	Stephen	Reginald	DD
30 Oct 1913	De Carteret	George Frederick Cecil	DD
25 Nov 1913	Beaven	Frederic Hicks	DD
16 Feb 1914	Ditchfield	John Edwin Watts	DD
4 Jan 1915	Taylor	Samuel Mumford	DD
4 Nov 1915	Owen	Charles Mansfield	DD
21 March 1916	Willson	John Basil Wynne	DD
8 Oct 1917	Penfold	John Brosher Vernon	BD
8 June 1917	Floyd	Alfred Ernest	DMus
8 June 1917	Wentworth-Sheilds	Wentworth Francis Wentworth	DD
27 June 1917	Palmer	George Herbert	DMus
27 June 1918	Cranswick	Harvard George	DD
27 June 1918	Sadlier	William Charles	DD
6 March 1918	Ingles	Charles William Chamberlayne	DD
12 Nov 1919	Jones	Frank Melville	DD
12 Nov 1919	Linton	James Henry	BD
27 June 1919	Willink	John Wakefield	DD
2 Feb 1920	Mccormick	Joseph Gough	BD
18 May 1920	Roach	Frederick	DD
12 Nov 1920	Brown	Francis Ernest	DD
16 Nov 1920	Duppuy	Charles Ridley	DD
19 Nov 1920	Crowther	Davideson Coates	DD
26 March 1920	Jarvis	Alfred Charles Eustace	BD
19 Aug 1921	Elsey	William Edward	DD

Date	Surname	First name(s)	Degree
18 Nov 1921	Richards	Isaac	DD
19 Nov 1921	Hull	Percy Clarke	DMus
28 Nov 1922	Errington	Francis Henry	DCL
28 Nov 1922	Luscombe	Samuel	MA
31 Oct 1923	Moody	Charles Harry	DMus
31 Oct 1923	Wright	George William	DD
1 Feb 1924	Aglionby	John Orfeur	DD
12 May 1924	Woodward	George Ratcliffe	DMus
3 July 1924	Stuart	Henry Vener	BD
14 July 1924	Carpenter-Garnier	Mark Rodolph	DD
2 May 1925	Jarvis	Alfred Charles Eustace	DD
3 Oct 1925	Birley	Thomas Howard	DD
3 Oct 1925	Simpson	John Basil	DD
28 Oct 1925	Lavis	Sidney Warren	DD
20 April 1925	Fogarty	Nelson Wellesley	DD
6 Jan 1926	Forde	Lionel George Bridges Justice	DD
8 Jan 1926	De Candole	Henry Lawe Corry Vully	DD
17 May 1926	O'Ferrall	Ronald Stanhope More	DD
8 Sep 1926	Ekanayake	George Benjamin	DD
9 Feb 1927	Lea	Edward Howard	BD
13 Oct 1927	Chambers	George Alexander	DD
23 June 1927	Lovett	Ernest Neville	DD
11 March 1927	James	Melville Charles	DD
1 Feb 1928	Baker	Donald George	DD
21 May 1928	Nicholson	Sydney Hugo	DMus
21 May 1928	Thomas	Richard	DD
17 Oct 1928	Johnson	Arthur Basil Noel	DMus
19 Oct 1928	Mosley	Henry	DD
7 Nov 1928	Macmillan	John Victor	DD
7 Nov 1928	Williams	Max	DMus
14 Oct 1929	Hubback	George Clay	DD
14 Oct 1929	Williams	Charles Leo Lee	DMus
8 Nov 1929	Gibbs	Kenneth Francis	DD
16 July 1929	Ellis	William	DMus
16 July 1929	Hunt	Hubert Walter	DMus
10 Jan 1930	Holmes	Ernest Edward	DD
10 Jan 1930	Levertoff	Paul Philip	DD
6 Dec 1930	Aitken	George Benjamin Johnston	DD
6 Dec 1930	Lewis	David	DCL
10 March 1930	Brown	Ernst Faulkner	DD
11 Feb 1931	Haight	Mervyn George	DD
3 Sep 1931	Noble	Thomas Tertius	DMus
10 Nov 1931	Thorold	Ernest Hayford	DD
4 Dec 1931	Dwelly	Frederick William	DD
9 June 1931	Grace	Harvey	DMus
13 Jan 1932	Shaw	Geoffrey	DMus

Date	Surname	First name(s)	Degree
13 Jan 1932	Shaw	Martin Edward Fallas	DMus
1 Feb 1932	Moreton	George Harry	DMus
10 Aug 1932	Hardie	William George	DD
27 July 1932	Underhill	Francis	DD
13 June 1932	Brown	George Francis Graham	DD
24 May 1933	Woodward	Clifford Salisbury	DD
26 Jan 1934	Cook	Edgar Tom	DMus
15 Feb 1934	Soar	Joseph	DMus
11 May 1934	Morgan	John	DD
5 Nov 1934	Harton	Frederic Percy	BD
5 Nov 1934	Havard	William Thomas	DD
23 March 1934	Henderson	Ralph Bushill	BD
11 Jan 1935	Towers	John Robert	DD
27 Nov 1935	Thalben-Ball	George Thomas	DMus
2 Dec 1935	Macassey	Ernest Livingston	DD
14 Jan 1936	Baker-Wilbraham	Sir Philip Wilbraham	DCL
5 Nov 1936	Curzon	Charles Edward	DD
6 April 1936	Frewen	Henry	DD
27 April 1936	Spurling	Clement Michael	DMus
15 June 1936	Lunt	Geoffrey Charles Lester	DD
15 June 1936	Partridge	Frank	DD
31 May 1937	Hamer	Alban	DMus
22 Dec 1937	Martin	Albert Charles	MA
10 June 1937	Bennett	Frank Selwyn Macaulay	DD
10 June 1937	Woods	Edward Sydney	DD
10 Jan 1938	De Labilliere	Paul Fulerand Delacour	DD
10 Jan 1938	Hellins	Edgar William James	DD
10 Jan 1938	Vale	Walter Sidney	DMus
8 Dec 1938	Hone	Campbell Richard	DD
14 March 1938	Eeles	Francis Carolus	DD
31 Jan 1939	Vaisey	Harry Bevir	DCL
1 May 1939	Reed	William Henry	DMus
18 Sep 1939	Symons	Charles Douglas	DD
18 Nov 1939	Williamson	Edward William	DD
1 Dec 1939	Wassell	Richard	DMus
13 Dec 1939	Batty	Basil Staunton	DD
12 July 1939	Douglas	John Albert	DD
12 July 1939	Jacques	Reginald	DMus
5 Sep 1940	Monaham	Alfred Edwin	DD
18 Nov 1940	Brown	Claude	DMus
18 Nov 1940	Sitters	Percy Henry Smart	MA
19 April 1940	Chavasse	Christopher Maude	DD
27 April 1940	Balfour	Henry Lucas	DMus
17 June 1940	Crick	Douglas Henry	DD
17 June 1940	Smith	Guy Vernon	DD
7 Nov 1941	Hudson	Noel Baring	DD

Date	Surname	First name(s)	Degree
13 March 1941	Brook	Richard	DD
2 Feb 1942	Anderson	William Louis	DD
29 July 1942	Skelton	Henry Aylmer	DD
19 Jan 1943	Gorton	Neville Vincent	DD
1 Sep 1943	Stewart	Weston Henry	DD
12 Oct 1943	Askwith	William Marcus	DD
12 Oct 1943	Taylor	John Ralph Strickland	DD
17 Nov 1943	Ackerley	Frederick George	DD
12 July 1943	Booth	Joseph John	DD
20 Jan 1944	Deane	Anthony Charles	DD
3 May 1945	Martin	Clifford Arthur	DD
7 June 1945	Arnold	John Henry	DMus
7 June 1945	Grimes	Cecil John	DD
11 Nov 1946	Bradfield	Harold William	DD
1 August 1946	Campbell	John McLeod	DD
21 Oct 1947	Allen	Walter Godfrey	MA
17 April 1947	Sumsion	Herbert Whitton	DMus
24 April 1947	Barry	Frank Russell	DD
24 April 1947	Greaves	Arthur Ivan	DD
7 July 1947	Halse	William Charles	DD
4 June 1947	Mcgowan	Henry	DD
7 April 1948	Hammond	Lempriere Durell	DD
30 July 1948	Harland	Maurice Henry	DD
30 July 1948	Moline	Robert William Haines	DD
18 March 1948	Maude	John Cyril	MA
30 May 1949	Brinton	Jacob	MA
19 Sep 1949	Hunter	Leslie Stannard	DD
14 Oct 1949	Oddie	Basil William	MA
20 June 1949	Longworth	Tom	DD
20 June 1949	Wilson	Roger Plumpton	DD
10 Jan 1950	Montgomery-Campbell	Henry Colville	DD
10 Jan 1950	Roper	Edgar Stanley	DMus
3 Feb 1950	Fleming	William Launcelot Scott	DD
13 Sep 1950	Bartlett	David Daniel	DD
13 Sep 1950	Jones	Edward Michael Gresford	DD
5 July 1950	Jones	John Charles	DD
5 July 1950	Morris	Alfred Edwin	DD
23 June 1950	Knight	Alan John	DD
2 March 1950	Paget	Edward Francis	DD
13 Feb 1951	Allison	Sherard Falkner	DD
13 Feb 1951	Oldroyd	George	DMus
21 Feb 1951	Stanway	Alfred	MA
5 Dec 1951	Marsden	Edwyn Lisle	MA
31 July 1951	Vining	Leslie Gordon	DD
16 June 1951	Roberts	Basil Coleby	DD
9 May 1952	Milner-White	Eric	DD

Date	Surname	First name(s)	Degree
17 Oct 1952	Owen	Reginald Herbert	DD
17 June 1952	Godfrey	Robert Samuel	MA
6 Oct 1953	Custard	Walter Henry Goss	DMus
6 Oct 1953	Pollard	Benjamin	DD
13 Oct 1953	Reeve	Arthur Stretton	DD
13 Oct 1953	Wilson	John Leonard	DD
27 Oct 1953	Barron	John Bernard	MA
17 March 1953	Chamberlain	Frank Noel	MA
17 March 1953	Wright	Leslie	MA
18 Jan 1954	Simon	William Glyn Hughes	DD
18 Jan 1954	Williams	Ronald Ralph	DD
15 Dec 1954	Lamb	Percy Charles	MA
28 Jane 1954	Clayton	Philip Thomas Byard	DD
28 June 1954	Morris	Arthur Harold	DD
17 Jan 1955	Baddeley	Walter Hubert	DD
17 Jan 1955	Morgan	Edmund Robert	DD
18 Oct 1955	Ellison	Gerald Alexander	DD
1 Dec 1955	Charles-Edward	Lewis Mervyn	MA
12 Dec 1955	Willink	Henry	DCL
3 March 1955	Bowen	Harry Duncan Storer	MA
16 Oct 1956	Bardsley	Cuthbert Killick Norman	DD
16 Oct 1956	Richards	John Richards	DD
16 Oct 1956	Watkins	Ivor Stanley	DD
9 July 1956	Willan	Healey	DMus
28 Jan 1957	Charles-Edwards	Lewis Mervyn	DD
28 Jan 1957	Williams	Gwilyn Owen	DD
18 Feb 1957	Riches	Kenneth	DD
18 Feb 1957	Stopford	Robert Wright	DD
19 Sep 1957	De Blank	Joost	DD
15 Oct 1957	Ashdown	Hugh Edward	DD
15 Oct 1957	Coggan	Frederick Donald	DD
5 Nov 1957	Woods	Frank	DD
12 April 1957	Allenby	David Howard Nicholas	MA
8 July 1957	Joyce	Cyril Alfred	MA
8 July 1957	Macinnes	Angus Campbell	DD
7 Feb 1958	Ridley	Mildred Betty	MA
7 Feb 1958	Snow	Diana Mary	MA
9 May 1958	Thorne	Frank Oswald	DD
7 Aug 1958	Barfoot	Walter Foster	DD
7 Aug 1958	Mukerjee	Arabinda Nath	DD
7 Aug 1958	Sherrill	Henry Knox	DD
7 Aug 1958	Yashiro	Michael Hinsuke	DD
19 Nov 1958	Brown	Charles Archibald	MA
2 July 1958	Ramsbotham	John Alexander	DD
11 July 1958	Lavis	Sidney Warren	DD
28 July 1958	Hughes	William James	DD

Date	Surname	First name(s)	Degree
28 July 1958	Kempthorne	Leonard Stanley	DD
10 June 1958	Healey	Kenneth	MA
21 March 1958	Thomas	John James Absalom	DD
28 Jan 1959	Waddington	John Albert Henry	MA
24 Feb 1959	Gough	Hugh Rowlands	DD
5 May 1959	Stockwood	Arthur Mervyn	DD
27 May 1959	Steer	Francis	MA
28 Sep 1959	Rogers	Aland Francis Bright	DD
19 Oct 1959	Abbott	Eric Symes	DD
3 July 1959	Paul	Leslie	MA
30 June 1959	Allen	Geoffrey Francis	DD
30 June 1959	Hebron	Tom	MA
9 Feb 1960	Pugh	Thomas Jenkin	MA
7 Nov 1960	Claxton	Charles Robert	DD
7 Nov 1960	Henderson	Edward Barry	DD
28 June 1960	Hodgkins	Michael Minden	MA
28 June 1960	Young	Stanley Edward William	MA
8 March 1960	Key	John Maurice	DD
24 March 1960	Phillips	John Henry Lawrence	DD
5 Jan 1961	Say	Richard David	DD
26 Jan 1961	Edwards	Quentin Tytler	MA
26 Jan 1961	Pace	George Gaze	MA
25 Feb 1961	Goddard	Leslie Thomas	MA
25 March 1961	Knight	Gerald Hocken	DMus
25 March 1961	Reindorp	George Edmund	DD
25 March 1961	Scott	John Arthur Guillum	DCL
25 March 1961	Tasker	Randolph Vincent Greenwood	DD
25 March 1961	Wigglesworth	Walter Somerville	DCL
10 May 1962	Binnall	Peter Blannin Gibbons	MA
10 May 1962	Deanesly	Margaret	DLitt
11 May 1962	Brown	Sir James	LLD
18 May 1962	Ewin	Ernest Thomas Floyd	MA
19 April 1962	Ward	Reginald Somerset	DD
24 July 1962	Beecher	Leonard James	DD
25 July 1963	Lesser	Norman Alfred	DD
28 June 1963	Patterson	Cecil John	DD
3 Nov 1965	Thompson	Edward	MA
18 Nov 1966	Davey	Francis Noel	DD
18 Nov 1966	Gill	John Clifford	MA
18 Nov 1966	Phillips	John Bertram	DD
25 July 1966	Skinner	Mildred	MA
24 Aug 1968	Strong	Philip Nigel Warrington	DD
29 Oct 1968	Gray	George Charles	DMus
25 Sep 1969	Browne	Charles Foster	DMus
21 Feb 1970	Wright	Edred John	BMUS
28 April 1970	Simpson	Rennie	MA

Date	Surname	First name(s)	Degree
25 Jan 1971	Browne	Elliott Martin	DLitt
20 Dec 1971	Surplice	Reginald Alwyn	DMus
April 1971	Jagger	Peter John	MA
17 March 1971	Vann	William Stanley	DMus
27 Sep 1972	Goodenough	Cecilia	DD
7 Feb 1973	Hewitt	Godfrey	DMus
16 May 1973	Huxtable	William John Fairchild	DD
7 Dec 1973	Eden	Conrad William	DMus
16 May 1974	Gabb	William Harry	DMus
20 May 1974	Rice	Francis George	MA
25 Oct 1974	Wicks	Allan	DMus
12 June 1974	Jones	Hugh LLewellyn	MA
17 Dec 1975	Lacey	Janet	DD
17 Dec 1975	Trevisick	John Otway	MA
24 April 1976	Beeson	Trevor Randall	MA
18 April 1977	Bancroft	Henry Hugh	DMus
18 April 1977	Guest	George Howell	DMus
18 April 1977	Howe	John William Alexander	DD
18 April 1977	Kent	Harold Simcox	DCL
18 April 1977	Saunders	Cecily Mary Strode	MD
25 Jan 1978	Carey	David Macbeth Moir	DCL
25 Jan 1978	Evans	Sydney Hall	DD
3 Oct 1978	Fisher	Reginal Lindsay	MA
3 Oct 1978	Whistler	Benedicta	MLitt
31 Oct 1978	Dakers	Lionel Frederick	DMus
10 Oct 1979	Carpenter	Edward Frederick	DD
31 Oct 1979	Adams	Kenneth Galt	MA
31 Oct 1979	Hickinbotham	James Peter	DD
31 Oct 1979	Howard	Rosemary Christian	MA
31 Oct 1979	King	Thomas George	DD
14 Jan 1980	Lepper	Barbara Helen	MA
16 May 1981	De Sausmarey	John Havilland Russell	MA
June 1981	Guest	Douglas Albert	DMus
June 1981	Kendall	Richard Elliott	MA
June 1981	Payton	Arthur Edward	MA
June 1981	Whitaker	Charles Edward	MA
22 June 1982	Green	Cecil Frederick	DD
22 June 1982	Grierson	Jane	MA
22 June 1982	Harvey	Francis William	MA
22 June 1982	Hoskins	Hubert Henry	BD
18 July 1983	Bill	Edward Geoffrey Watson	DLitt
18 July 1983	Chartres	Richard John Carew	BD
18 July 1983	Cole	Frederick Walter	MA
18 July 1983	Stott	John Robert Walmsley	DD
18 July 1983	Warters	Vivienne Violet Belle	MA
17 May 1984	Bubbers	David Bramwell	MA

Date	Surname	First name(s)	Degree
17 May 1984	Paul	Leslie Allan	DLitt
17 May 1984	Roper	Anne	MA
17 May 1984	Royle	Roy Joseph	MA
20 June 1985	Bailey	Sydney Dawson	DCL
20 June 1985	Feibusch	Hans Nathan	DLitt
20 June 1985	Green	Bryan Stuart Westmacott	DD
20 June 1985	Jones	Douglas Rawlinson	DD
20 June 1985	Morgan	Penelope Ethel	MA
20 June 1985	Royall	Arthur Robert	MA
29 June 1985	Clark	Barbara Jean	MA
28 July 1986	Scott	Edward Walter	DD
11 June 1986	Bird	Pamela	MA
11 June 1986	Green	Ronald Henry	MA
11 June 1986	Hill	Eric Claude Combe	DD
11 June 1986	Moore	Evelyn Garth	DCL
11 June 1986	Wakefield	Gordon Stevaens	DD
8 Sep 1987	Jakobovits	Immanuel	DD
17 June 1987	Baker	Thomas George Adames	DD
17 June 1987	Barber	Melanie	MA
17 June 1987	Dearnley	Christopher Hugh	DMus
17 June 1987	O'Brien	Richard	DCL
17 June 1987	Thomson	James Phillips Spalding	MD
16 June 1988	Bollom	David	MA
16 June 1988	Dufty	Arthur Richard	DLitt
16 June 1988	Fry	Christopher Arthur Hammond	DLitt
16 June 1988	Hoban	Deirdre Elizabeth	MA
16 June 1988	Tanner	Mary Elizabeth	DD
16 June 1988	Vanstone	William Hubert	DD
17 June 1988	Palmer	Barnard Harold Michael	DLitt
12 July 1989	Alves	Colin	MLitt
12 July 1989	Birch	John Anthony	DMus
12 July 1989	Clark	John Patrick Hedley	DD
12 July 1989	Livingstone	Elizabeth Anne	DD
12 July 1989	Marshall	Michael Leicester John	MA
12 July 1989	Nicholson	Peter Charles	MA
12 July 1989	Whitfield	William	DLitt
16 May 1990	Bevan	Maurice Guy Smalman	BMUS
16 May 1990	Coleman	Roger	MLitt
16 May 1990	Edwards	David Lawrence	DD
16 May 1990	Nicholls	Bernard Douglas	MA
16 May 1990	Nicholls	Doris Alma	MA
16 May 1990	Reed	Bruce Douglas	MLitt
16 May 1990	Royle	Roger Michael	MA
16 May 1990	Sanders	John Derek	DMus
10 Jan 1991	Baker	Derek John Davey	MA
10 Jan 1991	Baker	John Austin	DD

Date	Surname	First name(s)	Degree
10 Jan 1991	Dudley-Smith	Timothy	MLitt
10 Jan 1991	Gruber	Pamela Helen	MA
10 Jan 1991	Heaton	Eric William	DD
10 Jan 1991	Marsh	Bazil Roland	MLitt
10 Jan 1991	Massey	Roy Cyril	DMus
10 Jan 1991	Robson	Frank Elms	DCL
10 Jan 1991	Root	Celia Mary	MA
10 Jan 1991	Taylor	Robert Selby	DD
10 Jan 1991	Thimont	Bernard Maurice	MA
10 Jan 1991	Tyler	Anne Florence	MA
11 June 1992	Bax	Josephine Chloe	MLitt
11 June 1992	Beckwith	Roger Thomas	DD
11 June 1992	Craston	Richard Colin	DD
11 June 1992	Etchells	Dorothea Ruth	DD
11 June 1992	Nevile	Mildred Mary	MA
11 June 1992	Newton	John Theodore	MA
11 June 1992	Seal	Richard Godfrey	DMus
11 June 1992	Thorogood	Bernard George	DD
11 June 1992	Wright	William Hutchinson	MA
11 May 1993	Sutherland	Frank Nicholas	MA
12 May 1993	Buchanan	Colin Ogilvie	DD
12 May 1993	Buck	Richard Peter Holdron	MA
12 May 1993	Dykes Bower	Stephen Ernest	DLitt
12 May 1993	James	Eric Arthur	DD
12 May 1993	Lings	George William	MLitt
12 May 1993	Lowater	Peter Alexander	MA
12 May 1993	Oppenheimer	Laetitia Helen	DD
12 May 1993	Owen	John Arthur Dalzie	DCL
12 May 1993	Pearce	John Brian	MLitt
11 May 1994	Ray	Mary Eva Pedder	MA
7 June 1994	Thorold	Henry Croyland	MLitt
7 June 1994	Barratt	Anthony John	MLitt
7 June 1994	Bell	Robert Hunter	DMus
7 June 1994	Conway	David Martin	DLitt
7 June 1994	Crossland	Anthony	DMus
7 June 1994	Evans	Geoffrey Baibridge	MA
7 June 1994	Sweet	John McMurdo	DD
3 May 1995	Gunn-Johnson	David A	MA
31 May 1995	Boughen	Robert Keith	DMus
31 May 1995	Brown	John	MA
31 May 1995	Evetts	Leonard	DLitt
31 May 1995	Graham	Andrew Kenny	DD
31 May 1995	Lunn	George	MA
31 May 1995	Newton	John Anthony	DD
31 May 1995	Sims	Andrew Charles Peter	MD

5 A MISCELLANY OF ARTICLES ON LAMBETH DEGREES

These articles were originally published as follows:

1. Sylvanus Urban, "Correspondence of Sylvanus Urban: Lambeth Degrees", *The Gentleman's Magazine* (May 1864) 633–638

2. Sylvanus Urban, "Correspondence of Sylvanus Urban: Lambeth Degrees", *The Gentleman's Magazine* (June 1864) 770–774

3. Cecil Wall, "Nova et Vetera: The Lambeth Degrees", *British Medical Journal* 3904 (Nov. 1935) 854–855

4. Charles A. H. Franklyn, "Lambeth Degrees", *British Medical Journal* 3901 (Oct. 1935) 703

5. L. A. Parry, "Lambeth Degrees", *British Medical Journal* 3899 (Sept. 1935) 603–604

5.1 'CORRESPONDENCE OF SYLVANUS URBAN': LAMBETH DEGREES

Correspondence of Sylvanus Urban.

[Correspondents are requested to append their Addresses, not, unless agreeable, for publication, but in order that a copy of the GENTLEMAN'S MAGAZINE *containing their Communications may be forwarded to them.]*

LAMBETH DEGREES.

SIR,—The letter of W. E. L. in your March Number on Lambeth degrees touches a question which is of some antiquarian interest, and was once of considerable practical importance.

The circumstances which gave rise to the institution of these degrees were probably the attempts made both in Church and State, during the fifteenth century, partly to restrict the exercise of the papal power in opposition to the Statute of Provisors, by securing promotion to the graduates of the English Universities, and partly to advance and strengthen the Universities themselves by providing competently for their graduates. Examples of the measures taken for these purposes may be found in Wood's *Antiquitates* (ed. 1674), 197, &c., 216, 217, &c., Labbe and Cossart, *Concilia*, xiv. 347, &c. ; there are others in Wilkins, and among the official Correspondence of Bishop Beckington, shortly to be published by the Master of the Rolls, under the editorship of Mr. George Williams.

To evade the disabilities imposed by these acts on non-graduates, and to secure for themselves the privileges of graduates, it became usual towards the end of the century for clerks who had not been educated at the Universities to obtain dispensations from Rome, enabling them to hold pluralities, &c., and in some few recorded cases to obtain degrees from the Pope, on the strength of which they were incorporated in the English Universities with the same rights as the original graduates.

One or two cases of the incorporation of these Roman graduates are to be found in the Cambridge records ; e. g. "Frater Steele," of Rome, was incorporated in 1492; "Frater Raddyng," a doctor of Rome, in 1497 (MS. Lambeth, 1133) ; and in 1501 "Mr. Cabald" had a grace "ut admittatur ad eundem gradum in quo stat Romæ." It seems more probable that these degrees were granted by the Pope as a part of his ordinary power, than in any connexion with a University ; for the power of conferring degrees was at this time exercised by other bodies than the Universities, as by the Counts Palatine (*Comites Palatini Lateranenses*), who also could confer the power of making notaries by faculty. (See the seventh Decretal, lib. iii. tit. iv., and Battely's Somner's Canterbury, part i., App., 59, and Du Cange, sub voce *Comes Palatinus*). It was not necessary, however, to go to Rome for these degrees ; the power to confer them was bestowed upon the legates. Many examples of this may be found in the *Bullarium*, and one instance may suffice here. Cardinal Wolsey's Bull of Legation (Rymer, xiii. 739) allows him the power, "quascunque personas, sufficientes tamen et idoneas, volentes ad doctoratus, seu licentiaturæ, aut Baccalaureatus in utroque vel altero Jurium, et ad magistratus tam in Theologia quam in Artibus et Medicina vel alios gradus pro-movendi."

The statute of 25 Henry VIII. c. 21, invests the Archbishop of Canterbury with power to grant all manner such licences, dispensations, compositions, faculties, grants, receipts, delegacies, &c., as heretofore had been accustomed to be had and obtained from Rome. (See Mr. Workard's letter in the April Number.)

Degrees are not specified in this transfer of authority, but they are under-stood to be included in the term *faculties*. Bishop Gibson (*Codex, &c.*, ed. 1713, p. 105) has the following note on the subject :—

> " Among the other heads in which faculties had been customarily grantable, and were now made grantable by the Archbishops of Canterbury in virtue of this act, we find in the said Book of Taxation (see § xi.) the two that follow :—' Creatio Doctorum in quacunque facultate, £4. Creatio aliorum graduatorum in quacunque facultate, £4.' Which power as it hath not been abrogated or touched by any succeeding law, so hath it been exercised by the successive archbishops as a right vested in their see, by no less authority than that of Parliament, to which autho-rity as conveyed by this act special reference is made in the body of every faculty that is granted upon this head."

The right thus conferred, or presumed to be conferred, was exercised by the archbishops apparently without objection until in the reign of George I. it was disputed, and made the subject of a lawsuit. Gastrell, Bishop of Chester, refused to admit Samuel Peploe, a B.D. of Lambeth, to the Wardenship of Manchester College. The cause was tried first at Lancaster Assizes, on the 13th of August, 1722. The argument in favour of the Archbishop's right was conducted with great learning and research. The notes for the instruction of counsel may be found among Bishop Chandler's papers, Brit. Mus. MS. Add. 6489. The hearing occupied fifteen hours. "A prescriptive right was made out to general satisfac-tion, and a statutable right also so far as there was occasion to go into the Act of Parliament. But the jury of gentlemen gave a verdict to the right in general, without fixing it on any single foot." (MS. Lambeth, 1133.) It was then carried by appeal before the King's Bench, and there decided in favour of the Archbishop's right, May 22, 1725. (Notes and Queries, iii. 276.) This case is referred to by Blackstone, Comm., i. 381, (ed. 1829). He quotes it as "The Bishop of Chester's case, Oxon. 1721." This I have not seen.— So much for the origin of the right.

The *status* of the Lambeth graduates was always rather unsettled, and the few who are mentioned as incorporated at Cambridge, received that honour with the proviso that it should not be construed into a precedent. Baker (MS. 42, pp. 136, 137, 140, in the Public Library at Cambridge) objects to the practice of admitting them *ad eundem*, as inconsistent with the rights and privileges of the University, and, moreover, expressly guarded against by the oath taken by the inceptors in every faculty, viz. " Jurabis quod extra istam Universitatem, nusquam præterquam Oxoniis in illa facultate incipies, nec con-senties ut aliquis alibi in Anglia incipiens hic pro doctore vel magistro in illa facultate habeatur." I do not remember to have seen in Wood's *Fasti* any mention of a Lambeth graduate. It will be seen, however, from the list of degrees, that from the time of the Restoration to the end of the seventeenth century they were generally conferred on members of the Universities.

The right of conferring degrees was exercised by Archbishop Cranmer as early as 1539. In that year he commissioned Bishop Rugg of Norwich to confer the degree of Doctor of Divinity on Eligius Ferrers. He instructs him in the commission to proceed in the business with two other D.D.'s to be chosen by the Bishop, "si eum ad gradum antedictum suscipiendum, prævio examine debito, habilem reperietis." Accordingly in the Act of execution they represent "quia per debitam examinationem comperimus et invenimus memoratum E. F. ad gradum doctoratus in facultate Theologia suscipiendum habilem dignum et idoneum." (MS. Lambeth, 1133.) The documents connected with this transaction were adduced in Peploe's case, and copies of them are in Bp. Chandler's MS. B. Mus. Add. 6489.

Very few instances are to be found of Lambeth degrees granted before the Restoration. The records of the Faculty Office supply none, and the search made, in the Peploe case, in the Patent Rolls, in which by the 25 Henry VIII. c. 21, these faculties are required to be enrolled, disclosed only two or three. I have searched also the Dispensation Rolls at the Record Office, which extend from 1597 to 1641, and have found but one case, that of John Hillyard. The Cambridge records supply two or three more.

The earliest records of the Faculty Office are two paper books marked A and B, which contain memoranda of the dispensations, creations of notaries, marriage licences, licences of non-residence, of eating meat in Lent, of commendams, &c., from 1543 to 1548, and from 1567 to 1591 respectively. The only case which I have found in them bearing on this subject, and as it is the only one adduced in the Peploe case from them, I suppose it to be the only one—is an admission by Cranmer, of George Broke, B.A., of the University of Venice, to the rights and privileges of a B.A. in England, and to equality with other graduates.

Archbishop Parker granted the degree of B.D. to one Blage: the form of the act was adduced in Peploe's case, from a MS. of Bishop Pearson, in the Library of Canterbury Cathedral. A copy of this form will be found in the Chandler MS.

The list of degrees before the Restoration is then as follows :—

   1539, Feb. 17. Eligius Ferrers, D.D.
   1544, Dec. 6. George Broke, B.A. of Venice, *ad eundem.*
   1559—1575. ——— Blage, B.D.
   1615, Mar. 14. Samuel Purchas, M.A., made B.D.
   1617, Nov. 20. John Hillyard, M.A., made B.D.
   1619, June 28. William Neile, M.A.
   1635, Dec. 9. Edward Layfield, M.A., Archdeacon of Essex, made B.D.

All these were adduced in Peploe's case. Purchas, the author of "The Pilgrims," is mentioned by Wood in the *Fasti* as a Cambridge man, and by Baker and Cole in their "Cambridge Collections."

From the time of the Restoration the list is perfect, the loss of one book in the Faculty Office being supplied by the list adduced in the Peploe case, 1660 to 1716. By the kindness of the officers of the Faculty Office I am enabled to furnish you with a copy of the list from 1660 to the present day.—I am, &c.,

Navestock, April 9.   WILLIAM STUBBS.

GRADUATI LAMBETHANI.

Juxon (1660, Sept. 3—1663, June 4).

	Degree conferred.
1660, Nov. 24. John Sudbury, M.A.	D.D.
Dec. 24. Wm. Braborne, M.A. Oxon., Chap. to the Archbishop	D.D.
1661, Sept. 24. Robert Sanderson	LL.B.
1662, Feb. 23. Peter Berkenhead, B.A.	M.A.
1663, May 11. William Fyffe, M.A. Trin. Coll. Oxon.	M.D.
May 12. Edm. Freeman, alias King, incorp. at Cambridge 1671, Oct. 5	M.B.

Sheldon, (1663, Aug. 31—1677, Nov. 9).

1663, Sept. 9. Policarp Dakyn, M.B. of Derby	M.D.
Sept. 17. Alexander Cheeke	LL.B.
Sept. 21. John Clements	LL.B.
Sept. 22. Edward Exton	LL.B.
Sept. 24. Robert Thompson	LL.B.
Sept. 30. John Randolph, M.A., R. of Leverington	D.D.
Oct. 7. John Pell, M.A., Ch. to Abp.	D.D.
Oct. 31. Robert Thoroton, M.A.	M.D.
1664, Feb. 4. John Selleck, M.A., Archd. of Bath	D.D.
March 15. George Cary, M.A., Dean of Exeter	D.D.
May 2. Wm. Hawkins, M.A. Ch. Ch. Oxon.	D.D.
Oct. 25. John Pritchett, M.A.	D.D.
1668, June 17. John Dryden, Esq.	M.A.
1671, Jan. 3. Laurence Seddon, B.D. Brasenose Coll.	D.D.
1672, Oct. 22. Antony Saunders	D.D.
1674, Aug. 19. Samuel Woodford, B.A. Wadham Coll.	D.D.
1675, April 9. Wm. Rosewell, M.A.	M.D.
Nov. 3. Wm. Harrison, M.A. Wadham Coll.	D.D.
Dec. 7. John Eachard, M.A. Cath. H.	B.D.

Tillotson, Dean of Canterbury, sede vacante.

1677, Nov. 21. Robt. Taylor, St. John's, Oxon.	M.A.
Dec. 10. John Blow, of Newark	Mus.Doc.
Dec. 11. James Clifford, Succentor of St. Paul's	M.A.

Sancroft (1678, Jan. 27—1691, Feb. 1).

1678, Feb. 1. Gabriel Towerson, M.A. All Souls	D.D.
Feb. 5. Wm. Shippen, M.A. Univ.	D.D.
Feb. 6. Francis Barnard, incorporated at Cambridge	M.D.
Feb. 9. John Newell, Alban Hall	M.A.
March 9. Peter Dent, Trinity, Camb. incorp. at Camb. 1681, March 18	M.B.
May 13. Sam. Bishop, M.A. Ch. Ch.	D.D.
May 25. Geo. Thorpe, B.D., Ch. to Abp.	D.D.
June 4. Geo. Speed, Magdalen Hall	M.A.
June 28. Thos. Comber, M.A. Sidney Coll.	D.D.
1680, Sept. 29. Gilbert Burnet, Bp. of Sarum 1689	D.D.
Nov. 1. Wm. Batty, M.A., Ch. to the	

	Degree conferred.
King, incorporated at Cambridge 1681, June 22	D.D.
1680, June 4. John St. John	LL.D.
1685, Nov. 12. Wm. Stanley, Master of Corpus, Camb., incorp. at Camb. 1694, Jan. 18	D.D.
Dec. 6. John Marshall	LL.B.

Tillotson (1691, April 23—1694, Nov. 22).

1691, June 8. William Talbot, M.A.	D.D.
June 25. William Walmsley	LL.B.
July 2. Thomas Hobbs	M.D.
July 3. James Barker	M.A.
Aug. 13. John Patrick, M.A.	D.D.
Nov. 19. Ralph Barker, Ch. to Abp.	D.D.
Dec. 7. Robert Hooke	M.D.
Dec. 21. Thomas Manningham, M.A.	D.D.
1692, March 3. Caleb Coatsworth	M.D.
1693, Mar. 27. Jonathan Blagrave, M.A.	D.D.

Tenison (1694, Dec. 6—1715, Dec. 14).

1695, Jan. 18. Thomas Green, S.T.B., incorp. at Cambridge 1695	D.D.
Jan. 18. John Knighton	D.D.
Feb. 4. John Woodward, incorp. at Cambridge 1695	M.D.
Feb. 8. Edward Gee	D.D.
March 27. Richard Willis, Bp. of Gloucester, 1715	D.D.
April 16. Michael Geddes	LL.D.
June 6. Francis Bragge	LL.B.
1696, Sept. 22. John Robinson, Bp. of Bristol 1710	D.D.
1697, March 3. Edward Tenison	LL.B.
1698, Jan. 10. John Wilson	LL.D.
May 16. Edward Vernon	M.A.
1700, Jan. 26. George Nevell	LL.B.
1701, Sept. 1. Thomas Walte	LL.B.
Nov. 26. John Crompton	M.D.
1702, June 18. Edm. Gibson, Librarian at Lambeth, Bp. of London 1723	D.D.
May 13. John Moore	LL.B.
July 22. Richard Knipe	M.A.
1704, Feb. 1. Thomas Hayley, B.A.	M.A.
1705, Nov. 29. William Lloyd	D.D.
1706, July 10. John Harris	D.D.
1707, Feb. 18. John Benbrigg	M.D.
May 5. Posthumus Smith	LL.B.
1708, March 9. Wm Wotton, S.T.B.	D.D.
April 13. Richard West	D.D.
July 6. Joseph Barton	M.A.
1711, June 5. Dormer Parkhurst	LL.B.
1712, May 17. James Jones	M.A.
June 23. William Pearson, M.A.	LL.D.
1714, April 23. Edward Tenison, Bp. of Ossory 1731	D.D.
April 26. Charles Talbot, B.A. Oxon.	LL.B.
Oct. 1. Timothy Goodwin	D.D.
1715, Aug. 4. Richard Rider	LL.B.

Wake (1716, Jan. 16—1737, Jan. 24).

1716, Jan. 26. Benjamin Hoadley, Bp. of Winchester 1734	D.D.

II

	Degree conferred.
Jan. 28. Lancelot Blackburn, M.A. Oxon., Abp. of York 1724	D.D.
June 28. Thos. Bowers, M.A. Camb., Bp. of Chichester 1722	D.D.
June 28. David Trimmell, M.A.	D.D.
July 3. Thos. Cranmer, of Mitcham	M.D.
July 3. Richard Ibbetson	D.D.
July 23. William Whitfield	D.D.
Nov. 27. Thomas Tullie, M.A.	LL.D.
1717, Jan. 14. Henry Downes	D.D.
1718, March 10. Sam. Peploe, Warden of Manchester, and Bp. of Chester	B.D.
1720, March 19. Daniel Hill	D.D.
April 28. Chas. Cobb, M.A. Trin. Coll. Oxon., Abp. of Dublin 1742	D.D.
June 28. Wm. Bradshaw, M.A., Preb. of Canterbury	D.D.
Sept. 28. Wm. Birch, Chanc. of Worc.	D.D.
1721, Jan. 16. Samuel Lisle, M.A., R. of St. Mary-le-Bow, Bp. of Norwich	D.D.
March 27. John Henry Ott, Librarian at Lambeth	M.A.
1722, Aug. 10. Charles Lambe	D.D.
1723, June 24. Rich. Chicheley, M.A., Sec. to the Abp.	LL.B.
1724, Jan. 8. John Gilbert, M.A., Abp. of York 1757	LL.D.
March 5. Chas. Naylor, M.A., Chan. dioc. Sarum	LL.D.
March 12. James Horner	M.A.
June 1. Zachary Pearce, M.A. Camb., Bp. of Rochester 1756	D.D.
Oct. 6. Edward Wake, M.A. Oxon.	D.D.
1725, Feb. 13. Dennis Payne, R. of Aberley	M.A.
May 26. Rd. Lardner, Middle Temple	LL.B.
Nov. 20. John Walker, M.A. Camb., Chap. to the Abp.	B.D.
1726, Oct. 22. James Stillingfleet, M.A.	D.D.
1727, March 10. George Ffenning, Dean of Carlisle	LL.D.
1728, Feb. —. Richd. Chicheley, LL.B.	LL.D.
Feb. 2. John Heber, Oxford	M.A.
Feb. 13. John Newey, M.A. Oxford	D.D.
June 5. William Ayerst, B.D., Preb. of Canterbury	D.D.
1729, March 14. Stephen Sleeth, King's College, Camb.	M.A.
1731, Feb. 27. Mordecai Cary, Bp. of Clonfert 1735	D.D.
Sept. 9. John Howell, of Isleworth	M.D.
Nov. 11. Wm. Pownall, Cambridge	LL.B.
1732, May 10. Richard Bundy, M.A.	D.D.
1733, Feb. 12. Nathanael Lancaster, Chap. to Prince Frederick	D.D.
March 9. John Baron, M.A. Camb.	D.D.
Nov. 7. Peter Maurice, M.A., Dean of Bangor	D.D.
1734, Jan. 15. Robt. Bolton, M.A. Oxford	LL.D.
1735, May 20. John Abbot, New Coll. Oxford	M.A.
1736, July 26. John Metcalfe, M.A. Camb.	LL.D.

Potter (1737, *Feb.* 28—1747, *Oct.* 10).

1737, Aug. 17. John Billingsley	M.A.
1738, Jan. 31. Rich. Chandler, Oxford	M.A.

	Degree conferred.
April 10. Robert Eyton, M.A. Camb.	D.D.
1739, April 3. George England	M.A.
1741, May 1. Richard Bullock, M.A.	D.D.
May 2. Samuel Shuckford	D.D.
1742, March 15. John Jones, Trin. Coll. Camb.	M.A.
1747, June 3. James Cawthorn, Clare Hall, Camb.	M.A.
Oct. 8. Thos. Potter, M.A. Ch. Ch. Oxf.	LL.D.

Herring (1747—1757, *March* 13).

1748, Jan. 4. John Hoadley, C.C.C. Camb.	LL.D.
1749, Jan. 14. Edw. Cresset, M.A. Trin. Coll. Oxford, Bp. of Llandaff 1749	D.D.
Feb. 6. Roger Comborbach, of Chester	LL.B.
June 2. John Head, M.A. Archd. of Canterbury	D.D.
1750, April 18. Robert Brereton, Trin. Coll. Camb.	LL.B.
Sept. 7. John Aylmer, Univ. Coll. Oxf.	M.A.
1751, April 11. Hugh Hughes, M.A. Oxford, Dean of Bangor	D.D.
April 22. Wm. Herring, M.A. Camb.	D.D.
April 22. John Sam. Hill, M.A. Camb.	D.D.
May 1. Francis Hender Foote, Chap. to Lord Chesterfield	LL.B.
July 1. John Thomas, M.A. Camb., R. of St. Peter's, Cornhill	D.D.
July 19. Samuel Salter, M.A. Camb., Canon of Norwich	D.D.
Oct. 4. Thomas Gyll, of Durham	M.A.
Nov. 4. Thos. Lewis, Jesus Coll. Oxf.	M.A.
Nov. 6. Peter Johnson, B.A. Ch. Ch. Oxford	M.A.
1753, March 9. Thomas Birch	D.D.
May 14. Abraham le Moine	D.D.
1754, Jan. 10. Wm. Warburton, M.A., Preb. of Glouc., Bp. of Glouc. 1760	D.D.
Jan. 10. John Coulter, R. of Foxearth, Essex	M.A.
March 5. Ferdinando Warner, R. of St. Michael's, Queenhithe	LL.D.
1755, Jan. 8. Richard Blackett Jekyll	M.A.
April 7. Mark Hildesley, M.A., R. of Hitchin, Bp. of Sodor and Man 1755	D.D.
May 29. Richard Dayrell, R. of Lillingston Dayrell	D.D.
Aug. 27. William Worcester Wilson	M.A.
Sept. 1. John Jortin, R. of St. Dunstan in the East	D.D.
Sept. 4. George Jubb, B.D., Chap. to the Abp.	D.D.
Oct. 31. John Pery, M.A. Oxford, Chap. to the Abp.	D.D.
1756, April 14. Joseph Payne	M.A.
May 19. William Langhorne	M.A.
July 14. John Pettingal, M.A. Jesus Coll. Oxford, B.A. 1728	D.D.
Sept. 4. John Osborne, R. of Newtimber	M.A.
Nov. 29. Cutts Barton, M.A., R. of St. Andrew's, Holborn	D.D.
Nov. 29. Thomas Holme	LL.B.
Dec. 4. John Hawkesworth	LL.D.
1757, Jan. 1. Lionel Seaman, M.A., Arch. of Taunton	D.D.

638   *Correspondence of Sylvanus Urban.*   [MAY,

Hutton (1757—1758, March 19).

	Degree conferred.
1757, Sept. 8. Robert Gilbert, M.A.	D.D.

Secker (1758—1768, Aug. 3).

1758, Aug. 2. John Davis, M.A.	D.D.
Aug. 3. William Tattan, M.A.	D.D.
Aug. 3. Robert Adkin	M.A.
1759, May 26. Jas. Pitcairn, M.A. Glasgow	LL.B.
1760, June 30. William Murray, M.A. St. John's, Cambridge	D.D.
1761, May 18. Denison Cumberland, M.A.	D.D.
1762, June 1. Geo. Secker, M.A. Ch. Ch., Chap. to the Abp.	D.D.
1763, May 6. Reeve Ballard, M.A., Preb. of Westminster	D.D.
1764, Aug. 21. Nicolas Halhead, of Durham	LL.B.
Sept. 18. James Ford	M.D.
1766, May 16. Heneage Dering, Dean of Ripon	D.D.
June 4. Richard Sutton, M.A.	D.D.
June 12. Tomlinson Bunting, Esq. of York	LL.B.
Sept. 13. Henry Burrough	LL.D.
1767, June 15. Thomas Knowles, M.A.	D.D.
1768, April 28. Lionel Place, of York	LL.B.

Cornwallis (1768—1783, March 19).

1768, Dec. 23. John Crookhall, B.A. Queen's College, Oxford	M.A.
1769, Sept. 6. John James Majendie	D.D.
1770, Feb. 21. Joseph Matthew	M.A.
Sept. 6. Bennett Storer	D.D.
Sept. 6. Richard Palmer	D.D.
Sept. 6. John Benson, M.A.	D.D.
Dec. 24. John Arnold	D.D.
1771, Feb. 21. Fred. Wollaston, LL.B.	LL.D.
June 12. Peirson Lloyd, M.A.	D.D.
Nov. 9. Richard George Robinson	LL.B.

	Degree conferred.
1772, Aug. 13. Joseph Banks	LL.B.
July 27. Mark Foster	M.A.
Nov. 27. Peter Pinnell, M.A.	D.D.
1773, May 13. Nicolas Corsellis	M.A.
June 7. Samuel Berdmore, M.A.	D.D.
Aug. 10. Edmund Burton	M.A.
1774, June 28. John Jekyll	LL.D.
1775, May 23. Wm. Bromley Cadogan, B.A.	M.A.
May 30. Richard Stoup	LL.B.
July 21. Nicolas Wakeham	D.D.
1776, Oct. 27. John Lord Monson	LL.D.
Dec. 11. George Hayter	M.A.
1777, July 3. James Farish	LL.B.
July 26. Richard Lucas	D.D.
1778, Jan. 5. William Langford, M.A.	D.D.
Feb. 18. East Apthorpe, M.A. Jesus Coll. Camb.	D.D.
Sept. 1. Charles Walker	M.A.
1779, Feb. 16. William Ramsden, M.A. Jesus Coll. Camb., Master of Charterhouse	D.D.
May 20. Matthew Thompson	M.A.
1780, Feb. 19. John Jones	M.A.
March 1. Peter Bowlby	D.D.
April 27. Thos. Exon, C.C.C. Camb.	M.A.
Nov. 26. Sir Thomas Broughton	LL.D.
1781, Jan. 30. William Morice, M.A.	D.D.
Feb. 16. Thomas Carwardine	M.A.
April 23. Richard Snowe	M.A.
May 9. James Smith	M.A.
Dec. 1. James Ramsay	M.A.
Dec. 11. Joseph Spooner	M.A.
Dec. 17. John Hodgson, Esq.	M.A.
1782, April 12. Joseph Hudson	D.D.
June 8. David Bayford, of Lewes	M.D.
July 24. Osmond Beauvoir, M.A.	D.D.
July 24. Thomas Vyner, LL.B.	LL.D.

(*To be continued.*)

770   [JUNE,

Correspondence of Sylvanus Urban.

[Correspondents are requested to append their Addresses, not, unless agreeable, for publication, but in order that a copy of the GENTLEMAN'S MAGAZINE *containing their Communications may be forwarded to them.]*

LAMBETH DEGREES (*concluded from p.* 638).

GRADUATI LAMBETHANI.

Cornwallis (continued).

	Degree conferred.
1782, Aug. 12. Denny Mart. Fairfax, M.A.	D.D.
Aug. 29. Robert Hastings	M.A.
1783, Jan. 24. Robert Hallifax	M.D.
Feb. 11. Samuel Hoole	M.A.
Moore (1783—1805, Jan. 18).	
1783, July 3. Bryan Ianson Bromwich	M.A.
1784, May 16. John Thomas	LL.B.
Oct. 28. Percival Stockdale	M.A.
1785, May 14. Robert Sinclair	M.A.
May 30. Edward Vaughan	D.D.
July 25. John William Egerton	LL.B.
Aug. 2. Francis Knollis	M.A.
1786, May 29. William Roberts	M.A.
Oct. 13. Daniel Evans	LL.B.
1787, March 15. William Brown	M.A.
May 23. John Buckner, M.A., Bp. of Chichester 1798	LL.D.
July 13. Richard Browne Cheston	M.D.
Dec. 22. Michael Thos. Becker, B.A.	M.A.
1788, March 7. Charles Coates, M.B.	LL.B.
March 8. John Ford	M.D.
1789, Jan. 9. Thomas Myers	LL.B.
Jan. 10. George Crabbe (the Poet)	LL.B.
1790, April 8. Thomas Lloyd	M.A.
Sept. 1. Nicolas Vere, B.A. Queen's Coll. Oxford	M.A.
1791, April 20. George Heath, M.A. King's Coll. Camb.	D.D.
April 29. John Vardill, M.A. Oxford	LL.B.
July 19. Thomas Hey, M.A.	D.D.
1792, Jan. 23. John Montgomery	M.A.
April 26. Joseph Jefferson	M.A.
Dec. 5. Matthias Rutton	M.A.
1793, Jan. 9. Ffolliott Herbert Walker Cornewall, M.A., Bp. of Bristol 1797	D.D.
Jan. 29. William Henry Cooper	M.A.
July —. John Ireland, B.A.	
1795, Jan. 10. Chas. Mongan Warburton	M.A.
Feb. 20. William Jackson	M.A.
March 11. Samuel Gale	M.A.
May 11. Francis Randolph, M.A.	D.D.
May 29. John Goodwin	M.A.
June 30. John Luxmoore, M.A. Camb.	D.D.
June 30. William Cole, M.A.	D.D.
July 17. John Pretyman, M.A.	D.D.
Dec. 11. John Rowland Sproule	LL.B.

	Degree conferred.
1796, Feb. 27. John Hawkins, Vicar of Great Halstead	M.A.
April 28. Philip Baker	M.A.
Dec. 19. Henry Ingles, M.A.	D.D.
1797, April 24. John Moore, B.A.	LL.B.
Aug. 3. Robert Watts	M.A.
1798, Oct. 31. William Williams	M.A.
Dec. 3. Charles de Guiffardiere, Preb. of Sarum	M.A.
Dec. 15. Samuel Ryder Weston, B.D.	D.D.
1799, Jan. 10. William Tait	LL.B.
March 8. Nicolas Waite Robinson	M.A.
May 27. Isaac Wm. Webb Horlock	M.A.
1800, May 24. William Gomm	M.A.
Oct. 9. Henry Jenkins, Missionary in Caicos	M.A.
1801, Feb. 23. Thomas Bernard	M.A.
June 3. John Inglis, son of Bp. of Nova Scotia	M.A.
Nov. 9. Bernard Cracroft	M.A.
1803, Jan. 27. Hon. Geo. Pelham, M.A. Camb., Bp. of Bristol 1803	D.D.
March 4. Robert Pope, of Staines	M.D.
March 30. John Ireland, M.A. Oriel Coll. Oxford, Dean of Westminster	D.D.
April 1. Edward Barnard	M.A.
May 3. George Martin	M.A.
June 27. Charles Ekins, B.A. King's Coll. Camb.	M.A.
1804, Jan. 21. Robt. Darby Waddilove, Dean of Ripon	D.D.
Oct. 8. Jehosaphat Mountain	D.D.
Oct. 8. Jn. Nesbit Jordan, Emmanuel Coll. Camb.	M.A.
Dec. 5. Philip Fisher, B.D. Univ. Coll. Oxford	D.D.
Manners-Sutton (1805—1828, July 21).	
1805, March 18. Hen. Goddard, Merton Coll. Oxford	M.A.
1806, Jan. 14. Samuel Henley, Queen's Coll. Camb.	D.D.
Feb. 3. Hannyngton Elgee Boyd	M.A.
March 6. John Henry George Lefroy, B.A. Oxford	M.A.
Aug. 13. Fred. Gardiner, Balliol Coll.	M.A.
Aug 25. Thomas Day, Maidstone	M.D.

	Degree conferred.
1806, Dec. 10. Rob. Stanser, LL.B., St. Paul's, Halifax, N.S., Bp. of Nova Scotia 1816	D.D.
1807, April 7. Thomas Hughes, M.A. St. John's Coll. Camb.	D.D.
June 30. John Inglis, M.A., Bp. of Nova Scotia 1825	D.D.
1808, July 5. John Plumptre, M.A. King's Coll. Camb.	D.D.
1810, March 8. Gerald Valerian Welles-ley, M.A., Preb. of Durham	D.D.
March 19. Brownlow V. Layard	M.A.
June 14. Luke Heslop	D.D.
1811, Jan. 4. Henry Dison Gabell	D.D.
June 14. Andrew Bell, Master of Sherburn Hosp.	LL.D.
Aug. 21. Samuel Hudson	LL.B.
Aug. 27. Charles Burney	* D.D.
1812, April 27. Charles Goddard	M.A.
July 3. William Procter	M.A.
July 29. Edward Barry	D.D.
Aug. 20. William W. Dakins	D.D.
Sept. 19. William Preston	M.A.
1813, April 26. Stephen Saunders	D.D.
1815, Sept. 25. Robert Jones, M.A.	D.D.
1816, Aug. 16. Livingstone Booth	M.A.
1818, Feb. 7. John Day	M.D.
1819, March 11. Carr Ellison Lucas	M.D.
June 14. Henry Fardell	M.A.
1820, June 20. Jehoshaphat Mountain	D.D.
July 22. Christopher Hodgson	M.A.
1822, Feb. 18. Richard Smith	M.A.
Nov. 7. William Oliver Locke	M.D.
1823, April 22. Wm. Alleyne Barker	M.A.
1824, July 21. James Rumsey	M.D.
1825, Aug. 13. Fred. Jos. Cox Trenow	M.A.
Aug. 31. Daniel Jarvis	M.D.
1826, Jan. 10. Robert Willis	D.D.
Feb. 13. William Barnes	M.A.
April 13. William Thomas	D.D.
May 29. Edward Grimstone	M.D.
1827, June 12. Thomas Wharton	M.A.
Aug. 30. Richard Bagot, M.A. All Souls', Oxford, Bp. of Oxford 1829, D.D. of Oxford 1829	D.D.
Oct. 3. William Chandler	M.D.
Oct. 7. Geo. Kelly (aft. Holdsworth)	M.A.
Dec. 21. Chas. Mansfield Clarke	M.D.
1828, Feb. 27. William Roy	D.D.
March 25. A. Robt. Chas. Dallas	M.A.
May 28, Wm. Samways Oke	M.D.
Howley (1828–1848, Feb. 11).	
Dec. 30. William Hodge Mill, Prof. of Hebrew, Camb.	D.D.
1829, May 25. William Snowden	B.D.
Aug. 12. John Morgan	M.A.
Aug. 19. Joseph Hemington Harris	D.D.
Aug. 24. George Walter Wrangham	M.A.
Oct. 21. Joseph Samuel Stockwell	M.A.
1830, May 4. Robt. W. Bamford, M.A.	B.D.
1832, April 13. Archibald J. Stephens	M.A.
May 22. Thomas Pickthall	M.A.
July 3. James Mayne	M.A.
Sept. 12. Thomas Carr, Bp. of Bom-bay 1837	D.D.

	Degree conferred.
1832, Dec. 29. George Wallace	M.A.
1833, June 12. John Robinson	M.A.
July 29. William Walker	M.A.
Nov. 25. George Newby	M.A.
1834, April 15. Henry Heap	B.D.
July 30. Allan Macpherson	B.D.
Aug. 4. Samuel Maddock	M.A.
Oct. 20. John Wm. Drage Merest	B.D.
Dec. 19. Richard Hodgson	M.A.
1835, Feb. 24. John Jennings	M.A.
March 30. George Heathcote	M.A.
July 25. George Oliver, Inc. of Wol-verhampton	D.D.
1836, Jan. 14. John Wenham	M.A.
May 19. William Robert Griesbach	M.A.
Sept. 8. William Otter, M.A. Camb., Bp. of Chichester 1836	D.D.
Oct. 12. David Davies	M.D.
1837, Jan. 11. Valentine Knightley	M.A.
Feb. 3. Joseph Ditcher	M.A.
Feb. 23. Joseph Wardle	M.A.
1838, Jan. 19. Robert Taylor	M.A.
Feb. 1. John Richardson Major	D.D.
Feb. 10. William Buxton Marsden	M.A.
March 17. Charles Fletcher	M.A.
June 6. Richard Penderel Llewellyn	M.A.
Sept. 11. Joseph Jameson, Precentor of Ripon	B.D.
Oct. 11. Morgan Morgan	M.A.
Nov. 21. Robert Meek	M.A.
1839, Jan. 28. Robert Shittler	D.D.
Feb. 18. William Blanshard	M.A.
May 23. Henry Cooper	B.D.
July 8. Aubrey George Spencer, Bp. of Newfoundland 1839	D.D.
Oct. 4. William West Simpson	M.A.
Dec. 5. John Clark	M.A.
1840, Feb. 14. Thomas Jessop	D.D.
April 15. Thomas Garnier, Dean of Lincoln 1860	LL.D.
June 10. William Walton	M.A.
July 30. Connop Thirlwall, Bp. of St. David's	D.D.
Sept. 12. William Vernon	M.A.
Oct. 10. Robert Hull	M.D.
Oct. 31. Richard Thos. Tucker, B.A. Camb.	D.D.
Dec. 26. John Couch Grylls	M.A.
1841, April 21. James Greig Murray	B.D.
June 22. Sir Wm. Hyde Pearson	M.D.
Aug. 17. John Burt	M.A.
Aug. 17. John Winter	M.A.
Nov. 10. Michael Solomon Alexander, Bp. of Jerusalem	D.D.
1842, May 16. Grantham Munton Yorke, late of Queens' Coll. Camb.	M.A.
July 27. John James Gelling, Inc. of St. Catherine Cree, London	M.A.
1843, Jan. 21. Henry John Gauntlett, Chatham-place, London	Mus.Doc.
Jan. 25. William Cowper, Inc. of St. Philip's, Sydney, N.S.W.	D.D.
Jan. 27. William Bedford, Inc. of St. David's, Sydney, N.S.W.	D.D.
Jan. 27. Thomas Sharpe, Inc. of Ba-thurst, N.S.W.	M.A.

772   *Correspondence of Sylvanus Urban.*   [JUNE,

	Degree conferred.
Jan. 27. Henry Tarlton Stiles, Windsor, N.S.W.	M.A.
Jan. 27. Robert Forrest, Camden, N.S.W.	M.A.
Jan. 27. Thomas Hassall, Cobbity, N.S.W.	M.A.
Jan. 27. William Horatio Walsh, Ch. Ch., Sydney, N.S.W.	M.A.
March 29. William Strachan, R. of Ch. Ch. Nassau	D.D.
April 22. Thos. Pierce Williams, B.A., late Fell. of St. John's Coll. Camb., R. of St. Elizabeth's, Jamaica	D.D.
May 27. Chas. Lyne, Preb. of Exeter	M.A.
June 14. Duncan Campbell	M.A.
June 17. Wm. Garrard, New Norfolk, Van Dieman's Land	M.A.
July 7. F. Robert Braithwaite, Archdeacon of St. Christopher's	M.A.
July 7. John M'Cammon Trew, Archdeacon of Bahamas	D.D.
Aug. 2. Thos. Samuel Wallis, Polytechnic Institution	Mus.Doc.
Dec. 13. Wm. Hayes, King's Coll. London	M.A.
1844, Jan. 10. John Fothergill, Archdeacon of Berbice	M.A.
Feb. 22. John Rushton, Archdeacon of Manchester	D.D.
May 21. Chas. Blackman, Principal of Theol. Inst., Newfoundland	M.A.
July 10. Samuel Paynter Musson, R. of St. Catherine's, Jamaica	D.D.
July 16. Richard Panton, B.A. Camb., Rural Dean of Surrey, Jamaica	D.D.
1845, Jan. 31. Francis Robert Raines, Inc. of Milnrow	M.A.
March 18. Alf. Pet. Lovekin, Scholar of King's Coll. London	M.A.
April 8, John Campion, Clerk	M.A.
Aug. 11. Fredk. William Trevannion, Inc. of Whitby, Yorkshire	M.A.
Nov. 29. William Broadley, St. Dorothy's, Jamaica	M.A.
Dec. 2. Wm. Rowe Lyall, M.A., Archdeacon of Maidstone	D.D.

	Degree conferred.
1846, Feb. 6. Geo. Undy Withers, M.A. Camb., Princ. of Bps. Coll. Calcutta	D.D.
Feb. 6. Thomas Dealtry, Archdeacon of Calcutta	D.D.
March 31. Samuel Johnson, Rector of Hinton Blewitt	M.A.
May 9. Edward Cheere, King's Coll. London	M.A.
June 30. Samuel Gobat, Bp. nominate of Jerusalem	D.D.
Aug. 28. Thomas Rochford Redwar, P. C. of St. Thomas', Rolls	M.A.
Oct. 21. Thos. Wm. Johnes, Licent. Theol. Univ. Durham	M.A.
Oct. 22. Thos. Eyre Poole, Chaplain of Sierra Leone	D.D.
Nov. 20. Fran. Bell Grant, St. Peter's, Antigua	M.A.
Dec. 11. John Congdon Shapley, R. of Carriacou, Granada	M.A.
1847, Jan. 13. Benjamin Bailey, Archdeacon of Colombo	D.D.
March 23. James Bardaley, Curate of Burnley	M.A.
July 2. Edw. Jackson, St. James's, Leeds	M.A.
July 21. George Mackie, B.A. Pemb. Coll. Camb., Ch. to Bp. of Montreal	D.D.
July 28. Daniel Newham, Emmanuel Coll. Camb.	M.A.
Aug. 31. William Baldwin, Inc. of Mytholmroyd	M.A.
Sept. 17. Hugh Martin Short, Inc. of Wortley, Yorkshire	M.A.
Oct. 26. Colin Maclaverty, dioc. of Jamaica *	M.A.
Nov. 15. Thomas James Boardman, Stockwell, Middlesex	Mus.Doc.
Nov. 24. John Campbell Stone, R. of Portland, Jamaica	M.A.
1848, Jan. 6. Thos. Watts, Haverfordwest	M.A.
Jan. 22. James Prince Lee, Bp. of Manchester 1848	D.D.
Feb. 1. Samuel Roffey Maitland, Librarian at Lambeth	D.D.

LAMBETH DEGREES.

SIR,—The following notes have been suggested by the first portion of Mr. Stubbs's valuable and interesting communication.

It appears that Pope Alexander VI. empowered Jasper Pon, his orator and commissary for the jubilee, to create doctors in both the laws, or in the one of them. See the "Articles of the Bull of the holy Jubilee of full remission and great joy granted to the realm of England, &c., to be distributed according to the true meaning of our Holy Father

unto the King's subjects, by the hands of his dear and well-beloved William Butts, Student in the University of Cambridge." (Gairdner's Letters and Papers illustrative of the reigns of Richard III. and Henry VII., ii. 100.)

Eligius Ferrers (D.D. 1539) was Abbot of Wymondham in Norfolk 1532, Vicar of Wymondham 1538, Canon of Norwich 1539, and Archdeacon of Suffolk 1541. He died in 1548, and was buried on the south side of the altar of Wymondham Church, under a fine monument, but which has neither arms nor inscription.

Blage, who was made B.D. by Archbishop Parker, was no doubt Thomas Blagne, who became a pensioner of Queens' College, Cambridge, in 1568. He seems to have removed to Oxford, where it is probable he became B.A. He was instituted to the Rectory of Little Braxted, Essex, Sept. 9, 1570; Archbishop Parker, to whom he was Chaplain, collated him to the Rectory of St. Vedast, London, Sept. 2, 1571, at which time he was B.A. He was also Chaplain to Archbishop Whitgift, and in 1578 resigned St. Vedast's. On June 20, 1580, he was instituted, on the presentation of the Queen, to the Rectory of Ewelme, Oxfordshire. He was one of her Majesty's Chaplains in Ordinary at or soon after this period. On April 2, 1582, he supplicated the University of Oxford for the degree of D.D.; it was not granted, but on Jan. 24, 1588-9, the University of Cambridge passed a grace that he might have that degree there on keeping the usual exercises and being incorporated, and he was created D.D. at the following commencement at Cambridge. He was installed Dean of Rochester Feb. 1, 1591-2, resigned the Rectory of Ewelme 1596, and became Rector of Bangor Monachorum with the chapels of Worthenbury and Orton, Flintshire, Dec. 26, 1604. His death occurred in October, 1611. He published, "A Schole of Wise Conceytes, translated out of divers Greke and Latin Wryters," Lond., 8vo., 1569; "A Sermon preached at the Charterhouse before the King's Majestie, on Tuesday the tenth of May, 1603," Lond., 12mo, 1603. There is reason also to believe that he assisted Archbishop Parker in his *Antiquitates Britannicæ.*

Robert Thoroton (M.D. Oct. 31, 1663), well known as the historian of Nottinghamshire, was of Christ's College, Cambridge, B.A. 1642-3, M.A. 1646, having in the latter year a licence from his University to practise physic. He died in Nov. 1678.

Sir Edmund King, M.D. Lambeth,

was incorporated at Cambridge in 1671, (Munk's Coll. of Physicians, i. 415). We do not observe his name in Mr. Stubbs's list.

Peter Dent (M.B. March 9, 1678) practised as an apothecary in Cambridge, and had a considerable knowledge of botany and natural history. He was buried at St. Sepulchre's, Cambridge, Oct. 5, 1689. His widow, Elizabeth, died in 1708; and his son, of the same name, who was also an apothecary, and had been a sizar of Trinity College, died June 12, 1717, aged 80.

Edward Tenison (LL.B. March 3, 1697, D.D. April 23, 1714) was incorporated LL.B. at Cambridge, where he had taken his B.A. degree in 1694-5 as a member of Corpus Christi College.

Timothy Goodwin (D.D. Oct. 1, 1714), who was a native of Norwich, was a member successively of Trinity and Corpus Christi Colleges in Cambridge. On Jan. 22, 1696-7 (being then D.D. of Utrecht), he became M.A. at Oxford as a member of St. Edmund Hall. In 1697 he was incorporated M.A. at Cambridge. He was Archdeacon of Oxford Feb. 1, 1706-7; became Bishop of Kilmore and Ardagh Dec. 19, 1714; and Archbishop of Cashel June 3, 1727. He died at Dublin Dec. 13, 1729.

William Ayerst (D.D. June 5, 1728) became Fellow of Queens' College, Cambridge, in 1716. He was B.A. at Oxford Oct. 21, 1703, and M.A. there by diploma Nov. 7, 1707, being incorporated in the latter degree at Cambridge in 1715. He proceeded B.D. at Oxford June 25, 1717, and was in the same year incorporated in that degree at Cambridge. He affords a remarkable instance of a fellow of a Cambridge College who obtained all his degrees elsewhere. He died May 9, 1765.

Stephen Sleeth [or rather *Sleech*] (M.A. March 14, 1729) took the degrees of B.A., B.D., and D.D. at Cambridge. His M.A. degree was evidently given as a qualification for a fellowship at Eton, of which college he ultimately became Provost. (See Harwood's *Alumni Etonenses,* 30, 84, 87, 310).

William Murray (D.D. June 30, 1760) was a native of Middlesex, took the degree of B.A. at Pembroke College, Oxford, Feb. 18, 1726, became a pensioner of St. John's College, Cambridge, April 11, 1738, and was in the same year created M.A. at Cambridge. He had the prebend of Coringham in the church of Lincoln, and died in Nov. 1778.

Heneage Dering (D.D. May 16, 1766) is called Dean of Ripon; this is a mistake. Heneage Dering, Dean of Ripon, died April 8, 1750, in the eighty-sixth year of his age, having been created LL.D. at Cambridge by royal mandate as far back as 1701. The D.D. of 1766 was his second son, of the same name, Canon of Canterbury, and Rector of Middleton Keynes, in Buckinghamshire, who died May 19, 1802, aged 84. He was originally of St. John's College, and afterwards Fellow of Peterhouse, Cambridge, in which University he took both degrees in arts.

William Ramsden, Master of Charterhouse (D.D. Feb. 16, 1779), was admitted a sizar of St. John's College, Cambridge, July 3, 1738, and took both his degrees in arts at that college, viz. B.A. 1741-2, M.A. 1745. We suspect that there is a mistake in describing him as of Jesus College, Cambridge.

Thomas Exon (M.A. April 27, 1780) was a native of Devonshire, and was admitted of Corpus Christi College, Cambridge, in 1776. He took no degree in that University.

      C. H. and THOMPSON COOPER.
Cambridge.

Nova et Vetera

THE LAMBETH DEGREES

BY

CECIL WALL, D.M., F.R.C.P.

In the early part of the ninth century Charlemagne's concessions to Leo III enabled the Papacy to establish a monopoly in teaching in all the countries brought under its influence. Universities and colleges were under Papal control until the Reformation, and degrees were granted by the Pope's delegates. In England in 1351 was passed the Statute of Provisors, which denied the Papal claim to dispose benefices. This statute forbade anyone to receive or execute any letters of provisions for preferment, but the law as it stood carried all dependent questions to the courts at Rome. Consequently in 1353 the Statute of Praemunire was enacted prohibiting the questioning of any judgement of the King's courts by any foreign court.

According to William Stubbs (*Gentleman's Magazine*, 1864, i, 633):

"During the fifteenth century attempts were made to restrict the exercise of the Papal power in opposition to the Statute of Provisors by securing promotion to the graduates of the English universities and to advance and strengthen the universities by providing competently for their graduates. To evade the disabilities imposed thus on non-graduates and to secure for themselves the privileges of graduates it became usual towards the end of the century for clerks who had not been educated at the English universities to obtain dispensations from Rome enabling them to hold pluralities, etc., and in some few recorded cases to obtain degrees from the Pope, on the strength of which they were incorporated in the English universities with the same rights as the original graduates. It seems probable that these degrees were granted by the Pope as a part of his ordinary power and not in any connexion with a university. It was not necessary to go to Rome for these degrees: the legates could confer them. For instance Cardinal Wolsey's Bull of Legation in 1529 gave him the power to admit suitable persons to be doctors, licentiates, bachelors, masters, etc., in Law, Theology, Arts, and Medicine."

In 1534 an Act was passed " concerning the exoneration of the King's subjects from exactions and impositions heretofore paid to the see of Rome and for having Licences and Dispensations within this realm without suing further for the same." This Act provided that the Archbishop of Canterbury should have power to grant " all manner of such licences, dispensations, compositions, faculties, grants, receipts, delegacies, instruments, and all other writings for causes not being contrary or repugnant to the Holy Scriptures and laws of God as heretofore hath been used and accustomed to be had and obtained by your Highness or any of your noble progenitors or any of your or their subjects at the see of Rome." It enacted, further, that where the dispensations, etc., should be " of such importance that the tax for the expedition thereof at Rome extended to the sum of £4 or above," they must be confirmed by letters patent under the great seal to be enrolled in chancery." Both these clauses apply to degrees in divinity, law, and medicine granted by the Archbishop of Canterbury, it being assumed that degrees were included in the term " faculties " of the Act. In the book of Taxation, Section XI, the fee for the creation of a doctor in any faculty was £4. Bishop Gibson stated that the Archbishops had claimed and exercised the right to confer degrees under this Act, and their right was not challenged until the reign of George I, when Gastrell, Bishop of Chester, refused to admit Samuel Peploe, B.D.Lambeth, to the wardenship of Manchester College. The decision was given in the Archbishops' favour in the King's Bench in 1725.

The right of the Archbishop of Canterbury to grant the doctorate in any faculty, established in 1534 by the Act of Supremacy and Succession, persists and is not infrequently exercised in faculties other than that of medicine, and it is customary for the doctor thus created to wear the hood and robes of the university to which the Archbishop belongs. The doctorate, however, is an academic distinction, and in the faculty of medicine did not directly confer the right to practise. In Oxford and Cambridge it was customary for the regius professor of medicine to grant to bachelors of the faculty a licence to practise after they had conducted a certain number of cures. This licence was operative in the university towns and presumably throughout England, except in London, where the College of Physicians, under its charter confirmed by statute, claimed an exclusive right to permit practice. In 1606 Thomas Bonham, who had proceeded M.D. at Cambridge in 1595 without any grace, when summoned by the College replied that he had practised and would practise physic in London without their leave. He was fined £10 and committed to prison pending payment. He brought an action against the President and Censors for illegal imprisonment and won the case ; Coke, Warburton, and Daniel, the judges in the Court of Common Pleas, ruling that the College had not the power to commit Bonham to prison for any of the causes mentioned.

It was left undecided whether Oxford and Cambridge graduates could practise in London without the leave of the College. Instead of instituting another test case the College agreed with the universities in 1675[1] to restrict their licence to English graduates in medicine, and the universities seem to have agreed not to grant their licence except with the approval of the College. The College was chiefly perturbed by the practising apothecaries. In 1633 John Buggs was summoned to the Censor's Board and fined. He promptly went to Leyden, and after a sojourn of two months returned with an M.D. degree : on the strength of this he received from Cambridge in 1634 a licence to practise physic, and in 1635 he was incorporated M.D. at Oxford. The College did not take any further proceedings against him, but as he died in 1640 he did not live long to enjoy his victory.

The ease with which Continental degrees could be obtained, and the custom of the universities to incorporate such doctors *ad eundem* and thus render their holders eligible for the College licence, opened an opportunity for the Lambeth graduates. The records of the degrees granted by the Archbishops are preserved in the library at Lambeth Palace and deserve full investigation. Stubbs gives a list of those conferred since 1660. In some cases the M.D. degree was conferred on one who was already a graduate in arts. Thus William Fyffe, M.A. of Trinity College, Oxford, was granted the M.D.Lambeth in 1663, and in the same year Archbishop Sheldon conferred the degree on Robert Thoroton, the historian of Nottinghamshire, who was an M.A. of Cambridge and had received the university licence to practise medicine. The Archbishop, however, did not always require that those he honoured should have had a university education. Edmund Freeman, or King, became M.D.Lambeth in 1663, and was incorporated *ad eundem* at Cambridge in 1671. Francis Bernard, the apothecary to St. Bartholomew's, who did such good work during the plague, was granted the M.D.Lambeth by Sancroft in 1678 : after incorporation at Cambridge he became a Fellow of the College of Physicians.

The list of the Lambeth doctors seems to show that the degree was usually granted as a reward for eminent service to those who had not been able to conform with the university regulations for internal degrees. Robert Hooke, the secretary of the Royal Society, received it at the hands of Tillotson in 1691. John Woodward, the geologist and Gresham Professor of Physic, was honoured by Tenison in 1695 and Sir Charles Mansfield Clarke by Manners-Sutton in 1827 ; but it is not always easy to recognize the claim to the distinction. Edward Cronin, a well-known homoeopath, received the degree in 1858 just before the Medical Act came into force, and thus secured admission to the *Register*. Since 1858 the degree has been granted occasionally, but merely as a decoration. In 1880 it was conferred on Mr. James Rogers, a medical practitioner of Swansea, who was Mayor at the time of the Church Congress. The expense was said to have been about eighty guineas, and was defrayed by public subscription.

---

[1] Mason Good gives the date as 1637, but I cannot confirm this.

LAMBETH DEGREES CONFERRED SINCE 1660. (*Compiled from Stubbs's List and other Sources*)

Juxon, Archbishop:
1663, May 11th: William Fyffe, M.A., Trin. Coll., Oxford.
1663, May 12th: Edmund Freeman, alias King, incorporated at Cambridge October 3rd, 1671. (Sir Edmund King.)

Sheldon, Archbishop:
1663, September 9th: Policarp Dakyn, M.B., of Derby.
1663, October 31st: Robert Thoroton, Christ's Coll., Camb., B.A. 1642, M.A. 1646, L.M. 1646, Historian of Nottinghamshire.
1675, April 9th: William Rosewell, M.A.

Sancroft, Archbishop:
1678, February 6th: Francis Bernard, incorporated at Cambridge, Charter Fellow of the College of Physicians, 1687.
1678, March 9th: Peter Dent, an apothecary and botanist of Cambridge. Incorporated at Cambridge March 18th, 1681.

Tillotson, Archbishop:
1691, July 2nd: Thomas Hobbs.
1691, December 7th: Robert Hooke, Secretary, Royal Society.
1692, March 3rd: Caleb Coatsworth, F.R.S., formerly a surgeon, Physician to St. Thomas's Hospital.

Tenison, Archbishop:
1695, February 4th: John Woodward, Gresham Professor of Physic. Incorporated at Cambridge 1695.
1701, November 26th: John Crompton.
1707, February 18th: John Benbrigg.

Wake, Archbishop:
1716, July 3rd: Thomas Cranmer of Mitcham.
1731, September 9th: John Howell of Isleworth.

Hutton, Archbishop:
1764, September 18th: James Ford.

Cornwallis, Archbishop:
1782, June 8th: David Bayford of Lewes.
1783, January 24th: Robert Hallifax.

Moore, Archbishop:
1787, July 13th: Richard Browne Cheston, Surgeon, Gloucester Infirmary.
1788, March 8th: John Ford.
1803, March 4th: Robert Pope of Staines.

Manners-Sutton, Archbishop:
1806, August 25th: Thomas Day of Maidstone.
1818, February 7th: John Day.
1819, March 11th: Carr Ellison Lucas.
1822, November 7th: William Oliver Locke.
1824, July 21st: James Rumsey of Amersham.
1825, August 31st: Daniel Jarvis.
1826, May 29th: Edward Grimstone.
1827, October 3rd: William Chandler.
1827, December 21st: Charles Mansfield Clarke (" The Divine Doctor " of Wakley in the *Lancet*).
1828, May 28th: William Samways Oke of Southampton.
    (N.B.—In the *Lancet* (1864, ii, 229) it is stated that when Manners-Sutton, the Speaker, was M.P. for Scarborough Mr. Dunn, a surgeon, did him some acts of political kindness. Manners-Sutton asked his father, the Primate, to reward Mr. Dunn by granting an M.D. degree. Another letter, on page 257, states that the degree was given, not to Mr. Dunn, but to his partner Travis. Neither name appears in the list of graduates.)

Howley, Archbishop:
1836, October 12th: David Davies.
1840, October 10th: Robert Hull.
1841, June 22nd: Sir William Hyde Pearson.

The following have had degrees conferred upon them since the death of Archbishop Howley:

Joseph Laurie (1849) ; William Bayes of Cambridge (1850) ; Edmund Charles Johnson (1851) ; Frederick Gilder Julius of Richmond, Surrey (1851) ; John Green Bishop (1851) ; George Canney (1854) ; John Hodgson Ramsbotham of Leeds (1855) ; Ralph Barnes Grindrod of Great Malvern (1855) ; Edward Cronin (1858) ; William Baker (1858) ; Edward Westall (1861) ; John Rayner (1861) ; William Sherwin (1862) ; James Rogers of Swansea (1880).

In the seventeenth century there was considerable confusion between the bishops' licences to practise medicine or surgery and the Lambeth doctorate. The licences could be bought for a small sum at the vicar-general's office. (Hodge's *Vindiciae Medicinae*, 1666, p. 80.)

" His money's current and will pass,
    Though he who's licens'd is an ass."

These licentiates began to style themselves M.D., and some, like William Salmon, when asked to explain, interpreted the letters as indicating " Medicinae Donator."

5.3 THE LAMBETH DEGREES, CHARLES A H FRANKLYN

British Medical Journal: October 12, 1935.

LAMBETH DEGREES

SIR,

I have read with great interest "A. H.'s" letter in your issue of October 5th. I, too, have collected various notes about these degrees called "Lambeth." Very few even well-informed people seem aware of the actual procedure or what they really are. I have copies of one or two actual documents. – Actually "Lambeth" is a misnomer, for they are in fact Royal degrees granted by the Sovereign, and thus take precedence over all other degrees. The Archbishop merely issues an instrument nominating a certain person to a certain degree, but the final clause makes it null and void of effect unless it receives the Sovereign's Royal Letters Patent in confirmation thereof. The Letters Patent repeat this fact and confirm the degree, which is then registered in the House of Lords. The degree is actually per litteris regis.

I am, etc.,
CHARLES A. H. FRANKLYN.
Lincoln, Oct. 5th.

5.4   LAMBETH DEGREES, L A PARRY

Lambeth Degrees

SIR,—The recent book of Bloom and James, *Medical Practitioners in the Diocese of London, Licensed under the Act of 3 Henry VIII, c. 11,*[1] is of much interest to the medical historian. The Act deals with the licensing of medical practitioners by the Bishop of London in order to prevent ignorant quacks from practising. Though the Act has never been repealed, the Bishop has ceased to exercise his authority since 1745.

The Archbishop of Canterbury, under another old Act (25 Henry VIII, c. 21), has the right to grant M.D.

[1] Noticed in the *Journal* of August 24th, 1935 (p. 342). London: Cambridge University Press. (5s.)

degrees, commonly known as Lambeth degrees. Section 4 of this Act authorizes the Archbishop to grant licences such as the See of Rome had been wont to do. It was a remnant of Papal authority, transferred to the English Church at the time of the break with the Pope.

The Medical Act of 1857 abolished any right to practise with these degrees, unless they were granted prior to the Act. In the trial of Dr. Smethurst in 1859 for the poisoning of his wife, Dr. Julius, one of the medical witnesses, was asked if he were a doctor of medicine and if his degree was a London one. His answer was that it was an Archbishop of Canterbury's degree. Mr. Serjeant Parry exclaimed, '' What! can he make a Doctor of Medicine?'' The Lord Chief Baron, the Judge, observed, '' Yes, and he can make a Master of Arts.'' When Dr. Julius was asked if he had taken his degree as a matter of course, he replied that it was a very uncommon procedure. He had had to get a certificate from two members of the College of Physicians, stating that they had known him for a length of time and that he was a fit and proper person. It would be interesting to know if the Archbishop still grants these degrees. I fancy not. If this is correct, when was the last one issued?—I am, etc.,

Hove, Sept. 23rd.   L. A. PARRY.

STUDIES

6 CHARLES FRANKLYN ON LAMBETH DEGREES

WILLIAM GIBSON

Charles Franklyn was a man of strong opinions, and especially so on the subject of universities and academic dress, or academical dress as he insisted on calling it. Chapter Thirteen of his 1970 monumental work, *Academical Dress From the Middle Ages to the Present Day including Lambeth Degrees*, was devoted to the issue of Lambeth degrees.[1]

Franklyn noted that for centuries archbishops of Canterbury had conferred degrees in any Faculty but principally the degrees of MA, BD, DD, DCL, and DMus. He quoted Lord Davidson, formerly the Archbishop Randall Davidson, as saying 'I am a University'. Franklyn also noted that some archbishops had held examinations for the various degrees, especially MA, and he regretted that Archbishop Randall Davidson had discontinued the practice.

Franklyn claimed that 'the question of the academical dress that Lambeth graduate should wear is a vexed one, and calls for immediate enquiry and overhaul.' He suggested that there was no clear opinion at Lambeth or at Oxford and Cambridge of what should be done. This was not strictly true, since there was a settled practice that the robes were those of the university the archbishop awarding the degree had attended, at that point exclusively the universities of Oxford and Cambridge. Franklyn pressed this position further by suggesting that some people thought that the recipient of a Lambeth degree should wear the corresponding academic dress of that degree at whichever university from which the archbishop graduated. So if the archbishop was a London University, a DD Lambeth awarded by that archbishop should wear a London DD hood. Franklyn speculated that 'it would be interesting to hear what that University has to say upon the subject in the event of a London man succeeding to the Primacy!' This is something that Graham Zellick's contribution to this collection addresses.

Franklyn also reported that there was the opinion of the Rev. Thomas W. Wood in 1882 that if the recipient was already a graduate, when given the DD Lambeth, he should wear the DD academic dress of his own university irrespective of which university the archbishop attended. This raised the question of what would be done if the recipient was not already a graduate. In this case, Franklyn proposed that the recipient *should* wear the robes of the archbishop's own university. Franklyn claimed that this was the view of Strickland Gibson, Keeper of the Archives of the University of Oxford. Franklyn summed up the principle that 'The Archbishop creates a man DD, and if already a member of a University should wear his own University symbolism of that degree so conferred.' He complained that for so long archbishops were Oxford graduates that wearing Oxford robes for Lambeth degrees had become an established custom. But he pointed out the confusion it sometimes led to. In 1941, William Anderson, the new Bishop of Portsmouth, who was a Cambridge MA, wore an Oxford DD hood, having been a Lambeth DD by Archbishop Davidson. To avoid confusion, Davidson suggested that when in Cambridge Anderson should wear his MA Cambridge hood, but the University of Oxford did not approve of its DD hood being worn by a Cambridge man who actually held neither an Oxford or Cambridge DD; Franklyn commented: 'it is time that the two Universities came to some arrangement with Lambeth in this matter'; his own suggestion was that adding a one inch edging of purple on the cape of the hood to all Lambeth graduates would make the matter clear.

Franklyn was aware that, despite his view of how Lambeth academic dress ought to be reformed, the existing system was that, all recipients of Lambeth degree wear Oxford robes, because the overwhelming majority of archbishops were Oxford graduates, although at the time he wrote this Michael Ramsey was Archbishop and had graduated from Cambridge. Franklyn's view was also that recipients should regard a Lambeth degree as 'a promotion' and therefore should wear the robes of the corresponding degree of their own university. What Franklyn did not consider is what would be done in the case of a graduate whose

---

[1] C. A. H. Franklyn, *Academical Dress From the Middle Ages to the Present Day including Lambeth Degrees*, W E Baxter, Lewes (1970).

university did not award degrees in music or divinity – probably he did not regard such an institution to be a university. Franklyn gave the example of the previous Bishop of Portsmouth (Dr. Frank Partridge), who held a B.A. from the University of London, who was granted a Lambeth DD in 1936. Partridge would (under Franklyn's proposed system) have worn the London DD academic dress. But under the existing system, he wore the robes of an Oxford DD. In November 1938 London University awarded Partridge an honorary DD because he was the first London University graduate to be promoted to a diocesan see. Franklyn 'had the great pleasure' of making Partridge's London DD hood and chimere for him. This was a piece of invention on Franklyn's part since the chimere did not figure in the London University academic dress regulations. Partridge, Franklyn noted, therefore had an Oxford DD robe for garden parties, and two chimeres and two hoods for church use. Franklyn, in mischievous mood, suggested that Partridge could also mix his robes, wearing a London hood with an Oxford chimere and vice versa, 'so as to show both degrees.'

Franklyn also paid some attention to the nature of Lambeth degrees in a characteristically opinionated way. He started with the rather extravagant — and implausible — claim that 'the true nature and significance of these degrees is almost entirely unknown and it is doubtful whether half-a-dozen people in the world really know anything definite or accurate about them.' Franklyn claimed that he had spent forty years investigating 'the true nature of these degrees'. He claimed to have collected all sorts of materials on how they were conferred and consequently made the grand claim that he was 'now in a position to make the whole subject clear' – though he conceded that there were aspects of the conferment which were controversial and required further research.

Franklyn advanced three 'findings' – in reality these were all widely known. First, the term 'Lambeth degree' was merely a phrase to show the origins of the degrees; secondly that they were not — Franklyn claimed — conferred by the archbishop alone and thirdly that they were validated by confirmatory letters patent, issued under the great seal (or what Franklyn called *per litteras Regis*) and registered in a roll in the House of Lords, which was the location of the Crown Office. In fact, Franklyn was referring to practice in the mid-twentieth century, which he assumed had been in place since the inception of the degrees. But there was no evidence that this had been the practice for longer than the previous century.

Franklyn concluded, based on the confirmation by letters patent, that Lambeth degrees were therefore conferred by the Sovereign. They clearly were not awarded by a university and, in Franklyn's deeply royalist mind, would consequently take precedence over other degrees. So a Lambeth DD would take precedence over all other DDs, and a Lambeth DMus would take precedence over all other degrees of DMus or MusD, irrespective of whether conferred regularly or *honoris causa*.

Franklyn claimed that this issue of who awarded the degrees and their seniority 'have never been stated or brought forward before, nor do they seem to have been ever realised previously.' But for Franklyn the issue was incontrovertible:

> there could be no question at all, no question whatsoever, that a degree conferred by the Sovereign and registered in the Crown Office of the House of Lords would be superior to, and would take precedence over all other degrees …

He claimed that a degree 'bestowed' by letters patent (here Franklyn made a sleight of hand by suggesting that the degree was 'bestowed' by the monarch) was superior to a university degree 'because the Crown is the sole fountain of honour, and a university can only confer a degree in virtue of power and authority derived from the Crown.' Franklyn claimed therefore that a university degree was 'two removed from the source' whereas Lambeth degrees were only one place removed from the source of honour. There was of course in reality no distinction such as Franklyn sought to make between proximity to the source of all honours.

At this point, Franklyn helpfully summarised the ways in which a degree could be awarded. He identified seven methods for the award of a degree. First by letters patent – either to a university to confer a degree, or via a Lambeth award initiated by the archbishop of Canterbury. The former system was common in the early modern period when Tudor or Stuart monarchs visited the universities. Second was 'the ordinary way' of earning a degree through a course of study. Thirdly was the award of a degree by diploma, such as the award of a DD on a newly nominated bishop or the conferral of a DCL on the chancellor or vice-chancellor or an MP. Franklyn also claimed that the award of DDs to public school headmasters in the Victorian period was common and these degrees were awarded by diploma. The use of the term 'by diploma', claimed Franklyn, showed that the certificate of the award was sent to the recipient and there was no formal ceremony of admission to the degree. Franklyn cited the degree conferred on Franklin Roosevelt: 'in the summer of 1941 the University of Oxford acted unusually by conferring the degree of DCL upon …President Roosevelt by Diploma, but actually by ceremony too at a special Convocation of the University held in America! He was thus created a Doctor in Civil Law by Diploma and Convocation, but, I think, was not actually present at the ceremony!' Fourthly was an award by a decree by a university. This was the way in which degrees *ad eundem* were granted, recognising a degree at Oxford or Cambridge was equivalent to the university's own award. Fifthly by *jure dignitatis* by a university. This was, claimed Franklyn commonly used by Trinity College, Dublin when a bishop was nominated or a surgeon was appointed to a chair in surgery — in both cases a doctorate would be awarded *jure dignitatis* — to recognise the status that they had achieved as bishop or professor. Franklyn's view was that every professor of surgery ought at hold at least a M.Ch, every bishop a DD and every judge a DCL or LLD. The sixth method was by making an award *honoris causa*. Franklyn had strong views on such awards, it was

> a most abused method of conferment. It would be correct to create a bicycle manufacturer an honorary DCL, but it would be wrong to create a learned judge an honorary DCL, since of all people he is expected to know a great deal about Law; similarly a learned physician an MD or DM.

The final means of awarding a degree was by a university commission – often awarding a degree away from the seat of the university. The example Franklyn gave was the award of a DCL on the President of Portugal in 1941 when members of the House of Convocation of the University of Oxford travelled to Lisbon to confer the degree. In reality it is not clear what the distinctions were between the third, fifth and sixth methods.

The examination of the method of conferring degrees enabled Franklyn to assert that Lambeth degrees were not honorary degrees, but were regarded as full 'earned' degrees. This was because an 'earned' degree was conferred as a result of training, vocation, or profession, or by original work. Such a definition would include those who received Lambeth degrees. Moreover Franklyn asserted that 'a Lambeth degree is a full degree conferred by legal procedure by document, registered in the House of Lords, and probably superior to any Diploma or Certificate from a University or degree granting College.'

Then Franklyn returned to the issue of who actually conferred Lambeth degrees. His 'original thesis' was that a Lambeth degree was conferred by the Crown, because they were confirmed by letters patent. To Franklyn, 'it would seem plain logic' that if an archbishop's award of a Lambeth degree required confirmation by letters patent, 'the essential step' in awarding the degree was an act of the sovereign, although it was referred to as ratification, approval and confirmation. Franklyn argued that if, for example, the king or queen refused to issue the letters patent, or was advised not to do so, or a recipient died before the letters patent had been issued, the archbishop's legal instrument on its own would be regarded as insufficient and the degree would not have been conferred. While there might have been a degree ceremony at Lambeth Palace, without the confirmation of letters patent the degree would be invalid.

Franklyn set himself the task of trying to clarify this issue in 1942 and wrote to Cosmo Gordon Lang, the previous archbishop of Canterbury, who had been ennobled as Lord Lang of Lambeth. He seems to have sent Lang the whole typescript of Chapter Thirteen of his *Academical Dress From the Middle Ages to the Present Day including Lambeth Degrees*. Lang replied on 11 March 1942:

> The summary of your conclusion as contained in p. 143 (of the then typewritten text) has in my judgement no foundation in fact. The Degrees are *conferred* by the Archbishop at his own complete discretion. They are only confirmed by the Crown as indeed the documents which you quote abundantly testify. The Crown merely confirms the recipient of the Degree in his possession of it. The conferring of the Degree is entirely in the hands of the Archbishop.

Three days later, Lang's chaplain, the Rev. Ian White-Thompson, writing at Lang's request:

> As to your main conclusion, His Grace can only say that you and he must agree to differ. He cannot accept the argument that letters patent confirming a degree which has already been conferred by the Archbishop of Canterbury implies that it is the Crown and not the Archbishop who confers the degree.

Lang sent Franklyn's opinion to H. T. A. Dashwood, Registrar of the Faculty Office, who wrote to Franklyn on 4 May 1942:

> I read your Chapter XIII of your book at the request of Lord Lang, and returned it to him with a full letter in February last. In my letter I stated that there is no foundation in your statement that these Degrees are conferred by the Crown.

Franklyn was not abashed by these responses. He saw that the Archbishop, his chaplain and the registrar supported the claim that the degrees were awarded by the archbishop. But Franklyn was not convinced by their claims. He cited the phrase in the archbishop's award of each degree, which was "Provided Always, that these Presents do not avail you anything, unless duly conferred by the King's letters patent."

Franklyn pressed on with his research. He consulted a Lord Justice of the High Court of Appeal, who was also a member of the Privy Council. However Franklyn claimed that he did not have not the authority to quote him by name. But he quoted a letter dated 29 March 1943, from the Lord Justice of Appeal:

> I have read your M.S. with interest and have had an opportunity of talking it over with Mr. Kenneth Mead Mac'Morvan, KC, MA, LLB, (Cantab), who knows much more than I do about these matters. He has not been able to give much time to it, but the point interest him very much.

> A difficulty which suggests itself is that apparently Royal letters patent are not issued in the case of degrees lower than that of a Doctor, *e.g.* an MA degree. This suggests that it is not the Crown that grants the degree, although in the case of a doctorate the issue of letters patent is necessary. It seems clear that the granting of the degree must be on the initiative of the Archbishop, and unless it can be established that he merely nominates and recommends a candidate (as, *e.g.* the Lord Chancellor recommends the appointment of someone as a High Court Judge), it may be difficult to say that the Archbishop does not in truth confer the degree. This is the only criticism I am able to make. Please do not quote me, as I am not an ecclesiastical lawyer. Mr Mac'Morvan thought your thesis very interesting, and regarded the subject as one eminently suitable for research.

Franklyn then consulted the Crown Office of the House of Lords. On 2 April, the Clerk told him that the Lambeth BD was also confirmed by letters patent. Franklyn concluded that there were two classes of degrees conferred at Lambeth Palace. First was the MA, which was not confirmed by letters patent, but merely endorsed and registered in the Crown Office. The second type of degrees were the BD, DD, DCL, DM and DMus, which were confirmed by royal letters patent.

Despite the Archbishop's and the legal opinions, Franklyn continued to pose the question, 'Is a Lambeth degree duly conferred and valid if it lacks the sovereign's confirmatory letters patent?' After all, the Lambeth MA appeared to be conferred without letters patent. Yet Franklyn pointed out that the Lambeth MA seemed to require letters patent, according to the formal instrument, but did not receive it, and appeared to be valid without it; but the other Lambeth degrees receive confirmation by letters patent, even though the Archbishop felt them to be conferred before confirmation.

Franklyn felt that the solution to the situation lay in the history of the Lambeth degrees. He claimed that until the Reformation, the Church in England was part of the Western or Roman Church, having split (Franklyn called it 'a heretic section') from the Orthodox, or Greek Church. The Pope, as supreme head of the Roman Church, exercised jurisdiction over the Church in England, for which purposes he sent papal legates to England. The archbishop of Canterbury and sometimes the papal legate conferred degrees from the Pope. The archbishop conferred these degrees on behalf of the pope. When Henry VIII broke with Rome and established the Church of England, which was independent from Rome, he placed himself at the head of the Church of England. In this capacity he took over the various ecclesiastical functions formerly exercised by the Pope. Degrees continued to be conferred by the archbishop, but instead of being ratified by the pope, were confirmed by the king. Of course Franklyn did not notice the technical distinction between the monarch as 'supreme governor' of the Church and the archbishop as head of the Church, a distinction which came in during Elizabeth I's reign. An issue on which Franklyn was silent is the exercise of the power to award degrees by other primates. There is some evidence that in Ireland the archbishops of Armagh had this power, though they seem to have usually exercised it by the practice of asking Trinity College Dublin to grant a degree on their behalf.

In relation to this, Franklyn cited a letter from Canon J. M. J. Fletcher to Dr. L. H. Dudley Buxton and Strickland Gibson dated 12 August 1938:

> The Statutory authority to enable the Archbishop to confer these degrees was given to the then Archbishop of Canterbury (Thomas Cranmer) and his successors in 1534 under the "Peters Pence Act" (25 Henry VIII, c.21) The Act was passed for the exoneration of exactions paid to the See of Rome. By this Act the power of the Pope, who formerly used to grant dispensations and confer degrees was superseded; and the statutory authority to do so in his place was conferred upon the Archbishop of Canterbury. (But in all cases costing £4 or more in Tax on the Expedition to Rome, and the Tax on degrees amounted to £4, require confirmation by the great seal).
>
> Since the Universities of Oxford and Cambridge have ceased giving the DD degree *honoris causa*, to Bishops who were graduates of these Universities, the Archbishop seems to have conferred, in its place, the Lambeth Degree upon Diocesan Bishops.
>
> The present custom (I do not know whether the Rev. Thomas W. Wood was mistaken or whether the custom was different when he wrote his book) certainly is for the Archbishop to confer the degree of his own University, whether the recipient is a member of that University or not, *e.g.* our own Bishop of Salisbury, who is a Cambridge man. The Bishop of Portsmouth, who is also I think (but I am writing this away from books of reference) a Cambridge man; and Canon E. W. J. Hellins, who was an MA of Cambridge but a DD of Lambeth.

Franklyn's citation of Fletcher meant that he had to correct two points: first archbishops never conferred any degree of their own university, they nominated to the degree, which degree, Franklyn stubbornly maintained, 'is not of any university but of the realm.' Secondly the Bishop of Portsmouth referred to in the correspondence was in fact a London BA.

Franklyn also noted the case of Samuel Peploe (which is covered in *The Bishop of Chester's Case With Relation to the Wardenship of Manchester* in this collection). Franklyn recited at some length the details of the Peploe case. From this, Franklyn concluded that Lambeth degrees conferred under the statute 25 Henry 8, cap 21 were at least doubtful. This was partly because the archbishops had not exercised the right to confer degrees continually even though Archbishops Laud and Juxon did so. Moreover Lambeth degrees could never be claimed to be any more than 'bare titles of Honour' which conferred 'no Legal or Canonical Effect'.

Franklyn also argued that even before the Reformation, papal degrees were never treated as 'good and effectual in Law, and beneficial to persons in England'. So degrees conferred by archbishop upon the precedent of papal authority could have no value. Franklyn continued that in Peploe's case, 25 Henry 8, cap 21 did not mention the power to award degrees at all so the power claimed by archbishops must be derived from the general powers transferred to the king. But the act was only supposed to grant to the archbishop the powers that the Pope had exercised. While it is clear that popes did award degrees, they were never entitled to do so in order to legally qualify clergy for ecclesiastical preferment in England. This was because the pope exercised spiritual jurisdiction, but not temporal jurisdiction, which Franklyn felt the conferment of a degree was.

Franklyn also cited the claim that in 1604 a dispute arose over precedence between Serjeants at Common Law and Doctors of Civil Law. To resolve the dispute it was argued that Doctors were made by letters patent under the great seal because the universities deriving their power from the Crown. So Doctors won the case.

Franklyn sided with the Bishop of Chester in questioning whether the archbishops had the power to confer degrees. The issue of whether proper records had been kept, or whether the archbishops had exercised the power continuously, or whether the Lambeth degrees were of any value. But in the end Franklyn had to concede that in court the case was decided against the Bishop of Chester. The Lambeth BD conferred on Samuel Peploe, was upheld as fulfilling the Statutes of Manchester College.

Franklyn however stuck to his view that, although the Archbishop confers the Lambeth Degrees, they are all Registered in the Crown Office of the House of Lords, an MA degree being merely endorsed, all the Doctorates and BD degrees being duly confirmed and ratified by the Sovereign's letters patent under the great seal of the realm as well. The Doctors are admitted into the number of the Doctors of the realm, Masters into the number of Masters, and Bachelors in Divinity into the numbers of Bachelors in Divinity of the realm. What is not clear is whether this practice existed before the late nineteenth century.[2] Having

---

[2] Dr Nick Groves, FBS, has kindly sent me the wording of the warrant issued in 1853 for the award of a DMus to Zechariah Buck, which is given in: T. Roast, *Zechariah Buck, Organist of Norwich Cathedral 1819–1877; a Bicentenary Memoir*, Gateway Music, Norwich (1998):

> Having thought fit to Confer on Zechariah Buck of the City of Norwich Gentleman the Degree of Doctor in Music:

> These are to Order and require that you issue forth Letters Testimonial of his creation in that Faculty under your Seal of Office according to the usual and accustomed form in the like cases observed, and for your so doing this shall be your Warrant.

> Given at Lambeth Palace this Eighth day of July in the Year of Our Lord One thousand eight hundred and fifty three.

> To the Right Worshipful Sir John Dodson, Knt, LLD, Master of the Faculties or his Surrogate.

The silence of this warrant on the issue of registering the degree in the Crown Office or confirmatory letters patent suggests that they may have developed in the twentieth century.

ignored the judgement of the archbishop and legal authority, Franklyn turned to the way in which the degree was conferred. By this point he had started to refer to the degrees as 'so-called Lambeth degrees.' Franklyn indicated that the process began when an archbishop decided to confer a degree on a candidate. Usually this was for 'some work which he has done, for some eminent service which he has rendered, or because of some office or appointment to which he has been preferred.' Often when a cathedral statute required a dean to be a DD he would make such an award to ensure that the candidate met the requirements of the statutes. The other frequent case was when a clergyman was made a diocesan bishop, if the bishop lacked a doctorate and was not offered one by his own university.

The archbishop of Canterbury then informed the candidate of his nomination and, if the recipient agreed to accept the degree, a date for the conferment was set at Lambeth Palace. At the ceremony of conferment, the candidates knelt before the Archbishop, and was hooded in the Palace Library, certain Latin Prayers being read by the Archbishop. Franklyn went on:

> one of the chaplains is also in attendance and places the hood over the recipient's shoulders at the moment when the Archbishop actually caps him. After the Latin Prayers have been offered, the candidate then also signs the Oath. The candidate kneels, and the Archbishop reads the Instrument.

Franklyn had received permission from Lord Lang to reproduce a specimen Instrument.

> Cosmo Gordon, by Divine Permission Archbishop of Canterbury, Primate of All England, and Metropolitan, by the Authority of Parliament, lawfully empowered for the purpose herein written, to our Beloved in Christ, [name] WHEREAS in Schools regularly instituted the laudable Usage and Custom hath long prevailed, and that with the Approbation as well of the pure reformed Churches as of the most learned Men for many Ages past, that they who have with Proficiency and Applause exerted themselves in the Study of any Liberal Science, should be graced with some eminent Degree of Dignity: And whereas the Archbishops of Canterbury, enabled by the public Authority of the Law, do enjoy, and have long enjoyed, the Power of Conferring Degrees and Titles of Honour upon well-deserving Men, as by an authentick Book of Taxations of Faculties confirmed by Authority of Parliament, doth more fully appear: WE THEREFORE, being vested with the authority aforesaid and following the Example of our Predecessors, have judged it expedient, in consideration of your Proficiency in Study, Uprightness of Life, Sound Doctrine, and Purity of Morals, that you be dignified with the Degree of (*e.g.* Doctor in Divinity) and We do by these presents, so far as in us lies, and the Laws of this realm do allow, accordingly create you an actual (Master of Arts, Doctor, etc.). And We do also admit you into the numbers of the (Masters of Arts, Doctors etc.) of this realm, the Oath (written above) having been by Us first required of you and by you duly taken and subscribed.

Sticking tenaciously to his earlier argument, Franklyn wrote that the Archbishop's Instrument concluded with the words: "these Presents do not avail you anything unless duly confirmed by the King's letters patent".

After the conferment, the archbishop signed the fiat which was given to the Master of the Faculties, the recipient and the archbishop signed the register. The event is concluded with three other Latin prayers.

The Instrument was then sent to the Clerk of the Crown Office in Chancery, at the House of Lords, and eventually the letters patent were issued, the Instrument and letters patent were fastened together. After these were signed and sealed with the great seal, and registered, they were delivered to the recipient of the degree.

Franklyn had also received permission to reproduce the instruments and letters.

Copy of Instrument and of letters patent creating the Rev. Mervyn George Haig, MA, Bishop of Coventry-designate, a Doctor in Divinity.

GEORGE THE FIFTH by the Grace of God of Great Britain Ireland and the British Dominions Beyond the Seas King Defender of the Faith TO ALL TO WHOM THESE PRESENTS SHALL COME GREETINGS We have seen certain letters of Creation to these Presents annexed which and everything therein contained according to a certain Act in that behalf made in the Parliament of Henry the Eighth heretofore King of England Our Predecessor We have ratified and approved and confirmed and for Us Our heirs and successors We do ratify approve and confirm by these Presents so that [name] in the Letters aforesaid named may use take and enjoy freely and quietly with impunity and lawfully all and singular the things in the same specified accordingly to the form and force and effect of the same without any impediment whatsoever although express mention of the certainty of the premises or of any other gifts or grants by Us heretofore made to the said [name] be not made in these Presents or any other thing cause or matter whatsoever in anywise notwithstanding IN TESTIMONY whereof We have caused these Our Letters to be made Patent WITNESS Ourself at Westminster the day of   in the   year of our Reign   (sgnd.) SCHUSTER.

HAIG, M.G.   DEGREE: DD

COSMO GORDON, by Divine Providence, ARCHBISHOP OF CANTERBURY, Primate of All England and Metropolitan, by Authority of Parliament, lawfully empowered for the purposes herein written. To our beloved in Christ, The Reverend MERVYN GEORGE HAIG, Clerk, Master of Arts, One of the Six Preachers in Our Cathedral and Metropolitan Church of Christ Canterbury, Chaplain to His Majesty the King, and lately Our Principal Chaplain and Private Secretary, now Bishop Designate of Coventry HEALTH AND GRACE in Jesus Christ our Saviour. WHEREAS in Schools regularly instituted the laudable Usage and Custom hath long prevailed, and that with the Approbation as well of the pure reformed Churches as of the most learned Men for many Ages past, that they who have with Proficiency and Applause exerted themselves in the Study of any Liberal Science, should be graced with some eminent Degree of Dignity: AND WHEREAS the Archbishops of Canterbury, enabled by the public Authority of Law, do enjoy, and have long enjoyed, the Power of conferring Degrees and Titles of Honour among well-deserving Men, as by an authentick Book of Taxations of Faculties, confirmed by Authority of Parliament, doth more fully appear: WE THEREFORE, being vested with Authority aforesaid, and following the example of our Predecessors, have judged it expedient that you whose Proficiency in the Study of Divinity, Uprightness of Life, Sound Doctrine, and Purity of Morals, are manifest to Us, be dignified with the Degree of Doctor in Divinity And we do by these presents, so far as in Us lies, and the Laws of this realm do allow, accordingly create you an actual DOCTOR IN DIVINITY jure dignitatis And We do also admit you into the Number of the Doctors in Divinity of this realm; the Oath hereunder-written having been by our Master of the Faculties first required of you, and by you duly taken and subscribed.

I, MERVYN GEORGE HAIG, Clerk, Master of Arts, Bishop Designate of Coventry the person to be admitted to the Degree of Doctor in Divinity by the Most Reverend Father in

God COSMO GORDON by Divine Providence, Lord Archbishop of Canterbury, Primate of All England and Metropolitan, do swear by Almighty God that I will be faithful and bear true allegiance to His Majesty King George, His Heirs and Successors, according to Law. PROVIDED ALWAYS that these Presents do not avail you anything, unless duly confirmed by the King's Patent.

GIVEN under the Seal of our OFFICE OF FACULTIES at Doctors Commons this eleventh Day of February in the Year of our Lord One Thousand Nine Hundred and thirty one and in the third year of Our Translation.

L.S.   (sgd.) ARTHUR W.D. MOORE
                                                               Registrar.

CONFIRMATORY PATENT

GEORGE THE FIFTH by the Grace of God of Great Britain Ireland and the British Dominions Beyond the Seas King Defender of the Faith TO ALL TO WHOM THESE PRESENTS SHALL COME GREETINGS We have seen certain letters of Creation to these Presents annexed which and everything therein contained according to a certain Act in that behalf made in the Parliament of Henry the Eighth heretofore King of England Our Predecessor We have ratified and approved and confirmed and for Us Our heirs and successors We do ratify approve and confirm by these Presents so that MERVYN GEORGE HAIG Clerk Master of Arts One of the Six Preachers in Our Cathedral and Metropolitan Church of Christ Canterbury Our Chaplain and lately Principal Chaplain and Private Secretary to the Most Reverend Father in God Our right trusty and well beloved Councillor Cosmo Gordon by Divine Providence Lord Archbishop of Canterbury in the Letters aforesaid named (since appointed to be Bishop of Coventry) may use take and enjoy freely and quietly with impunity and lawfully all and singular the things in the same specified according to the form force and effect of the same without any impediment whatsoever although express mention of the certainty of the premises or of any other gifts or grants by Us heretofore made to the said Mervyn George Haig be not made in these Presents or any other thing cause or matter whatsoever in anywise notwithstanding IN TESTIMONY whereof We have caused these Our Letters to be made Patent WITNESS Ourself at Westminster the 17th day of Feby in the twenty first year of Our Reign.

(The great seal affixed)   (sgd.) SCHUSTER.

This concluded Franklyn's analysis of Lambeth degrees.

7 Dispensations, Privileges, and the Conferment of Graduate Status: With Special Reference to Lambeth Degrees

Noel Cox

This article was originally published as:

Noel Cox, "Dispensations, Privileges, and the Conferment of Graduate Status: With Special Reference to Lambeth Degrees", *Journal of Law and Religion* 18.1 (2002–2003) 249–274

Reproduced by permission of Cambridge University Press.

DISPENSATIONS, PRIVILEGES, AND THE CONFERMENT OF GRADUATE STATUS: WITH SPECIAL REFERENCE TO LAMBETH DEGREES

Noel Cox[†]

I. INTRODUCTION

Since 1533 archbishops of Canterbury have conferred academic degrees by virtue of the power invested in them by the Ecclesiastical Licences Act 1533-1534, also known as the Peter's Pence Act.[1] Legally these so-called Lambeth degrees, named after the principal residence of the archbishop, survive as an aspect of the medieval papal authority to grant dispensations. This is, in individual cases of hardship, the see of Rome might exercise the jurisdiction vested in him as patriarch of the west—though not necessarily in other patriarchs[2]—to confer upon an appropriate recipient the academic degree which he would have received but for some impediment.[3]

But properly speaking, these degrees were not just an exercise of papal dispensation, they also sometimes had the character of a grant of a privilege. For example, the papacy might confer a degree upon a recipient to enable that person to hold an office that the canon law, or a specific institutional rule, limited to graduates. The power claimed and exercised by the papacy to confer the status of graduate to someone who had not earned it in the traditional way was never limited solely to true dispensations, but always included positive privilege as papal degrees granted for political reasons clearly illustrate.

---

† LLM (Hons) PhD. Barrister of the High Court of New Zealand, and of the Supreme Courts of Tasmania, New South Wales, and South Australia. Lecturer in Law at the Auckland University of Technology.

1. 1.25 Hen. 8, c. 21 (Eng.).

2. In the east, the concept of economy (οικονομια) is generally equated with dispensation, though there are important differences, both in theory and practise. For dispensations generally, *see* the "Report of a Commission appointed by the Archbishop of Canterbury," *Dispensation in Practice and Theory* (SPCK 1944).

3. Such impediments included non-residence, non-fulfilment of a prescribed minimum course of study, or other regulation imposed by the code of canon law, papal documents such as the encyclical *Pascendi*, or relevant decrees issued by the Holy See.

250   *JOURNAL OF LAW & RELIGION*   [Vol. XVIII]

In post-Reformation England, Lambeth degrees replaced papal degrees and degree status. Awarded to this day, Lambeth degrees are, generally speaking, lineal descendants of the medieval papal or legatine degrees. But their nature has perhaps been misunderstood: they should not be thought of as merely honorary degrees. Like the papal degrees they replaced, they are best understood as privileges rather than dispensations, though they reflect aspects of both papal powers, and more broadly, the influence of the canon law and the papacy upon medieval higher education.

After outlining the early evolution of the universities as canonical institutions and briefly covering the nature of medieval university degrees, this article will review the nature of the dispensation and the role of papal privileges in medieval society. The article will then examine post-Reformation ecclesiastical jurisdiction in England and review the history of the Lambeth degrees, as bestowed from the Reformation to the nineteenth century, as well as describing modern Lambeth degrees. I will consider whether Lambeth degrees have continued to serve as examples of dispensation or privilege, or survive as merely a form of honour, and assess Lambeth degrees as they now stand.

II.   THE RISE OF THE MEDIEVAL UNIVERSITIES

After the intellectual nadir of the Dark Ages, centers of learning grew up in many leading cities of the west, often originating in the monastic and cathedral schools. In all, some twenty-three universities were founded in Europe prior to 1300.[4] The earliest universities to form were however in Italy, at Salerno[5] in the ninth century, and Bologna[6] in the eleventh century. The rise of the university in other countries soon followed. Towards the end of the twelfth century, a few of the greatest schools, including Salerno and Bologna, claimed international standing, largely on the basis of their excellent teaching.

The more ancient and customary term for these institutions was *studium* and subsequently *studium generale*, the specific term

---

4. There were eleven in Italy, five in France, two in England, five on the Iberian Peninsula. *See* Denys Hay, *Europe in the Fourteenth and Fifteenth Centuries* 361 (2d ed., Longman 1989).

5. Although it was never anything than a medical school, so could not be said to be a *universitas litterarum*, though its wide standing made it a *studia generalia* even if only in the field of medicine. A modern university was established at Salerno in 1970.

6. Bologna began as a law school but widened its scope to become a true *universitas litterarum*, something that Salerno never did. The University of Bologna remains, probably the oldest still extant.

universitas being confined to the scholastic guild within the *studium*. The *universitas* often meant simply the student body, usually called the nation, organised for the communal protection of the foreign student body, men who otherwise, being aliens, were at the mercy of local inn-keepers and tradesmen.

In the early thirteenth century, and for long afterwards, superior schools were classified as either general or particular. By the end of the thirteenth century, the general schools began to be called *studia generalia*, or places to which scholars flocked from all parts of Europe.[7] The particular schools remained limited to educating regional students in the "primitive" sciences, grammar and philosophy. They did not teach arts, medicine, law and theology, nor were they universally considered to confer the same qualifications by the best scholars.[8]

The fusion of the *universitates* into a single *universitas* was a gradual process,[9] but by the close of the medieval period however these distinctions had been lost sight of, and the term *universitas* was used alone. A precise definition of those schools that were recognized as universities, particularly in this early period, is difficult; but an essential feature was that a university was incorporated as such by a sovereign power,[10] or at least received recognition from the sovereign. University attributes scarcely less important included admission of students from all parts of the world, plurality of masters, provision for the study of one at least of the higher faculties,[11] the provision for residence, and the right to confer degrees. In almost all cases, the earliest universities evolved as scholastic guilds, developed on an analogy with the tradesmen's guilds and the later guilds of aliens that sprang up in the thirteenth and fourteenth centuries in most of the great European cities. Formal

---

7. There has always been some difficulty in ascertaining a seniority list for the earliest universities. It is impossible to do so with any degree of precision, largely because the first universities- those having their origins in the eleventh to thirteenth centuries, were the outcome of spontaneous social developments. As the earliest universities grew out of associations of students, many of them came into existence as result of the migration of students from one centre to another. Thus scholars from Bologna created Padua. Paris, the earliest of the northern type of university, was unusual in that it was created by its masters.

8. Reverend Fr. Benedict Hackett, *The Original Statutes of Cambridge University: The Text and Its History* 176 (Cambridge U. Press 1970).

9. Christopher Lucas, *Our Western Educational Heritage* 234 (Macmillan Publg. Co. 1972).

10. Sir William Blackstone, *Commentaries on the Laws of England* vol. 1, 472 (Richard Burn ed., Garland Publg. 1978); *St David's College, Lampeter v Ministry of Education*, 1 All E.R. 559, 560 (Ch. D. 1951).

11. The higher faculties were divinity, law (including canon law), and medicine. Arts (or philosophy) was regarded as a lower faculty as all men had to pass through its doors before they would be permitted to study for a qualification from the higher faculties. At Oxford it was however possible to study civil law after four years without taking the BA.

252   *JOURNAL OF LAW & RELIGION*   [Vol. XVIII

recognition might soon come to a successful school, but they were generally recognised as universities by the sovereign power only after their successful formation.

The papacy soon exercised the sovereign's prerogative to recognize a university. In a bull of 1225, Emperor Frederick II purported to confer upon his new school at Naples the prestige that earlier *studia* had acquired by reputation and general consent, and Pope Gregory IX followed this example for Toulouse in 1229. Other *studia generalia* were subsequently founded by papal or imperial bulls. In fact, by the second half of the thirteenth century, jurists commonly held that a *stadium generale* possessing the right of conferring degrees and licences to teach could only be founded by a *potestatis generalis*, or sovereign authority, particularly the pope or emperor. As a consequence the more prominent of the long-established universities which lacked a papal bull of foundation set about seeking *de jure* recognition or confirmation of their titles from the Holy See.[12] For example, in 1292 the Universities of Paris and Bologna found it desirable to obtain similar bulls from Pope Nicholas IV. However, a few schools such as Oxford were too well established to be seriously questioned for lack of papal recognition, and these were always regarded as *studia generalia ex consuetudine*.

The recognition of the privileges of a university of masters, which freed it from control by local ecclesiastical or civic authority, created a new type of higher education in Christendom.[13] But universities were not completely beyond the control of Rome. As an example, a charter from the papal legate to Oxford in 1214 confirmed the clerical status of the student members of the university.[14] If students were clerics, the church could exercise at least some control over their actions. Expanding this trend toward the clericalization of university education, by the mid-thirteenth century it was taken for granted that canons and other higher clergy would be released from their benefices for study.[15] Under Pope Boniface VIII, it became customary for the parochial clergy to obtain dispensations for study, thus allowing members of the wider Church educational facilities.[16] Since so many members of the student

---

12. G.L. Haskins, *The University of Oxford and the 'Ius Ubique Docendi',* 56 English Historical Rev. 281, 282-283 (1941).

13. Colin Morris, *The Papal Monarchy—The Western Church from 1050 to 1250* at 505 (Clarendon Press 1989).

14. *Id.* at 506.

15. Leonard Boyle, *The Constitution "Cum ex eo" of Boniface VIII,* 24 Mediaeval Stud. 263 (1962); J.R.H. Moorman, *Church Life in England in the Thirteenth Century* 31, 96 (Cambridge U. Press 1946); M. Gibbs & J. Lang, *Bishops and Reform* 184 (Clarendon Press 1934).

16. Leonard Boyle, *The Constitution "Cum ex eo" of Boniface VIII,* 24 Mediaeval Stud. 263

body were clerics, it was natural that the church should continue to exercise some degree of oversight over the universities.

From the very beginning, both civil and ecclesiastical authorities that chartered colleges and universities, and gave them broad powers to grant "the usual degrees." The degrees of the *studia generalia* were publicly conferred by a general power, the pope or emperor, though the power to confer degrees was also exercised by authorities other than the universities, such as the Counts Palatine, as late as the sixteenth century. But the pope claimed particular oversight of the universities and the conferral of academic degrees.[17] Indeed, in the Roman Catholic Church, the Holy See today has the right to establish and govern universities,[18] and still exercises the power of conferring degrees, particularly in the fields of theology, philosophy, Scripture, and canon law.[19]

III. The System for Granting Medieval Degrees

The medieval higher education system was rather different from that with which we are familiar today. Latin was the language of instruction throughout the middle ages, and beyond. As previously suggested, the university scholar was usually a cleric, that is a man in holy orders, or one who at least had received the tonsure, although many students did not advance beyond deacon and forsook the religious vocation for a secular career.[20]

After preliminary qualifications in the faculties of arts or philosophy,[21] students were awarded degrees in theology, law,[22] and

---

(1962).

17. Canon 817 of the Roman Catholic Code of Canon Law (1983) provides that only a university or a faculty established or approved by the Apostolic See may confer academic degrees which have canonical effects in the Church. The Canon Law Society of Great Britain & Ireland, *The Code of Canon Law in English Translation* 149 (Collins Liturgical Publications 1983).

18. *See id.* at 147-149, canons 807-821.

19. The papal universities are canonically erected, and are governed by the Code of Canon Law, papal documents, and decrees issued by the Holy See. Among the most important of these have been the encyclical *Pascendi*, issued by Pope Pius X 8 Sept. 1907, and the apostolic constitution *Deus Scientiarum Dominus*, issued by Pope Pius XI 24 May 1931.

20. For the clerical status of medieval university students, *see* the Very Revd. Rashdall Hastings, *The Universities of Europe in the Middle Ages* (F.M. Powicke & A.B. Emden eds., Clarendon Press 1936).

21. The MA or BA might be the only qualification ever obtained by most students.

22. At Oxford, bachelors of canon law were styled BCanL, and doctors of canon law DCanL (or doctor of decrees, the *decretorum doctor*). The bachelors and doctors of civil law, the sole type remaining, were styled BCL and DCL, the former being *licencia legendi aliqina cursorie in iure ciuli*. At Cambridge, a single degree included both canon law and civil law, as LLB and LLD stand for bachelor and doctor of laws respectively. Civil Law was taught at Oxford at least as early as 1145, when Vacarius was giving lectures. Although teaching was disrupted at the Reformation, the regius professorships of civil law at Oxford and Cambridge, established 1540,

medicine.[23] The Church was especially concerned with the conferral of degrees in theology, and exercised a considerable influence, both direct and indirect, over the faculties of theology or divinity.[24] In particular, the papacy promoted the school of theology in Paris, and one in canon law in Bologna. As a subject in which degrees could be awarded, the discipline of music had a post-medieval arrival.[25]

Historically, the award of an academic degree meant that the recipient was accepted into a scholarly fraternity, the university. But for centuries, aspiring scholars sought alternative means of obtaining the degree, which was a necessary pre-requisite to teaching in a university[26] and for many official posts and offices, especially in the Church.[27] Where a student or other individual failed to obtain a regular degree, for whatever reason, the pope might be persuaded to deviate from the strict requirements imposed by those institutions upon their students,[28] not by directly dispensing with the requirements of an individual university,[29] but by himself conferring a degree, or equivalent status as a privilege or dispensation.

In England, the practice of granting these dispensations began during the time when attendance at Oxford or Cambridge, the only universities at that time, was frequently disrupted by social or political disorder, or perhaps by outbreaks of the plague. Perhaps more importantly, many men were unable to complete the full requirements

---

ensured that the civil law was not altogether abandoned.

23. The faculty of physic only developed at Oxford as late as *c*.1450-*c*.1500.

24. For any aspect of the development of the universities, the starting point must still be the Very Revd Rashdall Hastings, *The Universities of Europe, supra* n. 20.

25. Cambridge MusB 1500-1501, MusD 1463 (Thomas Saintwix or Saint Just); Oxford BMus 1505, DMus 1515 (Robert Porret or Perrot).

26. Indeed, in its original form the degree was nothing but a warranty of fitness to teach.

27. *Corpus Iuris Canonici* 1917, canon 1378, outlining the general and special rights and privileges of degrees, specified that, all other aspects being equal, graduates were to be preferred for certain ecclesiastical offices (such as bishop, canon, lector). The actual exclusion of non-graduates from certain offices is found still in the Roman canon law, though the degree of licentiate now suffices for all offices previously requiring a doctoral degree, excepting certain judicial offices. Declaration of the Congregation of Seminaries and Universities 23 May 1948, *Acta Apostolicae Sedis* 40:260.

28. The requirements of the universities included attendance at a prescribed course of study, for example, encyclical *Pascendi*, issued by Pope Pius X 8 Sept. 1907 provided that no one could receive the degree of DTh or DCnL without first completing the prescribed course in scholastic philosophy. This encyclical was confirmed 29 Apr. 1927 by the Congregation of Seminaries and Universities. *Acta Apostolicae Sedis* 19:194. Although an 11 Apr. 1928 ruling of the Congregation of Seminaries and Universities exempted laymen from this requirement, religious were still bound, unless they received a dispensation. *Acta Apostolicae Sedis* 20:157.

29. The chancellor, and at times the regents, had the power to dispense with certain elements of the constitutions of the universities of Oxford and Cambridge. *See generally* Hackett, *supra* n. 8.

DISPENSATIONS

for the award of degrees due to the exigencies of the time, including the needs of the Church for personnel.[30] The archbishop of Canterbury as permanent legate, or an ad hoc papal legate, was therefore empowered by the pope to grant exemptions from the residential and other requirements then necessary for taking a degree in England.[31] Papal degrees, or the grant of the status of a graduate, could also be conferred upon those with overseas qualifications not then recognised in England, something that was really a privilege, though it might be termed a dispensation and justified by the need to provide qualified personnel for the Church.[32]

In all cases the archbishop of Canterbury, where he was empowered to confer degrees, acted solely in the role of papal legate (permanent or ad hoc—when he was given a specific additional task by the pope), and appears to have claimed no inherent or plenary powers to confer degrees as archbishop.[33] These degrees were not awarded "in prejudice of the universities"[34]—though the pope claimed an overriding jurisdiction over all the universities; but because failure to confer a degree in the particular circumstances would be to work an injustice and might harm the Church by denying her the services of a worthy cleric.

During the fifteenth century, attempts were made to restrict the exercise of papal power in England through the Statute of Provisors 1351,[35] which sought to prevent papal interference with rights of presentation to livings, by securing promotion to the graduates of the English universities alone. The Act was, however, ineffective in

---

30. Once the structure of the university was firmly established, the study of Latin grammar (including literature), rhetoric (which also covered law) and logic (or dialectic) took some four to seven years. This led to the BA; The first recorded award of the baccalaureate was at Paris, in 1231; David Lockmiller, *Scholars on Parade* 209 (Macmillan 1964). The awarding of the baccalaureate could be followed by the course of studies known as the *quadrivium*. This involved the study of arithmetic, geometry (including geography and natural history), music (chiefly that of the Church), and astronomy (to which astrology was often added). This was normally followed by Hebrew, and Greek philosophy and history. After at least three years of study the degree of Master of Arts was awarded. In the fourteenth and fifteenth centuries less than half of the matriculated students proceeded to the BA, and much less than half of these completed the MA. Specialist qualifications in law and theology required even lengthier periods of attendance.

31. For the papal authority to confer degrees *see* Canon Law Society, *supra* n. 17, at 58 & 257, canons 333 § 3 & 1442.

32. Faculty Office records supply no records of pre-Restoration degrees. Rt. Revd. William Stubbs, *Lambeth Degrees* 1 Gentleman's Magazine & Historical Rev. 633, 635 (May 1864).

33. The rule that the archbishop acted only as delegate of the pope applied also for the creation of notaries public (who were however also appointed by the Emperor).

34. The Lambeth degrees were not awarded "in prejudice of the universities." Blackstone, *supra* n. 10, at vol. 1, 381.

35. 25 Edw. 3, c. 22 (Eng.).

limiting the numbers of clergy appointed from abroad,[36] because toward the end of the century, clerics not educated at English universities[37] who suffered disabilities imposed by the Act simply obtained dispensations from Rome enabling them to hold pluralities (more than one benefice), and in a few cases to obtain degrees from the pope.[38]

IV.   THE ROLE AND PURPOSE OF THE DISPENSATION

Dispensation is the suspension by competent authority of general rules of law in particular cases. Its object is to modify the hardship often arising from the rigorous application of general laws to particular cases, and its essence is to preserve the law by suspending its operation in such cases. In canon law theory, the dispensing power is the corollary of the legislative.[39] The dispensing power, like the legislative, was formerly invested in general councils and even in provincial synods.[40] But in the west, with the gradual centralisation of authority at Rome, it became ultimately vested in the pope as the supreme lawgiver of the Church.[41]

Despite frequent crises in the diplomatic relations between the Holy See and temporal governments in the later Middle Ages, the authority of the papacy as the dispenser of grace and spiritual licences remained largely unchallenged.[42] In the early thirteenth century Pope Innocent III (1198-1216) fostered the extension of papal political power. He emphasised, "as had no pope before him, the pope's *'plenitudo potestatis'* (fullness of power) within the Church."[43] Since the Church comprised the whole of mankind, medieval jurists were accustomed to what we might call shared sovereignty, and freely accepted that the pope

---

36. The king lacked the will to enforce the Statute of Provisors more stringently. C. Davies, *Statute of Provisors of 1351*, 38 History 116, 118-119 (1953).

37. It was also possible to obtain a degree from one of the English universities by incorporation. For example, Frater Steele of Rome, was incorporated at Cambridge in 1492; Frater Raddyng, a doctor of Rome, incorporated Cambridge 1497; Mr. Cabald, "ut admittatur ad eundem gradum in quo stat Romæ" 1501. Stubbs, *supra* n. 32, at 633.

38. *Id.*

39. For the view that in canon law the dispensing power is the corollary of the legislative. *See* Canon Law Society, *supra* n. 17 at 12-13, canons 85-93.

40. The dispensing power of the provincial synods only developed as the synods become more active, in the centuries after the conversion of Emperor Constantine the Great.

41. The pope was invested with *plenitudo potestatis*. The papacy of Urban II (1088-1099) marks the development of the use of dispensations. The majority of canonists conceded that the pope enjoyed a general and superior right over bishops. *See Corpus Iuris Canonici* 1959, canon 16, causa 25, quaesio 1.

42. A.D.M. Barrell, *The Papacy, Scotland and Northern England, 1342-1378* 230 (Cambridge U. Press 1995).

43. Kenneth Pennington, *The Prince and the Law, 1200-1600: Sovereignty and Rights in the Western Legal Tradition* 45 (U. Cal. Press 1993) (emphasis added). Canon 81 of the new *Codex* restricts the right of dispensation to the pope, a logical result of the *plenitudo potestatis*.

had a concurrent jurisdiction with temporal sovereigns.[44] The temporal princes could administer their own laws, but the princes of the Church, and especially the pope, administered the canon law (so far as it was subject to merely human control).

In the decretal *Proposuit*, Innocent III proclaimed that the pope could, if circumstances demanded, dispense from canon law, de jure, with his plenitude of power, on the basis that *princeps legibus solutus est* (the prince is not bound by the laws). Because the pope was above the law,[45] time or precedent did not limit his power, and he could dispense with any law.[46] Such a dispensation was not, strictly speaking, legislative, but rather a judicial, quasi-judicial, or executive act.[47] It was also, of course, subject to the proviso that his jurisdiction to dispense with laws was limited to those laws which were within his jurisdiction or competence. "[T]his principle would have been a commonplace to anyone who had studied in Bologna."[48]

By this power of dispensation the pope could release clergy and laity from the obligations of the canon law in all cases that were not contrary to *ius divinum* and even in a few cases that were.[49] This power was most frequently invoked to enable laity to marry notwithstanding impediments of affinity or kinship, and to enable persons labouring under an irregularity (such as of bastardy, servitude, or lack of age) to take orders or become regulars.[50]

Dispensations awarded might be classified into three categories.[51] The first two categories, rules concerning the procedure of taking holy orders, and dispensations concerning tenure of benefices, applied only to clergy. The third category, dispensations regarding marriage, concerned only the laity. Beside the three main classes of dispensation, the papal curia was ready to grant miscellaneous positive concessions to

---

44. The papal doctrine of *potestas absoluta*, as advocated by Hostiensis, was soon adopted by secular monarchs. Francis Oakley, *Jacobean Political Theology: The Absolute and Ordinary Powers of the King*, 29 J. of History of Ideas 323 (1968).

45. *Supra ius.*

46. *"Possumus supra ius dispensare;"* Pennington, *supra* n. 43, at 58 (quoting Hostiensis, *Lectura Super Decretalibus* (1512)).

47. For dispensation as a judicial, quasi-judicial, or executive act *see for example* the *Corpus Iuris Canonici* 1983, canons 85ff.

48. Pennington, *supra* n. 43, at 57.

49. Medieval canonists treated privileges and dispensations as further sources of law, alongside customs and decretals. *See* Gabriel Le Bras, Charles Lefebvre & Jacqueline Rambaud, *L'âge classique, 1140-1378: sources et théorie du droit* vol. 7, 487-532 (Sirey 1965).

50. Regulars were bound by a religious rule, as by belonging to a religious order.

51. David Chamber, *Faculty Office Registers, 1534-1549: A Calendar of the First Two Registers of the Archbishop of Canterbury's Faculty Office* xiv-xv (Clarendon Press 1966).

applicants who could afford the necessary fees.[52]   This host of dispensations, faculties, and indults[53] included permission to eat flesh during Lent, the celebration of offices in chapels of ease and private oratories, and the granting of degrees.[54] Those dispensations relating to academic degrees were mostly issued under the sanction of the canon law as stated in the constitution of Boniface VIII beginning "Cum ex eo."[55]   Strictly these "dispensations" were more properly special exercises of jurisdiction rather than responses to anything unusual in a case arising under the pope's regular jurisdiction.

If the papal degree is properly seen as a dispensation rather than a privilege, then there were strict limits upon its exercise. For the pope could only exercise his jurisdiction to dispense from the strict requirements of the canon law if the matter were a proper one for the canon law.[56] "The pope dispensed with many things that others could not, but his dispensation must always be 'with cause'."[57] This cause invariably required that there be some benefit to the Church, as well as any to the individual concerned.[58]

V.   CONCERNING PAPAL PRIVILEGES

Papal privileges resembled dispensations, since both involved exceptions to the ordinary operations of the law.   But whereas "dispensations exempt[ed] some person or group from legal obligations binding on the rest of the population or class to which they belong,"[59] "[p]rivileges bestowed a positive favour not generally enjoyed by most people."[60] "Thus licences to teach or to practise law or medicine, for example,"[61] were "legal privileges, since they confer[red] upon

---

52. Wilfrid Hooper, *The Court of Faculties*, 25 English Historical Rev. 670, 671 (1910).

53. The terms dispensations, faculties, and indults were synonymous, though dispensations were generally reserved for grants by the archbishop of Canterbury in respect of a more important matter. Sir Edward Coke, 4th *Institutes of the Laws of England* 337 (Garland Publg. 1979). The degrees awarded by the archbishop of Canterbury come under the general term "faculties."

54. Chamber, *supra* n. 51, at xvi.

55. Sexti Decretalium Lib I, *De electione et electi potestate*, tit vi cap xxxiv.

56. The question of what could be dispensed with, and what was immutable, was the subject of on-going debate.

57. Pennington, *supra* n. 43, at 196 (quoting Simone da Borsano, *Pastoralis*); Johannes Teutonicus, Glos. ord. to C. 1 q. 7 d. a. c. 6, v. *ut plerisque*.

58. In practice it was rarely difficult to show benefit to the Church, as the provision and encouragement of skilled personnel was always one of the main concerns of the Church. Recognition of graduate status benefitted both Church and individual.

59. James A. Brundage, *Medieval Canon Law* 161 (Longman 1995); *Decretum Gratiani*, D 3 c. 3.

60. *Id.*

61. *Id.* at 160. In the *Corpus Iuris Canonici* 1917, no cleric might practice medicine or

recipients the right to perform certain functions for pay, which the rest of the population [was] not [permitted to exercise.]"[62] Yet, such licenses might also involve what should properly be termed dispensation, if they waived canon law requirement that an individual hold a particular qualification to practice law or medicine, as, for example, a degree.

The distinction between privilege and dispensation was not always clearly observed, and the term dispensation rather than privilege was used, even when the nature of the act made it clearly a privilege. Indeed, medieval canonists treated privileges and dispensations as distinct, though related, aspects of the law.[63] The pope might confer a degree as a positive privilege in his capacity as a temporal sovereign, or he might do so by way of dispensation from the strict requirements of the canon law. In both cases his authority to do so was found in the canon law.[64]

As suggested, in some instances petitioners sought an academic degree because without one they could not hold a particular office.[65] In these cases, conferring the status of a graduate is the granting of a privilege, in that the recipient has received a positive favour not generally enjoyed by most people, but it also acted as a dispensation with the requirements of the canon law. Still, however they were justified, in canon law, the conferral of degrees or degree status gave substantial and substantive rights and privileges, and were not merely empty honours.

In the event of degree status being conferred, the recipient was not deemed to hold the degree in question, but would enjoy any privileges which might be attached to such a degree- including qualification for office. Conferring the degree itself would of course would mean that the recipient enjoyed the style and not merely the privileges of a degree. They might also, for example, be thereafter admitted or incorporated to the same degree *ad eundum* at Oxford or Cambridge- though few seem

---

surgery without an apostolic indult; canon 139.2 9 (reviewer's translation).

62. Brundage, *supra* n. 59 at 160-161.

63. Privileges and indults were both special favours. Some writers hold that the former are positive favours, while indults are negative. Amleto Giovanni Cicognani, Joseph Michael O'Hara & Francis Brennan, *Canon Law* 477-486 (2d ed., Newman Bookshop 1947).

64. The pope's powers as a temporal sovereign are recognised in the Roman Catholic Code of Canon Law 1983. In practice matters of education are dealt with though the hierarchy of the Church, rather than through that of Vatican City State, the residual part of the Papal States.

65. Canons of certain cathedrals and Westminster Abbey were still required to be degree-holders until recent times. The dean of Westminster Abbey was required to be a doctor or bachelor of divinity as recently as the late twentieth century. W.R. Pullen, 'The Constitution of the Collegiate Church' in the Revd. Edward Carpenter; *A House of Kings* 455 (London Baker 1966).

to have been so distinguished. It was however often difficult to be certain whether the degree itself, or merely its status and privileges, which was being conferred. Given the ostensible purpose of the papal dispensatory jurisdiction, it would perhaps be more logical to view all of these "degrees" as strictly degree-status, and not substantive degrees. But the medieval—if not indeed modern—concept of the degree is of a grade or status. One achieves the status of master or doctor, which is conferred by one's university (or in rare cases, by the pope). It is not an award, but the recognition of a certain degree of learning. It is perhaps significant that in the records of the (post-Reformation) Court of Faculties, the early "Lambeth degrees" are described in terms of dispensation to enjoy the privilege of DCL or whatever the degree might be.[66]

The exercise of the authority to confer such a privilege was often a positive step by the pope to emphasise his spiritual, if not temporal, authority. We have already seen how, during the fifteenth century, attempts were made in England to restrict the exercise of papal power in opposition to the Statute of Provisors 1351.[67] To evade the disabilities imposed by that Act on non-graduates, it became usual towards the end of the century for those clerics not educated at English universities to obtain dispensations from Rome, including, in a few cases, degrees.[68] These were positive favours not generally enjoyed by most people, and that they were dispensing with the requirements of the canon law was a secondary consideration. They were also exercised for the good of the individual as well as the good of the church.

VI. POST-REFROMATION ECCLESIASTICAL JURISDICTION IN ENGLAND

The Statute of Appeals 1532[69] took away the right of English clergy and laity to appeal to Rome in causes testamentary and matrimonial and in regard to right of tithes and oblations. Instead, the power to hear final appeals was given to the archbishop of each of the two English provinces, Canterbury and York. In cases involving the king, final appeal was to the Upper Houses of Convocation of each province. The Act of Submission of the Clergy 1533-1534[70] took away

---

66. 20 Sept. 1537, Thomas Tasshe, BCL, dispensation to enjoy the privilege, etc. of a DCL, £4 (F I/Vv, fo. 175v). Chamber, *supra* n. 51, at 121.

67. *Supra* n. 35.

68. Stubbs, *supra* n. 32, at 633.

69. The Statute of Appeals 1532 is also called the Ecclesiastical Appeals Act, 24 Hen. 8, c. 12 (Eng.).

70. 25 Hen. 8, c. 19 (Eng.).

all appeals to Rome, and transferred further appeals "for lack of justice" from several courts of the archbishops to the king in Chancery.[71] Under King Henry VIII, his vicar-general, Thomas Cromwell, heard these appeals.[72] Commissioners heard appeals under King Edward VI.[73] Since then, the Privy Council has, in many causes been the highest appellate court, though it is not strictly an ecclesiastical court.[74]

After 1534, neither the king nor his successors, nor any subject, could sue for licences, dispensations, etc. to the see of Rome. The archbishop of Canterbury had exercised the *legatus natus*[75] that the pope enjoyed throughout all England before the Reformation. Since then the archbishop has been empowered by the Ecclesiastical Licences Act 1533-1534[76] to exercise certain powers of dispensation in causes formerly sued for in the court of Rome.[77]

Particularly relevant to this article, section 3 of the Ecclesiastical Licences Act 1533-1534[78] conferred upon the archbishop of Canterbury the power formerly vested in the pope to grant:

> all manner such licences, dispensations, compositions, faculties, grants, [receipts], delegacies, instruments, and all other writings, for causes not being contrary or repugnant to the holy scriptures and laws of God, as heretofore hath been used and accustomed to be had and obtained by your Highness, or any of your most noble

---

71. The Act of Submission of the Clergy 1533-1534, *supra* n. 70, did however assert the partial continuance of the authority of the canon law.

72. For Thomas Cromwell's appointment as vicegerent *see From Edmund Bonner's commission as bishop of London, 1538,* reprinted in Geoffrey Elton, *The Tudor Constitution* 367-368 (2d ed., Cambridge U. Press 1982).

72. Act of Supremacy, 1534, 26 Hen. 8, c. 1 (Eng.).

73. Commissioners were established under the Submission of the Clergy Act 1533, *supra* n. 70. For the history of the Court of Delegates *see* Blackstone *supra* n. 10, vol. 3, at 66; William Holdsworth, *History of English Law* vol. 1, 603-605 (7th ed., A.L. Goodhart & H.G. Hanbury eds., Methuen and Sweet & Maxwell 1972); G.I.O. Duncan, *The High Court of Delegates* (Cambridge U. Press 1971).

74. The Judicial Committee of the Privy Council (formally Her Majesty in Council), is the Court of Final Appeal, and replaced the Court of Delegates in 1833. His Majesty's Privy Council Act, 1833, 3 & 4 Will 4, c. 41 (Eng.). By the Appellate Jurisdiction Act, 1876, 39 & 40 Vict., c. 59 (Eng.), all archbishop and bishops were eligible to be members of the Judicial Committee, but they were not ex officio members. Order in Council dated 11 Dec. 1865, Rules for Appeals in Ecclesiastical and Maritime Causes, r. 3. *See* the Ecclesiastical Jurisdiction Measure, 1963, no. 1 (Eng.).

75. The legatine jurisdiction of the archbishop gave him a concurrent jurisdiction with that of all bishops within his province.

76. 25 Hen. 8, c. 21, § 3 (Eng.).

77. Diocesan bishops also retained whatever rights they possessed which then covered such diverse matters as residence, ordination outside the dioceses of birth, fasting, public reading of banns. *Id.* at § 4. These are but rarely invoked today, if at all.

78. *Supra* n. 1.

progenitors, or any of your or their subjects, at the see of *Rome*.[79] subject always to the authority of the Crown,[80] though part of this dispensation power became obsolete and part was curtailed by statute. The archbishop of Armagh was given similar powers.[81] These powers were confirmed by another Act of 1536.[82] Moreover, any dispensations that were so important that they were taxed at Rome at the sum of £4 or above had to be confirmed by letters patent under the great seal to be enrolled in chancery. Under this power, the archbishop continued to grant special licences to marry, to appoint notaries public, and to grant dispensations to clerics to hold more than one benefice.[83] He also continued to grant licences for preaching, teaching, or to practice medicine,[84] and, more infrequently, degrees or degree status.[85]

---

79. *Id.* at § 3, ¶ 4.

80. E.F. Churchill, *Dispensations under the Tudors and Stuarts*, 34 English Historical Rev. 409-415 (1919).

81. The archbishop of Armagh's powers were conferred indirectly. The powers conferred by the Ecclesiastical Licences Act (1533-1534) extended to Ireland. Some time in the course of the sixteenth century a permanent commission granted the jurisdiction to the archbishop of Armagh (as Primate of All Ireland), in virtue of which he took over the jurisdiction exercised by the Court of Faculties. Certainly, he exercised dispensing power by 1690. Wilfrid Hooper, *The Court of Faculties*, 25 English Historical Rev. 670, 685 (1910). The commissary of the Irish Court of Faculties was also judge of the Court of Prerogative, 1827, 7 & 8 Geo. 4, c. 44 (Eng.), and admitted Irish notaries. *In re Champion*, 1906 P. 86, 92 (citing *O'Brien v. Bennett*, Court of Faculties (Ireland) (not reported)). The power of making notarial appointments was abolished by the Irish Church Act, 1869, 32 & 33 Vict., c. 42, § 21 (Eng.), and vested in the Lord Chancellor. The Matrimonial Causes and Marriage Law (Ireland) Amendment Act, 1870, 33 & 34 Vict., c. 110, § 29 (Eng.).

82. The Ecclesiastical Licences Act, 1536, 28 Hen. 8, c. 16 (Eng.).

83. The power to grant dispensations to clerics to hold more than one benefice is now exercised in the Church of England in accordance with the Pluralities Act, 1838, 1 & 2 Vict., c. 106 (Eng.) and the Pastoral Measure. Bishops also received faculties from the pope to appoint notaries, but from the time of John Pecham (1279-1292) onwards it was usual for the archbishop of Canterbury to receive such apostolic faculties.

84. Only five licences to practise medicine were granted in England 1534-1549. *See generally* Chamber, *supra* n. 51. Civil registration of medical practitioners began in England with the Physicians and Surgeons Act, 1511-1512, 3 Hen. 8, c. 11 (Eng.). However, the administration of the scheme was entrusted to the bishops, each in his own diocese, advised by four medical men. In the seventeenth century there was considerable confusion between the bishops' licences to practise medicine or surgery and the Lambeth doctorate. Cecil Wall, *The Lambeth Degrees*, British Med. J. 854, 855 (1935).

85. The Lambeth degrees issued 1534 to 1549 numbered only four; 20 Sept. 1537, Thomas Tasshe, BCL, dispensation to enjoy the privilege, etc., of a DCL, £4 (F I/Vv, fo. 175v); 10 June 1538, Roger Colley, master of Grammar, Coventry and Lichfield diocese, dispensation to receive the privileges of his status in a university, £3 (F I/Vv, fo. 202v); 8 Feb. 1539, Ellis Ferrers, BTh, confirmation of faculty conceded by word of mouth of William bishop of Norwich for the above to enjoy the status of DTh, £4 (F I/VV, fo. 255r); 6 Dec. 1544, George Broke, student in Venice, natural son and legitimised son of George Broke, Lord Cobham, dispensation to hold the status and privileges of a BA. '*Concessa per litteras Rmi. dni. Archiepiscopi*,' 5s (F I/A, 92). *See generally* Chamber, *supra* n. 51.

The Master of the Faculties regulated all educational dispensations that fell under the Ecclesiastical Licences Act 1533-1534.[86] In the book of Taxation, Section XI, the fee for the creation of a doctor in any faculty was £4.[87] The Court of Faculties was in effect created by the Act, though it was not expressly named in that Act. It was—and still is—more than a court, and its functions were discretionary rather than ministerial,[88] the Master occasionally sitting *in iudicis* to hear argument.[89] Most ecclesiastical licences (such as marriage licences), and faculties appointing notaries public were also awarded by the Master under the inherent authority of the Ecclesiastical Licences Act 1533-1534.[90] The authority to confer Lambeth degrees was also based on this statute. Though degrees are not specified in this transfer of authority, they are understood to be included in the term faculties.[91]

Still, the status of the Lambeth graduates has always been rather unsettled, and the few who are mentioned as incorporated at Cambridge received that status with the proviso that it should not be construed as a precedent. Few Lambeth degrees seem to have been granted before the Restoration; although the Ecclesiastical Licences Act 1533-1534[92] required faculties to be enrolled, the Patent Rolls record only two or three,[93] and two or three more come from Cambridge records.[94] The Dispensation Rolls of the Public Record Office (1597-1641) record only one Lambeth degree.[95] Since the time of the Restoration, the list recording Lambeth degrees is perfect; though one book is missing from the faculty office, 1660-1716, its records were duplicated by list adduced in the *Peploe* case.[96]

---

86. *Supra* n. 76.

87. Wall, *supra* n. 84, at 854.

88. Wilfrid Hooper, *The Court of Faculties*, 25 English Historical Rev. 670, 676 (1910).

89. *See e.g. Champion, supra* n. 81, at 90.

90. *Supra* n. 76. Notaries are appointed under the inherent jurisdiction conferred by that Act and the later statutory authority of the Public Notaries Act, 1801, 41 Geo. 3, c. 79 (Eng.), the Public Notaries Act, 1843, 6 & 7 Vict., c. 90 (Eng.), and Courts and Legal Services Act, 1990, c. 41, § 57, ¶ 4 (Eng.).

91. Rt. Revd. Edmund Gibson, *Codex Juris Ecclesiastici Anglicani; or, the Statutes, Constitutions, Canons, Rubricks, and Articles of the Church of England Methodically Digested Under Their Proper Heads: With a Commentary, Historical and Juridical. Before It, Is an Introduction Discourse, concerning the Present State of the Power, Discipline and Laws, of the Church of England: and After It, an Appendix of Instruments, Ancient and Modern* vol. 1, 105 (J. Basket 1713).

92. *Supra* n. 76.

93. Stubbs, *supra* n. 32, at 635.

94. *Id.*

95. *Id.*

96. *Id.*

Power was conferred on the archbishop of Canterbury to act "for causes not being contrary or repugnant to the Holy Scriptures and the laws of God." This dispensation power partly fell obsolete, partly curtailed by statute.

Although the archbishop now enjoyed the authority hitherto confined to the pope, in the circumstances of his office there would have been little doubt where real power lay in the country. The Preface to the Thirty-Nine Articles of 1562, though somewhat later in date, reflects this state of affairs. It states that:

> Being at God's ordinance, according to our just title, *Defender of the Faith, and Supreme Governor of the Church, within these our Dominions*, we hold it most agreeable to this our kingly office, and our own religious zeal, to conserve and maintain the Church committed to our Charge in unity of true religion, and in the bond of peace .... We have therefore, upon mature deliberation, and with the advice of so many of our bishops as might conveniently be called together, thought fit to make this Declaration following:
> . . . .
>
> That we are Supreme Governor of the Church of England.[97]

Article 37 makes this claim to royal supremacy clearer:

> The Queen's Majesty hath the chief power in this Realm of England, and other her dominions, unto whom the chief government of all estates of this Realm, whether they be Ecclesiastical or Civil, in all causes doth appertain, and is not, nor ought to be subject to any foreign jurisdiction ....
>
> [W]e give not to our princes the ministering either of God's word, or of the Sacraments ... [b]ut that only prerogative which we see to have been given always to all godly Princes in holy Scriptures by God himself, that is, that they should rule all estates and degrees committed to their charge by God, whether they be Ecclesiastical or Temporal, and restrain with the civil sword the stubborn and evildoers ....
>
> The Bishop of Rome hath no jurisdiction in this Realm of England.[98]

The king's ecclesiastical authority may have been more circumscribed that that of the pope. But the subordinate position of the archbishop was clear. His duty lay to his king, rather to the pope, and

---

97. Edgar Gibson, *The Thirty-Nine Articles of the Church of England* 768 (8th ed., Methuen & Co. Ltd. 1912).

98. *Id.* at 759.

the exercise of his newly acquired legal authority was to reflect this political reality. This meant that in many instances the degrees were conferred for the benefit of state rather than church.

Some examples of the comparatively few degrees conferred by the archbishop of Canterbury in the first century after the Reformation still survive. For example, Samuel Purchas (c. 1575-1626), an author, was made a Bachelor of Divinity (BD) by Archbishop George Abbot 14 March 1615.[99] Although a graduate of the University of Cambridge, Purchas lacked the divinity degree thought appropriate for a chaplain to the archbishop of Canterbury, an office to which he was appointed in 1614. In this case, the exercise of the new archiepiscopal authority may be seen as the righting of a potential wrong (the exclusion of a worthy man from office due to a technical requirement), as a true dispensation.

On 9 December 1635 Edward Layfield, MA, archdeacon of Essex, was made a BD.[100] A graduate of Oxford, Layfield was also incorporated as MA at Cambridge.[101] But he did not have the BD required by the statutes of St Paul's Cathedral, London, of which he was made a canon in 1633. In the Purchas case, the Lambeth degree was awarded as a personal privilege to allow Purchas the status to which it was thought he was entitled, while in Layfield's case, it was given to avoid the consequences of a specific statute, thus allowing Layfield to hold an office to which he was strictly unqualified. The first was clearly not a dispensation, in the sense of the suspension by competent authority of general rules of law in a particular case, but the second appears to satisfy this test. We must conclude from these cases that even in the middle ages the precise nature of the papal degree as dispensation or privilege was uncertain; but whatever their precise legal nature, they were however undoubtedly either substantive degrees or degree status.

VII. Lambeth Degrees—Restoration to Nineteenth Century

From the time of the Restoration onwards the conferral of Lambeth degrees became more frequent. But as their numbers rose, their status became more uncertain. Sometimes Lambeth degrees were treated as substantive degrees, sometimes not. This was due in no small part, it

---

99. Stubbs, *supra* n. 32, at 635. Rt. Revd. William Stubbs, *Lambeth Degrees*, 216 Gentleman's Magazine & Historical Rev. 633 (1864). Adduced in Peploe's case, BM MS Add 6489. *Id. See The Dictionary of National Biography* vol. 16, 488-489 (Leslie Stephen & Sidney Lee eds., Oxford U. Press 1967).

100. Stubbs, *supra* n. 32, at 635. Adduced in Peploe's case, BM MS Add 6489.

101. Joseph Foster, 3 *Alumni Oxiensis* 890 (Kraus Reprint 1968). Incorporation meant that he was regarded as having the equivalent Cambridge degree.

would seem, to the increasingly varied reasons for which the degrees were conferred. As one example, on 11 May 1663, William Fyffe, MA, of Trinity College, Oxford, was created a Lambeth Doctor of Medicine (MD).[102] Fyffe, a Justice of the Peace and a Member of the 1661 House of Commons,[103] was a country gentleman; and his degree seems to have been more as an honour than a traditional dispensation or privilege. The next day, 12 May 1663, Sir Edmund Freeman, alias King, was also awarded an MD by Archbishop Sheldon. A surgeon, who later turned physician, Freeman was incorporated *ad eundem* at Cambridge 3 October 1671.[104] Unlike Fyffe, at least he was a medical man, and his Lambeth degree recognised his standing as such, in the way that a medieval scholar might be granted a degree by papal dispensation where he had failed to qualify through regular university study due to his service in the Church, or some other cause.

Similarly, later in the same year, on 31 October 1663, Robert Thoroton, of Christ's College, Cambridge,[105] was created an MD. Thoroton was a physician. He was also a country gentleman and noted historian of Nottinghamshire, who after the Restoration was made a Justice of the Peace.[106] In each of these cases, the recipient was being granted a positive privilege, but the benefit to the church or the general public was more difficult to discern.[107]

In some cases, the Lambeth degrees seem to have been conferred to give the recipients respectability as physicians. A few years after Thoroton's degree, on 6 February 1678, Francis Bernard, newly appointed Assistant Physician to St Bartholomew's Hospital, was created MD; and was incorporated MD *ad eundem* at Cambridge in the same year, becoming a Charter Fellow of the College of Physicians in 1687.[108] Also in 1678, Peter Dent, an apothecary and botanist of Cambridge, was granted a Lambeth MB.[109] He had been a member of Trinity College, but did not obtain a degree from that university. He was still incorporated as an MD *ad eundem* at Cambridge 18 March

---

102. Stubbs, *supra* n. 32, at 632.

103. Joseph Foster, 1 *Alumni Oxiensis* 541 (Kraus Reprint 1968).

104. 1629-1709. *Dictionary, supra* n. 99, at vol. 11, 127-128.

105. Robert Thoroton graduated BA 1642, MA 1646, licence to practise medicine 1646.

106. Robert Thoroton lived 1623-1678. *Dictionary, supra* n. 99, at vol. 19, 793-794.

107. That a benefit to the church was needed for the grant of a degree was a consequence of the nature of the degree as a dispensation; if seen as a privilege there would be no need for such a benefit. Pennington, *supra* n. 43, at 196 (quoting Simone da Borsano, *Pastoralis*); Johannes Teutonicus, Glos. ord. to C. 1 q. 7 d. a. c. 6, v. *ut plerisque*.

108. 1627-1698. *Dictionary, supra* n. 99, at vol. 2, 380.

109. Peter Dent died 1689. *Id.* at vol. 5, 828. Stubbs, *supra* n. 32, at 636.

1681.[110]

Sometimes Lambeth degrees clearly savoured more of honorary than of substantive degrees though this did not reduce the value of Lambeth degrees to the recipients in both social and professional respects. For example, on 8 December 1691, Robert Hooke, Secretary of the Royal Society, and an Oxford MA, was created an MD by warrant of Archbishop Tillotson.[111] On 4 February 1695, John Woodward, a geologist and physician and Gresham Professor of Physic, was made an MD by Archbishop Tenison.[112] He was incorporated an MD *ad eundem* at Cambridge on 28 June of the same year—subject to the usual proviso that it should not be construed as a precedent.

The right of the archbishops to confer degrees was not challenged until the reign of King George I, when Gastrell, bishop of Chester, refused to admit Samuel Peploe, BD *Lambeth*, to the wardenship of Manchester College. The statutes of the college required that the warden have a BD or LLD. Peploe was only an Oxford MA. Rather than seeking the requisite degree from his own alma mater,[113] he obtained a BD from Archbishop Wake. This was thought to have cast a slur upon Oxford, and was probably the real reason for opposition to his appointment to Manchester College.[114] Was a Lambeth degree sufficient to meet the requirements of the college statutes? The Court of King's Bench thought so when judgement was delivered in the archbishop's favour in 1725.[115] But the proper procedure—certainly the more politic—would perhaps have been for Peploe to have obtained a BD from Oxford.

The courts were clearly viewing the Lambeth degrees as full, though irregular (in that they were not conferred by the universities), degrees. Such a description could apply whether the degree were conferred as a privilege or by way of dispensation.

Sometimes the conferral of a Lambeth degree threatened considerable trouble for those who were perhaps not qualified to receive them. For instance, in 1756 John Hawkesworth obtained the degree of LLD from Archbishop Herring.[116] A prolific author, the degree was in

---

110. *Id.*

111. 1635-1703. *Dictionary, supra* n. 99, at vol. 9, 1177-1180.

112. 1665-1728. *Id.* at vol. 21, 894-896.

113. Samuel Peploe would have had to comply with the regulations of the university in order to have obtained a degree from Oxford.

114. *Dictionary, supra* n. 99, at vol. 15, 797-798.

115. Blackstone, *supra* n. 10, at vol. 1, 381.

116. E.H.W. Dunkin, *Index to the Act Books of the Archbishops of Canterbury 1663-1859* pt. 1, 388 (British Record Socy. 1929).

consideration of his literary talents, for Hawkesworth was a non-graduate. Yet Hawkesworth himself thought to practise in the ecclesiastical courts as an advocate, a project he soon abandoned.[117] Though he had once been apprenticed to an attorney, he would probably have been quite unsuited to the profession,[118] if, indeed, the dean of the Arches had sought fit to admit him as an advocate.[119]

VIII.   AN ASSESSMENT OF THE MODERN LAMBETH DEGREES

By the early years of the nineteenth century the tendency to regard the Lambeth degrees as honorific had become more pronounced. They were still used to confer social if not necessarily professional status upon men otherwise well-qualified. For example, on 21 December 1827, Sir Charles Mansfield Clarke, a fashionable accoucheur and for many years surgeon to Queen Charlotte's Lying-in Hospital, was made an MD. He had been educated at St George's Hospital and Hunterian School of Medicine, but was not a university graduate. At least Clarke became an MA at Cambridge in 1842.[120]

The list of recipients of Lambeth doctorates in the medical faculty shows that even those who had not been able to conform to the university regulations for internal degrees were usually granted the degree as a reward for eminent service.[121] However, Lambeth medical degrees awarded since 1858 do not confer the right to practise medicine,[122] and their function is more clearly that of an honour.[123]

---

117. The advocates were doctors of civil law (Oxford) or laws (Cambridge). Doctors were eligible for admission as advocates of the Court of Arches, whose dean admitted advocates on a rescript of the archbishop of Canterbury, if they had studied the civil and canon laws for five (and latterly three) years. Once admitted, they were qualified to practice in the other ecclesiastical courts and civil law courts, and to be appointed judges therein. Most were members of Doctors' Commons.

Prior to 1535 advocates were required to hold a degree in canon law or canon and civil law. After 1535 the degree awarded was solely in civil law, as canon law was no longer taught in English universities. In 1545 the Ecclesiastical Jurisdiction Act, 37 Hen. 8, c. 17 (Eng.), ended the legal requirement for ecclesiastical judges to possess a degree in canon law, but they were still required to have a doctorate in civil law. In the sixteenth century foreign degrees sufficed for this requirement, though such advocates invariably sought incorporation at Oxford or Cambridge. George Squibb, *Doctors' Commons: A History of the College of Advocates and Doctors of Law* 31, 41 (Clarendon Press 1977).

118. *Dictionary, supra* n. 99, at vol. 9, 203-205.

119. The procedure for appointment of advocates is given in *The King v. Archbishop of Canterbury*, 8 East 213, 103 Eng. Rep. 323 (K.B. 1807). Whether the dean had any discretion to decline to admit a candidate duly in receipt of an archiepiscopal rescript is however doubtful.

120. Sir Charles Mansfield Clarke lived 1782-1857. *Dictionary, supra* n. 99, at vol. 4, 419-420.

121. Wall, *supra* n. 84, at 855.

122. Medical Act, 1969, c. §§ 20 & 23(1), sched. 1 ¶ 13, sched. 2 (Eng.); Medical Act, 1956, 4 & 5 Eliz. 2, c. 76 § 7, sched. 3 (Eng.); Medical Act, 1858, 21 & 22 Vict., c. 90, sched. A ¶ 10; *R.*

Perhaps the most significant thing to reduce the practical benefits of obtaining a Lambeth degree and re-enforce the honorific aspects of the degree has been the opening of important posts to graduates of other schools. For example, the general privileges of graduates of the universities Oxford and Cambridge, and later London, with respect to offices open or exemptions granted to them by any Act of Parliament or regulation of a public authority, have been extended to graduates of other universities in England and Wales.[124]

The degrees currently granted by the archbishop are in divinity (DD,[125] BD,[126]) law (DCL or LLD[127]), arts (MA[128]), literature (DLitt), medicine (DM or MD[129]), and music (DMus or MusD,[130] BMus or MusB). Today the awards are generally made in recognition of the recipient's contributions to the life of the Church generally over many years.[131] Specifically, they recognise those persons who "have attained considerable eminence, both in art and science and in learning, without possessing that inestimable testimony to profound learning [a

---

v. Baker, etc., (Justices) & Clarke 66 L.T.R. 416 (Q.B. 1891). The privilege of practising was granted by the regius professor of medicine at Oxford and Cambridge to bachelors of the faculty after they had conducted a certain number of cures. This licence was operative in the university towns and presumably throughout England, though not in London, where the chartered College of Physicians claimed an exclusive right to permit practice. Wall, *supra* n. 84, at 855; *College of Physicians Case*, 2 Brownl. & Golds. 255, 123 Eng. Rep. 928 (C.P. 1609). Bishops licensed medical practitioners from 1511 till the mid-late eighteenth century, under the authority of the Physicians and Surgeons Act, 1511, 3 Hen. 8, c. 11 (Eng.).

123. An example of a Lambeth degree as an honour was the MD conferred on James Rogers, a medical practitioner of Swansea, who was Mayor at the time of the Church Congress. The expense was said to have been about eighty guineas, and was defrayed by public subscription. Wall, *supra* n. 84, at 855.

124. The graduates of the newer universities were expressly given equal privileges by the Victoria University Act, 1888, 51 & 52 Vict. c. 45, § 1 (Eng.), and similar later legislation.

125. The BD or DD were more usually given as BTh or DTh in the early faculty office registers. Chamber, *supra* n. 51.

126. Past recipients of the BD have included the Rt. Revd. Richard Chartres, then the archbishop of Canterbury's Domestic Chaplain, and now bishop of London.

127. Recent past recipients have included Sir John Owen, dean of the Arches; and Frank Robson, provincial registrar.

128. Recent recipients have included Bernard Thimont, former Controller of Her Majesty's Stationery Office; and the Revd. Rennie Simpson, precentor of Westminster Abbey, both non-graduates.

129. Past recipients of the MD have included Dame Cicely Saunders, medical director, St. Christopher's Hospice.

130. Recipients of the MusD have included Lionel Dakers, Director of the Royal School of Church Music; and Allan Wicks, Organist of Canterbury Cathedral.

131. The numbers of Lambeth degrees awarded since 1660 have been relatively small. Cecil Wall enumerated 43 MD to 1858 (after which the Lambeth MD ceased to be entered onto the medical register), from Stubbs' List and other sources. This is an average of less than one every five years, though the frequency varied, and there were as many as four in one year. Wall, *supra*, n. 84, at 855.

degree]."[132] In this respect they may resemble honorary degrees.

Recipients of the Lambeth degrees customarily wore robes of the same style as those of Oxford or Cambridge, whichever was attended by the archbishop conferring the degree.[133] Since the appointment of Dr Carey, a graduate of neither university,[134] new Lambeth graduates have worn Oxford academic dress of the appropriate degree, continuing the practice of the previous archbishop Dr Runcie, who was an Oxford graduate[135] All awards are made entirely at the discretion of the archbishop. In recent practice Lambeth degrees are awarded annually, in June. In practice, four to ten are awarded each year; for example, on 31 May 1995, for example, five doctorates[136] (two in divinity)[137] and two masters degrees were awarded.[138] In past years, doctorates in divinity were commonly awarded to all new diocesan bishops who were not already doctors of one of the universities,[139] *iure dignitatis*.[140] However,

---

132. 87 Parl. Deb., H.L. (5th ser.) (1933) 838, 839 (per Dr. Cosmo Lang, archbishop of Canterbury).

133. Wall, *supra* n. 84, at 854, 855. The exact status of the dress is uncertain, and it has been said that this rule only applied to non-graduate recipients, graduates wearing the robes of the appropriate degree of their own university. Charles Franklyn, *Academical Dress from the Middle Ages to the Present Day, including Lambeth Degrees* § 13 (Hassocks 1970). This latter interpretation has much to commend it, bearing in mind the nature of Lambeth degrees.

134. Dr. Carey himself wears the academical dress of his highest earned degree, the University of London PhD, rather than that of any of his several DD *honoris causa*.

135. Letter to the author from the Rt. Revd. Frank Sargeant, bishop at Lambeth, 8 Dec. 1995.

136. Professor Andrew Sims received an MD in recognition of his services to psychiatry, in particular in promoting the need to evaluate the religious and spiritual experience of patients. Leonard Evetts received a DLitt in recognition of his notable artistic contribution to the Church of England in the Northern Province as a designer of stained and clear glass and for his devoted service to the Newcastle Diocesan Advisory Committee for more than half a century. Robert Boughen was made a DMus in recognition of his outstanding contribution to the development of church music in Australia as Cathedral organist, teacher, conductor and composer for more than three decades; News Release from the Office of the Archbishop of Canterbury, 12 May 1995.

137. The Rt. Revd. Andrew Graham, bishop of Newcastle, received a DD in recognition of his services to the Church of England as theologian and teacher, and latterly as Chairman of the Doctrine Commission. The Revd. John Newton received a DD in recognition of his contribution to theological and historical scholarship and to the quest for Christian Unity; News Release from the Office of the Archbishop of Canterbury, 12 May 1995.

138. John Brown was made an MA in recognition of his services as Chapter Clerk, legal adviser and valued friend of Guildford Cathedral for more than thirty years. George Lunn was made a MA in recognition of his lifetime's contribution to the work, development and promotion of Christian communications and education throughout the world; News Release from the Office of the Archbishop of Canterbury, 12 May 1995.

139. Commonly, until the early twentieth century, diocesan bishop received doctorates from Oxford or Cambridge upon reaching episcopal dignity, by diploma or *honoris causa*. Parl. Deb., H.L., *supra* n. 132, at 840 (per Dr. Cosmo Lang, archbishop of Canterbury).

140. The practice of conferring degrees upon bishops was in furtherance of the very ancient custom that those who attain the status of a bishop should have a suitable degree in divinity. It was also used for those other Church dignitaries who were required, as by cathedral statutes, to hold a degree. *Id.* at 840-841.

these have been granted very sparingly since Archbishop Ramsey decided to change the policy when he became archbishop in 1961 and they are now awarded on the same criteria as other Lambeth degrees. The degrees do not, of course, confer the right of membership of any university.

IX.   MODERN LAMBETH DEGREES: DISPENSATION OR PRIVILEGE?

Lambeth degrees, also called Canterbury degrees (as 'DMus Cantuar') are still awarded under the original general authority of the Ecclesiastical Licences Act 1533-1534.[141] In the United Kingdom, the universities and other institutions which have the power to confer degrees are strictly controlled by legislation.[142] The continued authority for the archbishop of Canterbury to grant degrees can be found in the Education Reform Act 1988,[143] and the Education (Recognised Bodies) (England) Order 2000.[144]

Lambeth degrees are not honorary degrees,[145] though the candidates do not, in general, sit any examinations.[146] Indeed, to require examinations would have been contrary to the idea of a dispensation. Modern policy now requires that the recipients must be presumed to have the potential to have studied for the degree in question and to have been awarded it.[147] In many cases it is recognised that someone's service to the Church has precluded further academic study, and a Lambeth degree is a recognition of this sacrifice, as well as a sign of

---

141. *Supra* n. 76.

142. Only those universities, colleges or other bodies authorised by royal charter or Act of Parliament can confer degrees, which have official recognition. Education Reform Act, 1988, c. 40, § 214(2)(a) & (b) (Eng.). The older universities, the archbishop of Canterbury, the now defunct Council for National Academic Awards, Union Theological College, Royal College of Music, and the Royal College of Art are listed in the Education (Recognised Bodies) (England) Order, S.I. 2000, No. 3327 (Eng.) and earlier regulations. Polytechnics, which have now become universities, and the various degree-awarding colleges are provided for in separate legislation. Any award may by Order in Council be designated a recognised award. Education Reform Act, 1988, c. 40, § 214(2)(c); Education (Recognised Awards) Order, S.I. 1988, No. 2035 (Eng.). These include the Degree of the Utter Bar (Inns of Court), Degree of Barrister-at-Law (Inns of Court of Northern Ireland), and the Degree of Master of Horticulture of the Royal Horticultural Society.

143. *Supra* n. 142, at § 214(2)(a) & (b).

144. *Supra* n. 142.

145. Degrees are registered in the Crown Office of the House of Lords.

146. Examinations were conducted regularly for the MA from the 1860s until after the First World War. A limited number of candidates with good theology qualifications, who would otherwise register for the Diploma of Student in Theology, may still register for a Lambeth MA by thesis. The award of the degree is still subject to rigorous scrutiny. Parl. Deb., H.L., *supra* n. 132, at 838-839.

147. For the mode of exercise of the right to confer Lambeth degrees under Archbishop Lang, *see id.* at 838-841.

gratitude from the Church at large for someone's distinguished work and service.

In historical terms Lambeth degrees are a mixture of privilege and dispensation, through now conferred on statutory authority. They are of the nature of positive privileges, though they may potentially be conferred to meet some statutory requirement for office.[148] Indeed, Archbishop Lang appears to have accurately reflected the true nature of Lambeth degrees when he called himself a "one-man University."[149]

X. CONCLUSION

The papal dispensation was a suspension of the full rigours of the canon law, exercised, amongst other circumstances, where hardship or injustice to an individual would otherwise arise or continue. This is clear in the cases of dispensations for the ordination of illegitimate clerics, or the marriage of certain couples. But how does the theory of dispensation explain the miscellaneous powers of the papacy over such matters as the appointment of notaries public, or the conferral of degrees?

This wide range of additional positive concessions, miscellaneous faculties or licences was available to both clergy and laity. Each was intended to right a wrong. For example, the dispensations to practise medicine were to allow men who were barred, perhaps because they were monks, from the profession.[150]

By contrast, the confirmation or conferment of degrees by papal or later statutory authority is less clearly in the nature of a dispensation. However, these grants were always rare,[151] and sometimes occurred where the man concerned had failed to qualify for a degree because of a canon law impediment, such as illegitimacy.[152] Perhaps these grants are

---

148. Blackstone, *supra* n. 10, at vol. 1, 381.

149. Parl. Deb., H.L., *supra* n. 132, at 838.

150. The Faculty Office records give examples of a wide range of dispensations. Examples include: 10 Nov. 1536, Robert Browne, alias Broone, BM, of Oxford, licensed to practise by the university, dispensation to confirm this and permit him to practise anywhere, 40 s, *pro sigillo regis* (taxed for the Great Seal) 5 s (F I/Vv, fo. 104r); 10 Dec. 1536, Robert Moreton, OCist monk. Dispensation to practise medicine anywhere despite holy orders, £4 (F I/Vv, fo. 107v); 20 July 1537, Joseph Compton, priest, monk of Pershore, Worcester diocese, dispensation to hold a benefice and practise medicine anywhere, if granted his diocesan bishop's consent, £8 (F I/Vv, fo. 145r); 20 Sept. 1538, Joseph Hatfeld, Fellow of College of Bonshommes at Ashridge, Lincoln diocese, dispensation to practise medicine anywhere, £4 (F I/Vv, fo. 226v); 7 June 1547, Robert Porter, of Bedford, Lincoln diocese, dispensation to practise the art of medicine anywhere, 4 s 5 d (F I/A, 266). *See generally* Chamber, *supra* n. 51.

151. Only four Lambeth degrees were granted by the Court of Faculties 1534-1549. *See generally id.*

152. An example of a faculty granted because of a disability was when on 6 Dec. 1544, George

understandable because the possession of a degree was of course a necessary qualification for many offices, particularly in the Church.[153]

Yet, it was often difficult to see just what law was subject to dispensation. In earlier times, a faculty permitting a clerk in holy orders to hold an office which required a graduate, or the conferral of a degree upon such person would be a dispensation. But in most cases the ecclesiastical law no longer requires such qualifications. The award of a Lambeth MA to candidates with good theology qualifications—who would otherwise register for the Diploma of Student in theology and who complete a thesis—would appear to have nothing to do with dispensations.[154]

It would be stretching the definition given by Archbishop Lang to say that the object of dispensations is "to enable some responsible person, not bound by the strictness of regulation, to get things done which, if they were not done, would involve very real hardships and disabilities."[155] The current motivation seems to be to recognise persons who "have attained considerable eminence, both in art and science and in learning, without possessing that inestimable testimony to profound learning [. . . the degree]."[156]

The best explanation for the status of these degrees is that, although many degrees were granted to prevent harm, they were more properly classified as privileges rather than dispensations. Whereas dispensations exempt some person or group from legal obligations binding on the rest of the population or class to which they belong, privileges bestow a positive favour not generally enjoyed by most people. Both involved exceptions to the ordinary operations of the law, but privileges involved a more positive, individual act of favour. Thus a notary had certain rights not enjoyed by others with respect to taking evidence, and a degree conferred by faculty gave the recipient a status that he would not

Broke, student in Venice, natural son and legitimised son of George Broke, Lord Cobham, received a dispensation to hold the status and privileges of a BA (F I/A, 92). *Id.* at 248.

153. Although some modern ecclesiastical judges do receive Lambeth doctorates in law, this is no longer required to meet the requirements of the canon (or statute) law. Canon 127 of 1603 required that ecclesiastical judges be learned in the civil and ecclesiastical law, and at least a Master of Arts or Bachelor of Law, but did not require a degree in canon law. *Constitutions and Canons Ecclesiastical 1604: Latin and* English (Notes by J.V. Bullard, Faith 1934). The statute 37 Hen. 8, c. 17 has been repealed by SLR (Statute Law Provision) 1863. *See Chronological Table of the Statutes* 56 (The Stationery Office 2001).

154. The diploma of Student in Theology, established 1905, originally for women, and since 1944 for men also. The archbishop's examination in theology leads to a Lambeth diploma. This may be conducted by thesis for suitably qualified candidates.

155. Parl. Deb., H.L., *supra* n. 132, at 839 (per Archbishop Lang).

156. *Id.*

otherwise enjoy.[157]

Since 1533 the nature of the Lambeth degree has changed. Originally intended largely as an exercise of a papal jurisdiction to dispense with the strict requirements of the canon law, they are now largely conferred in much the same way as honorary degrees. But Lambeth degrees are not honorary degrees. The privilege has become much more important than an exercise of the right of dispensation, though the former terminology is often still used.[158] In the words of Archbishop Lang, the archbishop of Canterbury is a "one-man University,"[159] yet the degrees are not awarded "in prejudice of the universities."[160] He may be able to confer the privilege of a degree, but only in appropriate circumstances. Lambeth degrees awarded after examination were always, and remain, something of a conceptual enigma, and should perhaps be only sparingly conferred.

Currently, the awards of Lambeth degrees are usually made in recognition of the recipient's contributions to the life of the Church, generally over many years. They remain examples of the exercise of ecclesiastical jurisdiction in favour of men (and now women too) who are regarded as being worthy of such an exercise of dispensation or privilege. It is this idea that the award is for the good of the Church, as well as the good of the individual, which links modern Lambeth degrees with their ancient papal equivalents.[161]

---

157. Indeed, in the immediate post-Reformation period the Lambeth degrees awarded were all said to be by way of dispensation to enjoy the privilege, etc., of a [DCL]. *See generally* those listed in Chamber, *supra* n. 51.

158. The wording used by the Church of England suggests that the Church itself recognises that the nature of the Lambeth degree is rather more of a privilege than a dispensation. *See for example* the wording of the News Release from the Office of the Archbishop of Canterbury, 12 May 1995.

159. Parl. Deb., H.L., *supra* n. 132, at 838.

160. The view of Lambeth degrees as not being "in prejudice of the universities" was stated by Sir William Blackstone, *supra* n. 10, at vol. 1, 381.

161. Those instances where an individual has been awarded a Lambeth degree pursuant to examination are examples of the granting of a privilege, rather than a dispensation, though both aspects may be present.

8 Lambeth Degree Academical Dress

Noel Cox

This article was originally published as:

Noel Cox, "Lambeth Degree Academical Dress", *Transactions of the Burgon Society* 5 (2005) 65–75

Transactions of the Burgon Society, 5 (2005), pages 64–75

Lambeth Degree Academical Dress

by Noel Cox

In the United Kingdom the right of universities and other institutions to confer degrees is strictly controlled by legislation.[1] Lambeth degrees, also occasionally and perhaps misleadingly called Canterbury degrees (as in 'DMus Cantuar')[2] are still awarded by the archbishop of Canterbury under the general authority of the Ecclesiastical Licences Act 1533–1534,[3] although he is not a university nor an educational institution per se. The continued specific authority for the archbishop to grant degrees can however be found in the Education Reform Act 1988,[4] and the Education (Recognised Bodies) (England) Order 2003.[5] But unlike other degree-granting bodies, the archbishop of Canterbury does not prescribe a distinct set of academical dress for the recipient of his degrees. Instead the academic dress is either that Oxford or Cambridge. This is due, at least in part, to the history and nature of the degrees which he confers.

Lambeth degrees are not honorary degrees,[6] though the candidates do not, in general, sit any examinations.[7] Indeed, to require examinations as a regular course

---

[1] Only those universities, colleges or other bodies authorized by royal charter or Act of Parliament can confer degrees; Education Reform Act 1988 s 214 (2) (a) and (b). Polytechnics, which have now become universities, and the various degree-awarding colleges are provided for in separate legislation. Any award may by Order in Council be designated a recognized award. These include the Degree of the Utter Bar (Inns of Court), Degree of Barrister-at-Law (Inns of Court of Northern Ireland), and the Degree of Master of Horticulture of the Royal Horticultural Society.

[2] Letter to the author from the Rt Revd Frank Sargeant, bishop at Lambeth, 8 December 1995.

[3] 25 Hen VIII c 21 (1533–1534) s 3.

[4] s 216(1).

[5] SI 2003/1865. The older universities, the archbishop of Canterbury, the now defunct Council for National Academic Awards, Union Theological College, Royal College of Music, and the Royal College of Art are listed in the Education (Recognised Bodies) Order (England) 2003 (SI 2003/1865) and later regulations.

[6] The faculty awarding the degree states 'PROVIDED ALWAYS that these Presents do not avail you anything unless duly registered by the Clerk of the Crown in Chancery.' The wording of the Faculty expressly states that the Faculty is to 'create you an actual MASTER OF ARTS. And we do also admit you into the Number of the Master of Arts of

for these degrees would have been contrary to the idea of a dispensation (which Lambeth degrees have been said to represent), though its use was not altogether inconsistent with this notion, since the archbishop was empowered to use the privilege of conferring degrees or degree status for the good of the Church, or the benefit of an individual.[8] Some assessment of academic ability or education would therefore often have been appropriate.

The modern practice followed by the archbishop of Canterbury now requires that the recipients must be presumed to have the potential to have studied for the degree in question and to have been awarded it.[9] In many cases it is recognized that someone's service to the Church has precluded further academic study, and a Lambeth degree is recognition of this, as well as a sign of gratitude from the Church at large for someone's distinguished work and service. It is thus in these cases a combination of an honour and the recognition of academic standing— though perhaps rather more recognition of the latter than is usually the case for a degree awarded *honoris causa*. At the same time the Lambeth Master of Arts degrees by thesis—dating from 1990—and the Diploma of Student in Theology— dating from 1905—both reflect academic standing alone, since they are awarded purely on the basis of examination.[10]

In historical terms Lambeth degrees are a mixture of privilege and dispensation,[11] though now conferred on statutory authority. They are of the nature of positive privileges, though, like the Oxford MA by special resolution, they may potentially be conferred to meet some statutory requirement for office.[12] Indeed Archbishop Lang appears to have accurately described the true nature of Lambeth

---

this Realm' [from Faculty creating the author an MA, dated 3 May 2005, registered at the Crown Office of the House of Lords 18 July 2005].

   [7] Examinations were conducted regularly for the MA from the 1860s until after the First World War. A limited number of candidates with good theology qualifications, who would otherwise register for the Diploma of Student in Theology, may still register for a Lambeth MA by thesis. The award of the degree is still subject to rigorous scrutiny: (1933) 87 HL Official Report, pp. 838–39; Peter Beesley, *The Lambeth Degrees* (London: Faculty Office, 1992).

   [8] See Noel Cox, 'Dispensation, Privileges, and the Conferment of Graduate Status: With Special Reference to Lambeth Degrees' *Journal of Law and Religion*, 18.1 (2002–03), pp. 249–74; available online at:

   [9] For the mode of exercise under Archbishop Lang, see (1933) 87 HL Official Report pp. 838–41.

   [10] See Marjorie Thresher, *A Venture of Faith: History of the Lambeth Diploma, 1905– 1984* (London: S. Th. Association, 1989); Cox, 'Dispensation, Privileges, and the Conferment of Graduate Status'.

   [11] See Cox, 'Dispensation, Privileges, and the Conferment of Graduate Status'.

   [12] Sir William Blackstone, *Commentaries on the Laws of England*, ed. by E. Christian (New York: Garland Publishing, 1978), Vol. III, p. 381.

degrees when he called himself a 'one-man University'.[13] This dichotomy has had its influence upon the academical dress worn by the recipients of these degrees.

Lambeth academical dress

It would seem—subject to the absence of any systematic survey of records—that the recipients of the Lambeth degrees customarily wore robes of the same style as those of the ancient university (Oxford or Cambridge as the case may be) attended by the archbishop conferring the degree.[14] During the appointment of Dr Carey, who had not attended either university,[15] new Lambeth graduates continued the practice of the last archbishop (Dr Runcie), who was an Oxford graduate, and wore Oxford academical dress of the appropriate degree.[16] Under Dr Rowan Williams this practice has continued, though whether this is because of a desire for consistency or because Dr Williams's senior degree was from Oxford (he has degrees from Cambridge also) is unclear.

Degrees awarded by the archbishop are not those of the University of Oxford, or indeed those of Cambridge—so far as the regulations of these universities are concerned. But it is now the rule that recipients will wear the academical dress of the appropriate Oxford degree.[17] Since the degrees are awarded by the archbishop it would appear to be within his unrestricted authority to regulate academical dress. But let us set aside for a moment the variant rule established by Dr Carey, and look at the possible alternatives.

The choice may be influenced by a determination of what precisely is the legal nature of a Lambeth degree. Possibilities are (and these may not necessarily be exclusive):

---

[13] (1933) 87 HL Official Report, p. 838. The Education (Recognised Bodies) Order (England) 2003 (SI 2003/1865) lists the Archbishop of Canterbury amid a list of universities and colleges.

[14] Cecil Wall, 'The Lambeth Degrees', *British Medical Journal*, 2 (1935), pp. 854–55. The exact status of the dress is uncertain, and it has been said that this rule only applied to non-graduate recipients, graduates wearing the robes of the degree conferred by the archbishop appropriate to their own university; Charles Franklyn, *Academical Dress from the Middle Ages to the Present Day Including Lambeth Degrees* (Lewes: privately printed, 1970), Chapter 13 'Lambeth Degrees'. This latter interpretation has much to commend it, bearing in mind the nature of Lambeth degrees.

[15] Dr Carey himself wore the academical dress of his highest earned degree, the University of London PhD, to preference to that of any of his several DD *honoris causa*.

[16] Letter to the author from the Rt Revd Frank Sargeant, bishop at Lambeth, 8 December 1995. The current archbishop's senior degree is from Oxford, but his first degree is from Cambridge.

[17] Letter to the author from the Rt Revd Frank Sargeant, bishop at Lambeth, 8 December 1995. This has not always been the case, however.

(1)   a degree awarded by the archbishop as a university of himself

(2)   a 'generic' degree by dispensation or privilege (and not specific to any
       particular university)

(3)   a degree of Oxford or Cambridge by dispensation (irrespective of the
       absence of approval by the university authorities)[18]

(4)   a degree of the recipient's own university by dispensation (ditto)[19]

The origins of the Lambeth degree may lie in the ancient dispensatory powers
of the papacy,[20] but the degrees conferred by the archbishops of Canterbury are
clearly distinct degrees. This was certainly the view of Archbishop Lang,[21] and can
be seen reflected in the actual words of the fiat conferring the degree:

> WHEREAS in School regularly instituted that laudable Usage and Custom hath long
> prevailed, and that with the Approbation as well of the pure Reformed Churches as of
> the most learned Men for many Ages past, That they who have with Proficiency and
> Applause exerted themselves in the Study of any Liberal Science, should be graced with
> some eminent Degree of Dignity: AND WHEREAS the Archbishops of Canterbury,
> enabled by the public Authority of the Law, do enjoy, and long have enjoyed, the Power
> of conferring Degrees and Titles of Honour upon those considered deserving of such
> recognition, as by an authentic Book of Taxations of Faculties confirmed by Authority
> of Parliament, doth more fully appear:

> WE THEREFORE, being vested with the Authority aforesaid and following the
> Example of Our Predecessors have judged it expedient, that you whose Proficiency in
> the Study of Theology, Uprightness of Life, Sound Doctrine, and Purity of Morals, are
> manifest unto Us be dignified with the Degree of MASTER OF ARTS And We do by
> these presents, so far as in Us lies, and the Laws of this Realm do allow, accordingly
> create you an actual MASTER OF ARTS. And we do also admit you into the Number
> of the Master of Arts of this Realm: the Oath hereunder written having been by Us or
> Our Master of the Faculties first required of you, and by you duly taken and
> subscribed.[22]

---

[18] Beesley, *The Lambeth Degrees*.

[19] Franklyn argued that the degrees were conferred by the Crown, as they were invalid
without ratification (*Academical Dress*, Chapter 13). This argument is, however, untenable,
since the wording of the faculty is explicit that the recipient is being created a MA or
whatever by the archbishop. In ecclesiastical theory the dispensation or privilege is from
the archbishop in his ecclesiastical capacity and not as an agent of the Crown.

[20] Cox, 'Dispensation, Privileges, and the Conferment of Graduate Status'.

[21] (1933) 87 HL Official Report, p. 838.

[22] Author's MA, 3 May 2005. See also the fiats reproduced in Franklyn, *Academical
Dress*, which have virtually identical wording.

This is clearly a substantive degree, and not merely degree status (as 'MA status' at Cambridge). The key phrases include 'the power of conferring degrees', and 'create you an actual Doctor in Civil Law'. Nor is the archbishop purporting to act 'in prejudice of the universities',[23] since he is acting so as to create a new doctor (master or bachelor), but not of either university (that is, Oxford or Cambridge).

The first option (a degree awarded by the archbishop as a university of himself) would appear to be the most correct, though the third may reflect its historical nature more precisely. The archbishop is dispensing the recipient from the requirements of residence at a particular university, but not necessarily from the requirements for examination. The first option is also supported by the notion of the recipient as being admitted 'into the number of Doctors of Civil Laws of this Realm', since the wording suggests that 'Doctors of Civil Laws' are generic rather than particular to individual universities. The second option is also possible, though it may be unwise to rely too much upon the precise wording of faculties.

The third option however finds support from the argument that when the authority to confer degrees was confirmed in 1533 the only universities which existed were Oxford and Cambridge. However these institutions did not purport to confer Oxford and Cambridge degrees respectively, but rather generic degrees. A Master of Arts of Oxford was equally an MA at Cambridge, which was why these universities recognized the equivalent degrees of each other. Indeed from the earliest times degrees awarded by recognized universities have enjoyed the mutual recognition of other institutions throughout Christendom—and now globally. For some centuries the faculty awarding the Lambeth degree has clearly purported to award a degree, and not merely dispense from the requirements of a particular university. The fourth option might appear logical, but there is little evidence to suggest that it reflects actual practice or underlying theory.

This still does not tell us which academical dress Lambeth degree holders should wear; indeed it widens the range of choices. These would have been proportionately narrowed had Lambeth degrees been degrees of Oxford or Cambridge (or any other designated university) by dispensation.

There are at least eight possible positions with respect to academical dress for Lambeth degree holders:

(1)   A unique academical dress, distinct from Oxford or any other university

(2)   Oxford academical dress

(3)   Oxford or Cambridge academical dress, depending upon which university the archbishop himself attended

---

[23] Blackstone, loc.cit.

(4)   For a non-graduate, Oxford or Cambridge academical dress depending upon which the archbishop attended

(5)   For a graduate, the appropriate robes of their own university

(6)   For an Oxford or Cambridge graduate, the appropriate robes of their own university

(7)   Academical dress of Oxford, Cambridge or any other university depending upon that which the archbishop attended

(8)   For a non-graduate, academical dress of Oxford, Cambridge or any other university depending upon which the archbishop attended[24]

The first option, that of a unique costume, has much to commend it, and would clearly establish the uniqueness of these degrees. It has been advocated by a number of writers (as a change, rather than as reflecting contemporary practice).[25] But its institution would be a bold step, one which successive archbishops, mindful perhaps of the jealousy of the universities—and perhaps not wishing to attract undue attention to the archbishop's privilege of conferring degrees—have hesitated to take.[26]

The best argument for utilizing Oxford academical dress is that Oxford is the oldest university in the realm, and indeed one of the original *studia generalia*.[27] It also has the advantage of offering a degree of certainty—though it is perhaps to be regretted that the academical dress of Oxford has fallen into chaos, not having been properly revised since 1770.[28]

Where a candidate—or the archbishop—is a graduate of more than one university the senior degree would presumably determine the choice of academical dress.[29] There is some evidence, however, to suggest that it is the first degree which is important. The argument in favour of wearing the academical dress of Oxford or Cambridge, depending upon which university the archbishop himself attended, would appear rather curious. There seems to be little logical reason why this rule should ever have achieved currency, except convenience or expediency (for long

---

[24] Other options include the combinations 4 and 5; 4 and 6; 5 and 8; 6 and 8; 5 and 2 (for non-graduates) and so on.

[25] e.g. Franklyn, *Academical Dress*, Chapter 13.

[26] See however note 33 below about the hybrid Oxford/Cambridge academical dress of Dr Edmund Turpin.

[27] See Cox, 'Dispensation, Privileges, and the Conferment of Graduate Status'.

[28] *Oxford University Statutes*, ed. by G. R. M. Ward (Oxford: Oxford University Press, 1845–51), Vol. II, 1767–1850, pp. 9–10.

[29] Where the same degree is held in two or more universities, the senior is the first awarded. If the senior degree held is a Lambeth degree then we speculate on the alternatives.

the archbishops were graduates of one or the other, and indeed for much of the nineteenth century and into the twentieth century successive archbishops were Oxford men), unless indeed these degrees are dispensations from Oxford or Cambridge degree regulations. Nor is it especially helpful to observe that only these universities existed in 1533, since the Lambeth degree is but a continuation of a much older practice,[30] and not based upon any particular university.

The position of Lambeth degree academical dress is also complicated by the need for Lambeth degree recipients to utilize the academical dress of contemporary Oxford (or Cambridge)—and thus be affected by any changes in university regulations.[31] It does however appear to have the support of long practice.[32] It should also be remembered that prior to the seventeenth century the differences in the academical dress of the two old universities was less pronounced that it later became, and the importance of the choice was proportionately less. Moreover, it would seem that, in one instance at least, a hybrid Oxford/Cambridge academical dress was used.[33] This may well have been a deliberate attempt to return to the practice prevalent at a time that the academical dress of Oxford and Cambridge was in many particulars the same—though the dress of the DD of Oxford and Cambridge differed in the colours of the silk lining from at least the fourteenth century,[34] as did the MA.

For a graduate recipient of a Lambeth degree it might be appropriate to wear the robes of their own university—at least if the degree is seen as some form of dispensation or privilege. In the view of Franklyn, this was preferable as it approximated to a promotion theory, whereby the archbishop promoted a recipient within the recipients' own university.[35] But this could risk exciting the jealousy of

---

[30] And it could be argued that this means that the academical dress should be that of Oxford or Cambridge as it was in 1533, unreformed.

[31] When the archbishop introduced the MLitt he adopted not merely the degree title but also the academical dress of a new Oxford degree.

[32] W. N. Hargreaves-Mawdsley, *A History of Academical Dress in Europe until the End of the Eighteenth Century* (Oxford: Clarendon Press, 1963), p. 137, citing Wall, 'The Lambeth Degrees', p. 855. This view is also supported by Hugh Smith and Kevin Sheard, *Academic Dress and Insignia of the World* (Cape Town: A. A. Balkema, 1970), Vol. I, p. 802.

[33] For Dr Edmund Turpin's Lambeth DMus in the 1890s see: Nicholas Groves, *Theological Colleges: Their Hoods and Histories* (The Burgon Society, 2004), Section 7; Nicholas Groves and John Kersey, *Academical Dress of Music Colleges and Societies of Musicians in the United Kingdom* (The Burgon Society, 2002), Plate 3. This appears to have the sleeves of the Cambridge doctors other than those of music. See photographs on p. 64, above.

[34] See Hargreaves-Mawdsley, *A History of Academical Dress*, Chapters 3 and 4.

[35] Franklyn, *Academical Dress*, p. 217.

their own alma mater,[36] which might give the impression that the archbishop is interfering in their internal affairs. It is also at odds with the fact that the archbishops themselves normally ascribed to their degrees a rather firmer character than that of a mere dispensation.[37] It also does not appear to have been the customary practice.

A compromise would be to for a non-graduate to wear the robes of Oxford or Cambridge depending upon which university the archbishop attended, and for a graduate to wear the appropriate robes of their own university. This view is supported by several writers as the practice actually followed,[38] but is it unclear whether this is so. Certainly it was not consistently followed. It also involves two additional complications. The graduates would appear as though they were the recipient of a dispensation from the regulations of their own universities (which suggests an authority which the archbishops did not claim to possess); and not all archbishops can be presumed to be graduates of Oxford or Cambridge. Given that the majority of recipients of Lambeth degrees have been graduates, this usage would suggest that the degree is by way of dispensation from university regulations, which it is not (at least, not principally now).

Rather than resenting the use of their own robes by Lambeth degree holders,[39] the universities might welcome the use of their robes. It might be possible to allow the recipients to wear the academical dress of Oxford, Cambridge or any other university attended by the archbishop, or for graduates, the dress of the recipient's own university, if there is a dress for the applicable degree. This would assuage the understandable jealousy of the University of London, which missed the opportunity to see its own academical dress utilized, when Dr Carey, a London graduate, chose Oxford for his model.[40] However, some universities might resent what they might easily see as the usurpation of their academical dress by the archbishop. Nor is

---

[36] Where there is no equivalent degree, then presumably recourse would have to be had to Oxford.

[37] See the wording of the fiat, above.

[38] Frank Haycraft, *The Degrees and Hoods of the World's Universities and Colleges*, second edition (London: The Cheshunt Press, 1924), p. 18; Revd Thomas Wood, *The Degrees, Gowns and Hoods of the British, etc., Universities* (London: Thomas Pratt and Son, 1882); and strongly supported by Strickland Gibson, according to Franklyn, *Academical Dress*, p. 217.

[39] Oxford's response to the use of Oxford DD dress by the newly appointed Bishop of Portsmouth, a Cambridge man, in 1941, was not favourable (Franklyn, *Academical Dress*, p. 217). See also note 44, below.

[40] Beesley, *The Lambeth Degrees*, argued that the degrees are linked with the universities of Oxford and Cambridge since these were the only universities extant in 1533, and therefore the archbishop would not be able to award a degree purporting to be of one of the newer universities (not that they purport to the degrees of Oxford or Cambridge in any case).

there any sound reason why the archbishop should purport to confer the degree of any particular university.

Options 5 and 6 have an advantage in that the dress worn by graduates would be that of their own universities, rather than determined by the archbishop's choice of university. But this would result in an unsatisfactory lack of consistency of dress—something which has in recent decades been avoided simply because prior to Dr Carey for centuries all archbishops of Canterbury were Oxford or Cambridge graduates. The argument that graduates wore the dress of their alma mater also appears unsatisfactory unless the conferring of the degree is seen as a promotion[41]—which again raises problems in respect of the apparent usurpation of authority over individual universities. Although in some respects these might be seen as an exercise in dispensation, such a theory bears little relation to the practice of recent centuries.

On the available evidence, it seems that the academical dress of the universities of Oxford or Cambridge was always used, and possibly for some cases at least, a hybrid of the two, and the determining factor was the university of which the archbishop was a graduate. It could follow that this rule is not limited to Oxford and Cambridge, since there is no inherent reason why the archbishop must have attended either, though the current archbishop is a graduate of both universities.[42] Consequently, if the archbishop is a graduate of London, then any Lambeth degree recipients during that archbishop's episcopate should wear London academical dress.

However, there is a strong argument that the Act of 1533 does not confer any authority upon the archbishop to do what he could not do in 1533. Since only Oxford and Cambridge existed in that year, it would appear that he does not have the legal authority to confer London degrees, so the academical dress of London ought not to be worn.

The actual practice adopted appears to be entirely at the discretion of the archbishop.[43] Long-standing custom justifies the use of Oxford and Cambridge academical dress, not least because that is the only academical dress which appears to have been used for nearly five hundred years. No such history of customary use would justify the assumption of London academical dress, for example—at least, not without the consent of the university.[44] As remarked earlier, the result of broadening the usage would be less clarity.

---

[41] This would require research into what was worn by Lambeth graduates in the last century and earlier.

[42] MA (Cambridge), DD, DPhil (Oxford).

[43] Letter to the author from the Rt Revd Frank Sargeant, bishop at Lambeth, 8 December 1995.

[44] To use academical dress without permission could raise legal questions, including possible liability for the tort of passing off, or for breach of copyright. The addition of, for instance, a purple or violet stripe, might not suffice to escape liability. But it must be said

With the introduction of the Lambeth diplomas by examination from 1905 there has been some new and distinctive academical dress developed, namely the hood and gown of the Diploma of Student in Theology (STh).[45] However, since this is a distinct qualification without a university counterpart—though the hood is of Cambridge shape—this provides little guidance with respect to the Lambeth degree. It also is uncertain whether the innovation, inconsistent as it is with practice with respect to the degrees, was desirable.

With respect to the Lambeth degrees, since the archbishop is not acting 'in prejudice of the universities',[46] he must be presumed to be conferring a generic degree, or one of his own creation. Since the archbishop of Canterbury is a 'one-man university', a distinct academical dress, presumably based upon that of Oxford (as the senior university), would perhaps be desirable. It would be unsatisfactory to encourage the use of the academical dress of recipients' alma maters (even assuming such institutions approved what they might see as the usurpation of their academical dress), and far more sensible to emphasize the inherent unity of the degree.

In the absence of a truly generic pattern for academical dress that of Oxford must be preferred—despite the relatively confused state of Oxford academical dress, and the inherent difficulty involved in utilizing the academical dress of a university and the submission to its regulations which this would appear to require.

Franklyn's suggestion of adding a one inch purple stripe to the cape of the hood would appear sensible,[47] though there is no particular reason why that particular distinction ought to be adopted. The principal objection which might be raised is that it would be an innovation, and as such contrary to the fundamental nature of the Lambeth degree. At least the adoption of any innovations in Oxford academical dress has the authority of custom (long-standing adherence to Oxford practice), however unsatisfactory it might otherwise be.[48]

The principal difficulty remaining is the inherent dichotomy in the nature of the Lambeth degree. It is scarcely to be wondered if hybrids—such as Dr Turpin's

---

that it would be extremely unlikely for a university to take legal action, even if they had an arguable cause of action.

[45] Groves, *Theological Colleges*, p. 49. See also the Archbishop's Diploma in Church Music.

[46] Blackstone, loc. cit.

[47] Franklyn, *Academical Dress*, Chapter 13.

[48] Note also that the range of degrees which the archbishop may confer does not appeared to be limited, and in recent years the comparatively new degree of MLitt has been awarded. Cambridge adopted this degree in 1922, and Oxford in 1979 (the latter to replace the BLitt of 1895). It remains to be seen whether the archbishop will institute a degree which is not awarded by either Oxford or Cambridge, and what academical dress might be utilized in that case.

DMus gown—were not tried. But ultimately it might be desirable for an element of certainty to be achieved by an express statement of archiepiscopal policy.[49]

Dr Noel Cox is a barrister and Professor of Law at Auckland University of Technology, New Zealand. He is the holder of a Lambeth degree, having been awarded the MA by the Archbishop of Canterbury in 2005.

---

[49] It need hardly be added that such a policy (though not unalterable) would need to be the product of full and careful consideration from historical, legal, practical, ecclesiological and æsthetic perspectives.

9 The Centenary Eucharist and Presentation of the Lambeth Diploma and MA Degrees

Noel Cox

This article was originally published as:

Noel Cox, "The Centenary Eucharist and Presentation of the Lambeth Diploma and MA Degrees", *Transactions of the Burgon Society* 14 (2014) 12–15

Transactions of the Burgon Society, 14 (2014), pages 12–15

The Centenary Eucharist and Presentation of the Lambeth Diploma and MA Degrees

By Noel Cox

Ten years ago, on Tuesday, 3 May 2005, I was privileged to attend the Centenary Eucharist and Presentation of the Lambeth Diploma and MA Degrees in the Lambeth Palace Chapel. Looking back, it was an occasion of great moment, not just for me personally. We were fortune that the date of our graduation coincided with the centenary of the creation of the Lambeth diploma, a qualification now superseded by the MPhil and PhD—and indeed the MA itself was also later to be phased out.

Dr Rowan Williams, Archbishop of Canterbury, conferred MA degrees upon the Revd Vivienne Armstrong-MacDonell and me, and an STh (Diploma of Student in Theology) on Mark Ratcliffe. Mrs Armstrong-MacDonell, who was retired, had been the adult training adviser to the Diocese of Exeter. Her thesis was on 'Language, Power and Ministry'. At that time I was a senior lecturer in law and a barrister; I was ordained seven years later. My thesis was 'An exploration of the basis of legal authority of the Anglican Church in New Zealand'. Mark Ratcliffe, a reader in the Church of England in the Diocese of London and serving as a Sergeant in the Royal Air Force at RAF Uxbridge, wrote a thesis entitled 'Reader Ministry in the Church of England—where has it come from and where is it heading?'

The Archbishop presided at the Eucharist, assisted by the Revd Christine Hall, a deacon and a member of the Lambeth Degrees Committee. A couple of nuns were in attendance, and these assisted the Archbishop and Mrs Hall (who acted as deacon) during the Eucharist. Also in attendance were the Honorary Director of the Lambeth Diploma programme, the Very Revd Dr Martin Kitchen, the Lambeth Awards Officer (and Staffing Officer), Ms Karen Little, the Registrar of the Court of Faculties, Peter Beesley, the Chief Clerk and Sealer of the Court of Faculties, Stephen Borton, and the Secretary of the Lambeth Diploma Association, the Revd Alan Davies.[1]

All those involved in the graduation ceremony itself were dressed in academical dress as appropriate, with the Archbishop wearing over his black cassock an Oxford DD gown and black scarf. The Registrar wore court suit (single-breasted black suit jacket with waistcoat and grey striped formal trousers) with a solicitor's gown and a short wig. Dr Kitchen wore cassock, surplice and black scarf. Most of the clergy present were in choir dress (cassock, surplice and black scarf). I wore black gown and hood; without cap, as did Mr Ratcliffe and Mrs Armstrong-MacDonell. Ms Little, as a graduate in theology from King's College London, wore a black stuff gown with pointed sleeves gathered at the forearm and held in place with a cord and button, and a black stuff hood fully lined with white silk. The

---

1   A section of the University of London Church Choir, under its musical director, Bryan Almond, led the singing. The organist was Paul Dean. There were a number of interested individuals in the congregation, including friends and family of the graduands, and members of the Lambeth Diploma Association and Lambeth Degree Association.

cowl was faced inside for three inches and edged outside with 3/8 inch of faculty silk, in this case Sarum red. The neckband was similarly edged.

The two MAs wore Oxford MA gowns, and the STh a London BA gown. Academical dress for the STh was a Cambridge full shape hood of black stuff, the lining divided horizontally when worn, white over light blue. The gown was London BA with blue cord and button. Both MA candidates wore Oxford MA hoods; an Oxford Burgon shape, black silk, lined and bound ¼ inch crimson shot silk.[2]

The ceremony in the Lambeth Palace Chapel commenced, appropriately enough, with the hymn 'Come, ye faithful, raise the strain of triumphant gladness' (the words from St John of Damascus). Dr Kitchen read the first lesson (Proverbs 8. 22–31); the choir sang Psalm 19; and Deacon Hall read the Gospel (Matthew 13. 44–46, 52). The Archbishop's address was concerned with the Lambeth diploma programme, and the encouragement of education in the Church, especially for clergy.

After the conclusion of the Eucharist, and the hymn 'Teach me, my God and King', the stage, as it were, was changed (literally, as the Faculty Office officers placed a desk beside the altar). The Archbishop took his seat in front of the altar.

The Archbishop read a citation for the STh candidate, describing the nature of his work, and then called upon the Director of the Lambeth Degree programme (now wearing his Manchester PhD hood with his black scarf, over the surplice) to introduce him. A certificate was presented to the candidate, while he knelt before the Archbishop. Mr Ratcliffe then took his seat.

The second part of the ceremony was more formal, because, unlike the STh, the MA was a degree. The Archbishop continued his address, commenting on the scarcity of funding for advanced theological research, and giving a eulogy for the first MA candidate, who was me. He then called upon the Director to introduce me.

Martin Kitchen: 'Archbishop, I present to you Dr Noel Cox to be awarded the Lambeth MA in Theology'.

Archbishop: 'It now gives me very great pleasure to be able to use the right given to me by virtue of my historic office to grant dispensations, previously granted by the Pope, which means that I can dispense you, Noel Cox, from residence to qualify for the degree of Master of Arts for which you have shown evidence that you are worthy.'

Mr Beesley, the faculty office registrar, administered the oath of allegiance at a small table set to one side of the altar.

Now an MA, I knelt before the Archbishop, who read from the Instrument creating me 'an actual Master of Arts' and admitted 'into the Number of the Master of Arts of this Realm' for my 'Proficiency in the Study of Theology, Uprightness of Life, Sound Doctrine, and Purity of Morals'.

While the Archbishop read the Instrument, supported by the Registrar, I held the pendant wafer seal.[3] At the end the Archbishop capped me with a square cap (gently tap-

---

2   The academical dress of Oxford and Cambridge is of course very different. For more on the nature of Lambeth degree academical dress see Noel Cox, 'Lambeth Degree Academical Dress', *TBS*, 5 (2005), pp. 64–75.

3   This seal has been used since the time of Archbishop Cranmer in the reign of Henry VIII. On one side of the Seal is a representation of Moses lifting up the brazen serpent, with the motto 'Mundus transit' and the Arms of the See of Canterbury. The reverse side shows a representation of Christ's Crucifixion with St John. In Latin is a quotation from St John's Gospel (17. 3), which trans-

The Very Revd Dr Martin Kitchen, the author (MA), the Archbishop, the Revd Vivienne Armstrong-MacDonell (MA), and one step below, Mark Ratcliffe (STh).

ping the crown of the head), and then the Awards Office placed the hood over my shoulders. A newly created MA, I then stood and shook hands with the Archbishop, and the second MA was introduced.

Mrs Armstrong-MacDonell followed the same process as I had done.

The ceremony concluded with an anthem sung by the choir ('O praise ye the Lord, ye angels of his'), the Blessing, and a recessional hymn ('Now thank we all our God'). While the latter was being sung the Archbishop, the Director, the Registrar and Chief Clerk, and MAs and STh, and the awards officer, left the chapel in procession. This passed through the chapel, and through the Palace to the entrance hall, whilst the singing could still be heard from the chapel. A photo call was held outside the doors of the Palace.

Afterwards the MAs and STh signed the register and the MAs also signed copies of the faculties. The faculties were then put aside to be endorsed by the Clerk of the Crown in Chancery, a process which would take several months.

lates as: 'And this is life eternal, that they might know thee the only true God, and Jesus Christ whom thou hast sent'. One side is thus symbolic of the other: 'And as Moses lifted up the serpent in the wilderness, even so must the Son of Man be lifted up' (St John 3. 14).

14

Neither the MA nor the STh will be awarded in future. The MA has been replaced by the MPhil and a new higher qualification (the PhD) in the newly expanded Archbishop's Examination in Theology. The STh is being allowed to die out.

The graduation ceremony, accompanied by a nice lunch and a meeting of the Lambeth Degree Association, was particularly moving because it was a vivid reminder of the unique status enjoyed by the Archbishop of Canterbury,[4] as inheritor of the ancient legatine privilege to award degrees.[5] Archbishop Lang called himself a 'one-man University.'[6] Though a slight exaggeration of the nature of his powers, nonetheless it is memorable turn of phrase, and not wholly inaccurate, particularly with the recent expansion of the degree programme.

The day was also memorable for me because I had arrived in London at dawn that morning, and was to fly out again that night. Due to the difficulties of long-distance travel—I lived in New Zealand—I had left home on the Monday and got back home on Thursday.

---

4   Under the authority of the Ecclesiastical Licences Act 1533 (25 Hen VIII c 21), recognised, in accordance with s 216(1) of the Education Reform Act 1988, by the Education (Recognised Bodies) (England) Order 2003 (SI 2003/1865).

5   See Noel Cox, 'Dispensations, Privileges, and the Conferment of Graduate Status: With Special Reference to Lambeth Degrees', *Journal of Law and Religion*, 18(1) (2002-2003), pp. 249–274.

6   87 Parliamentary Debates, House of Lords (5th series) (1933) 838, 839 (per Dr Cosmo Lang, Archbishop of Canterbury).

10 LAMBETH ACADEMIC DRESS AND THE UNIVERSITY OF LONDON

GRAHAM ZELLICK

This article was originally published as:

Graham Zellick, "Lambeth Academic Dress and the University of London", *Transactions of the Burgon Society* 7 (2007) 39–47

Transactions of the Burgon Society, 7 (2007), pages 39–47

Lambeth Academic Dress
and the University of London

by Graham Zellick

Introduction

There were several references to the University of London in Professor Noel Cox's article in Volume 5 on 'Lambeth Degree Academical Dress',[1] since that is the only University apart from Oxford and Cambridge to have produced an Archbishop of Canterbury. Dr Carey, who holds the London degrees of BD, MTh and PhD, became the 103rd holder of that office in 1991.

Professor Cox speculates about the University of London's 'understandable jealousy'—a strange choice of word—on missing 'the opportunity to see its own academic dress utilized when Dr Carey, a London graduate, chose Oxford for its model'.[2]

Readers of Professor Cox's article may be interested in the protracted exchange of correspondence with Lambeth Palace between 1996 and 1998 initiated by me first as Deputy Vice-Chancellor of the University of London and eventually as Vice-Chancellor and President. The correspondence is summarized below and largely speaks for itself, but some commentary will follow.

The Correspondence

The correspondence began in June 1996 with the following letter from me to the Archbishop:

> I understand that the recipients of Lambeth degrees are wearing academic dress based on the University of Cambridge.[3] I had thought that the principle was that Lambeth graduates wore academic dress in the style of the Archbishop's own university, which in your case (for the first time) is the University of London.
>
> I should appreciate clarification of the situation.

---

[1] *Transactions of the Burgon Society*, Vol. 5 (2005), pp. 64–75.

[2] Ibid., p. 72.

[3] It was, in fact, Oxford.

A prompt response was received from the Archbishop's Research Officer, pointing out that Archbishops have always associated Lambeth degrees with Oxford or Cambridge—'the only universities in existence in England at the time of the 1533 Act'—because all (until Archbishop Carey) had attended either of these universities. She went on to explain that Archbishop Carey had followed the tradition of his predecessor, an Oxford graduate, and not used the robes of the University of London 'as he cannot use the robes of a university—even his own— which was not in existence at the time of the 1533 Act'.

In reply, I questioned the assertion that it was only the robes of universities in existence at the time of the Ecclesiastic Licences Act 1533 that could be prescribed by the Archbishop and I asked for the basis of this contention. I continued:

> I see nothing in the Act of 1533 which refers to the existence of any particular universities at that time, nor should there be, since we are talking about a power vested in the Archbishop which formerly reposed in the Pope. Nor do I see anything about the academic dress to be worn by the holders of Lambeth degrees. I assume that it is purely a matter of custom.
>
> *Halsbury's Laws of England* notes: 'The recipient is entitled to wear the academic costume of the university of which the archbishop himself is a member.' *Halsbury's Statutes* says: 'It is by virtue of this [s.3] and the following section [of the Act of 1533] that the Archbishop of Canterbury is empowered to grant . . . Lambeth degrees, which entitle the holder to wear the academic dress of the Archbishop's University without making him a member of it.' If, as I suppose, the wearing of academic dress by the holders of Lambeth degrees is purely a matter of custom and practice and not of law, then the basic principle noted in *Halsbury's* ought to be preserved and Lambeth degree-holders should now wear the academic dress of the University of London.

Over a month later, the Research Officer wrote to say that the points I had raised were being considered by legal advisers. Three months later, I enquired whether the legal advisers had completed their consideration of the matter and after a further delay of three weeks the Research Officer responded, making several points:

- 'London University' had contacted Lambeth Palace by telephone following Dr Carey's appointment and advised that the University's Statutes did not permit anyone but actual holders of its degrees to wear its robes: 'I was told therefore that under no circumstances would it be appropriate for recipients of Lambeth Degrees to wear London University robes, thereby creating the perception that the recipients were getting actual "London" degrees.'

- 'We therefore took the decision to continue the custom, followed from time immemorial, to use the robes of either Oxford or Cambridge—the only universities being in existence in England in 1533.'

- The two ancient universities accept the position and their statutes present no impediment.

- It would be difficult, five years into Dr Carey's archbishopric, to change what had become an established custom of using the robes of Oxford University.

I made the following points in reply:

First, there is the point you make about the University of London itself (which you have not mentioned hitherto). I have consulted officers of the University and no one can understand how this telephone call came to be made. Perhaps you could inform me who made this call so that we can ascertain on what authority it might have been done. As it happens, the information as you report it, is entirely inaccurate. Neither the Statutes of the University at the time, nor the present Statutes (for whose drafting I was responsible), contain any provision on academic dress at all, let alone stipulate that it could not be worn by Lambeth graduates. The only body at the time that could have given an authoritative ruling or indeed expressed any opinion on the matter was the Senate; it would now be the Academic Committee. Either then or now, my own view is that it is inconceivable that the University would have resisted the consequence of having one of our graduates as Archbishop of Canterbury. Indeed, how could it be anything but a privilege for the University's robes to be worn by Lambeth graduates?

In your earlier letter you said that the matter had been referred to your legal advisers and that, I believe, accounts for the substantial delay until now. However, I see little evidence of a legal analysis and nothing really adds to what you have already said and which I have questioned. You say that the ancient universities have accepted the position: I do not accept that the University of London would not also accept it if given the chance. There is certainly no impediment presented by our Statutes or any provisions made thereunder.

What have your legal advisers said about the statement in all the texts that the holders of Lambeth degrees wear the robes of the Archbishop's own university? By what authority are Lambeth graduates at present wearing the robes of the University of Oxford?

You say that, in any case, the position could hardly be changed now five years into Archbishop Carey's term of office. I do not agree.

I should be grateful if these points could be further considered.

The Research Officer replied by stating that my various points were being considered but an early reply was not likely since the Archbishop was preparing for

Christmas and shortly thereafter would be taking seven weeks' sabbatical leave. 'We are being asked not to bother him with issues which are not urgent.'

Three months later, the Research Officer wrote again, having consulted the Archbishop on his return. The Archbishop felt very strongly that the use of the robes of the two universities in existence at the time of the 1533 Act should be retained, since 'the link must be one of history and not related to any particular occupant of office'. There would, it was argued, be 'grave concern' if the robes of a particular university were being 'particularly advertised'. Moreover, the Archbishop would not wish his successors to have to be involved in a debate over the robes to be worn. The Research Officer concluded:

> '. . . I confirm that the Archbishop does not wish to vary the practice of ancient custom which is widely accepted to use the robes of either Oxford and [*sic*] Cambridge. I am sure no future Archbishop would wish to do so either.'

I replied seven months later, having assumed office as Vice-Chancellor, in the following terms:

> However strongly the Archbishop may feel on this issue, I have yet to hear from you any justification for departing from the principle that has been acknowledged by every authority on the subject, namely, that holders of Lambeth degrees wear the robes of the Archbishop's own University. You have produced no authority to confine this proposition to the two universities which were in existence in 1533.
>
> You say there would be 'grave concern if the use of the robes of any particular university was being particularly advertised' . . . Robes of particular universities are being used at present. Whether or not that gives rise to grave concern, I very much doubt.
>
> I do not understand your paragraph which says that 'this Archbishop would not wish his successors to have to be involved in a debate over the robes to be worn when they are giving their own degrees'. If Archbishop Carey were to adhere to the long-established rule, there would be no debate. Disquiet is caused now because the Archbishop is determined to disregard a principle what has been universally acknowledged.
>
> You conclude by saying that 'this Archbishop does not wish to vary the practice of ancient custom'. But this is precisely what he is doing. The ancient custom only limited the robes to those of Oxford and Cambridge because we have not previously had an Archbishop of Canterbury who was a graduate of another university. We now have a ludicrous situation in which each Archbishop, if he is not a graduate of either Oxford or Cambridge, will have to determine which of these two Universities will be used for Lambeth graduates, even where the Archbishop has no connection with either of them.
>
> The Archbishop's conclusion is not only insulting to his own University of London, but it derives no support from history, tradition, law or custom and I urge the Archbishop to reconsider the matter with care.

The reply, after just under two months, this time came from the Rt Rev. Frank Sargeant, Bishop at Lambeth, who made the following assertions:

- Neither the present Archbishop nor his successors would wish upon installation to become involved in a debate over the robes to be worn by Lambeth degree-holders.

- Successive Archbishops have rejected the suggestion that distinctive unique robes could be instituted for Lambeth degrees 'as this might well have the effect of seeing [*sic*] to create the Archbishop's own university'.

- No objections have ever been raised by Oxford or Cambridge and nothing in their statutes prevents it.

- There is no such 'long-established rule' but a convention or custom that the robes of one of the two English universities in existence in 1533 were to be used and 'generally, the preference would be for the present Archbishop's own university'. Although it was not possible to invoke the second part of the convention under Archbishop Carey, it was possible to adhere to the first part.

- The use of different robes could imply that the recipients were in fact holding degrees of a particular university which could jeopardise the Archbishop's power to grant degrees.

- The Archbishop wished to know whether my views were shared by a majority of the Council of the University but in any event 'the Archbishop's decision in this matter is final'.

After a further exchange of letters, in which Bishop Sargeant expressed Dr Carey's wholehearted support and affection for the University of London, the correspondence was closed without any convergence of views.

Commentary

First, as any lawyer with trial experience will say, a witness who shifts his ground from statement to statement is vulnerable. This correspondence illustrates the point nicely. In particular, an alibi needs to be advanced fully and early. The 'alibi' here—the mysterious telephone call referred to in the letter of 20 November 1996—surprisingly does not emerge until the second substantive letter and then is devoid of supporting detail. Had it been averred in the first reply, it might have been a clincher. Moreover, the inevitable request for further details as to who made the call elicited no response at all. Is it possible that no proper note was taken of the call and the file does not record to whom the office was speaking? If so, it betrays an unfortunate laxity in the administrative arrangements. Did Lambeth Palace really believe that such a message would be conveyed by telephone rather than in writing? And would not normal prudence dictate that the caller should have been asked to put the point in writing?

Dr Carey became Archbishop of Canterbury in 1991. In April of that year, Dr J. H. Pryor tabled the following question for answer at the next meeting of the University of London's Convocation (the body of the University's graduates, since abolished):

> (a) It has long been the custom, when the Archbishop of Canterbury grants Lambeth degrees, for the recipient of the degree to wear the academic dress of the Archbishop's university, Oxford or Cambridge. Now that we have the first Archbishop who is a London graduate, is the custom to be followed so that the grantees of Lambeth degrees in the present Archbishop's period of office may wear the academic dress of the University of London?

> (b) If so, will such graduates be eligible for membership of Convocation and/or to wear the distinctive Convocation dress?

Dr Pryor, a graduate of the University and Chairman of Convocation's Academic Dress Sub-Committee, died before the next meeting on 14 May and so the question went unanswered, but it is possible that it was he who made the telephone call referred to in the letter, purporting to speak for the University, though having no authority to do so and conveying wholly inaccurate information if the Research Officer's recollection is reliable.

The second part of Dr Pryor's question calls for comment. First, Lambeth graduates would obviously not have been eligible for membership of Convocation. As Professor Cox makes clear, the holder of a Lambeth degree does not become a member or graduate of the university whose robes he is disporting. Secondly, if Dr Carey had opted for London academic dress, the issue of what dress would have had to be confronted, because at that time what is variously called full academical dress, festal robes or doctors' scarlet was confined to members of Convocation, i.e. those graduates who had troubled to make the modest payment for lifetime membership of Convocation. This had always struck me as an odd and questionable practice and it was abandoned in my time as being offensive in principle and a crude device to promote membership of Convocation. Clearly, academic dress of the non-Convocation kind would hardly have been apt for the holders of Lambeth doctoral degrees.

Secondly, another oddity is the interval in the dialogue while the issue was referred to the legal advisers. Over four months later, when the conversation is resumed and the legal advisers have reported, the letter in November 1996 contains no legal points at all, which is perhaps hardly surprising since the question is not in fact a legal one. The legal advisers presumably reported as such, but Lambeth Palace was by this stage so committed to obfuscation and opacity that they could not bring themselves to say so. Or maybe the lawyers too couched their advice in impenetrable language to justify the long delay and a fat fee! The invocation of the Act of 1533 as limiting the academic dress to the only two universities in existence at that time is nonsense. Distinctive academic dress for different institutions did not in any event emerge for two centuries. If there were merit in this argument, it might mean that the actual academic dress current in 1533 should be used for Lambeth degrees without modification or adjustment. That has only to be stated to be rejected.

Thirdly, the correspondence does little to conceal the impatience, irritation and defensiveness of the writers, or the Archbishop, for pressing the point. Underlying this was, I believe, an anxiety that the press might become interested in the debate if it became public and throw a searchlight on Lambeth degrees and perhaps bring their continued existence into question.

Conclusions

Academic dress in Britain is not regulated by law. The power to prescribe academic dress does not even derive from university charters. The academical dress to be worn by the holders of Lambeth degrees is also not a matter of law but merely of custom or convention. After over four centuries, however, that custom or convention is neither clear nor settled. Lambeth Palace appears to believe that it is a matter for determination by each Archbishop individually, who will choose between Oxford and Cambridge. They seem unsure, however, whether his formal power to choose is broader than that.

Without wishing to rehearse Professor Cox's full discussion, the following seem to be the possibilities and all are clearly arguable:

- Only the robes of Oxford or Cambridge may be prescribed.

- An Archbishop who is a graduate of one of these will choose that University's robes.

- An Archbishop who is a graduate of both must make a firm election between them for the duration of his archiepiscopate.

- An Archbishop who is a graduate of both may use either, making the choice at each conferral.

- An Archbishop who is a graduate of neither is free to choose one of them or both, making the choice at each conferral.

- Where an Archbishop is willing to use either Oxford or Cambridge, the choice will be influenced by whether the recipient already holds a degree from one of them.

- An Archbishop who is a graduate of neither will continue the usage adopted by his immediate predecessor.

- An Archbishop who is a graduate of neither should normally choose the academic dress of the university of which he himself is a graduate (*quaere* whether that university would be able to refuse its consent[4]).

- An Archbishop may prescribe unique academic dress designed specifically for Lambeth degree-holders. This is already the case in respect of the Lambeth diploma of Student in Theology (STh).

- Any future Archbishop could alter this, or indeed any decision on academic dress taken by his predecessor.

- It is not a matter for determination by the Archbishop at all, but operates automatically, with the recipient 'entitled', as *Halsbury's Laws* and *Statutes* put it (see p. 40, above), to wear the academic dress of the Archbishop's own university.

One possibility absent from this list, though canvassed by Professor Cox,[5] is the use of the robes of the new Lambeth graduate's own university on the curious argument that the Lambeth degree may be said to represent some kind of advancement. This possibility, in my view, is devoid of logic or sound policy and it is without precedent.

Dr Carey or his advisers clearly came to the unexceptionable conclusion on his appointment that on grounds of expediency or policy it was preferable to adhere to the centuries-old custom of conferring Lambeth degrees in the dress of Oxford or Cambridge, both of which had long acquiesced in the practice, though the basis on which a non-Oxbridge Archbishop is to select between the two is unclear: perhaps he merely makes no change from his immediate predecessor, as with Dr Carey who continued Archbishop Runcie's use of Oxford robes.

The old stated principle that Lambeth degree holders wore the academic dress of the Archbishop's own University must therefore be read on the assumption that every Archbishop would be a graduate of either Oxford or Cambridge. The principle should apparently now read that each Archbishop will prescribe the robes to be worn, choosing between those of Oxford and Cambridge because of ancient usage and because it means that the consent of another institution does not have to be sought and obtained. After all, it is even possible that there could be an Archbishop who was not a graduate of any (British) university.

---

[4] See ibid., p. 73, n. 44.
[5] Ibid., pp. 71–72.

Despite the use of Oxbridge robes over the centuries, it is, however, difficult to see any basis on which an Archbishop could be prevented from prescribing other robes, whether of another university or designed specifically.

There is a substantive point that also arises in this connection which is not touched on in Professor Cox's article and which is arguably of greater significance. The choice of university determines not only the academic dress but also the range and nomenclature of degrees that can be awarded. There are differences between Oxford and Cambridge in this respect, as well as in how their degrees are abbreviated for post-nominal and other purposes. That is one reason why it does not seem desirable for any Archbishop to vary between the two universities as the mood takes him.

The main difference in terminology is in Law where Cambridge awards the near universal LLD but Oxford the fairly rare (though not unique) DCL (Doctor of Civil Law). The abbreviations for other degrees also differ considerably, with both universities adopting practices which are occasionally unusual and which usually differ from each other. Thus, for Science, Cambridge has the ScD, and in Medicine, Oxford the DM (instead of the universal MD) and the two universities have diametrically opposed practices in respect of their other degrees too: thus, in Music and Letters, Oxford has the DMus and DLitt while Cambridge the MusD and LittD. Only the DD is common to both.

I understand Lambeth is about to introduce a doctorate in philosophy, a degree unknown in 1533 and for several centuries thereafter. Not only do the Oxford and Cambridge robes for this degree differ fundamentally, but Oxford styles it DPhil and Cambridge the more usual PhD. Will this, too, alternate from Archbishop to Archbishop or even from graduate to graduate?

The use of Oxbridge degree titles, terminology and academic dress is unexceptionable. Perhaps some of us in London were disappointed (though certainly not jealous) when Lord Carey eschewed our robes for Oxford's. The Archbishop's degree-awarding power is a quaint historical relic, inappropriate and incongruous but inoffensive and benign. I recently had the pleasure of observing Dr Williams' admission of Rabbi Tony Bayfield, Head of the Movement for Reform Judaism, to the degree of Doctor of Divinity—a gesture warmly appreciated in Rabbi Bayfield's community. I understand Rabbi Bayfield wore a Cambridge DD gown, in recognition of his own membership of that University. Dr Williams seems to be alternating between Oxford *and* Cambridge robes. Can that be in conformity with the convention as Lambeth understands it? Perhaps someone would like to initiate correspondence with Lambeth Palace on this point!

Graham Zellick, MA, PhD, LLD, LHD, AcSS, CCMI, FRSA, Hon FRAM, Hon FSALS, is an Honorary Fellow of the Society. He is a Barrister and Master of the Bench of the Middle Temple, Honorary Fellow of Gonville and Caius College, Cambridge, Emeritus Professor of Law in the University of London, Honorary Professor in the School of Law, University of Birmingham and Visiting Professor of Law at Queen Mary, University of London.

THE BURGON SOCIETY

The Burgon Society was founded in 2000 in response to a growing interest in the subject of academical dress. It is named after John Burgon (1813–1888), sometime Dean of Chichester Cathedral, Fellow of Oriel College, Oxford, and the only person to have a shape of academical hood named after him.

The aims of the society are:

- to coordinate the study of academical dress in all its aspects: design, history and practice;

- to preserve details of the past and present practices of institutions regarding academical dress;

- to act in an advisory capacity to film and television companies, and to those who wish to ensure correctness in the usage of academical dress.

Membership of the Society is open to anybody who is interested in academical dress. Fellowship of the Society is awarded to members on the successful submission of a suitable piece of original work.

The Society meets several times a year to receive newly submitted fellowship papers and to discuss other matters related to academical dress. It publishes a scholarly journal, *Transactions of the Burgon Society*, containing research papers submitted during the year; and organises exhibitions of academical dress and study visits. The Society also possesses a substantial collection of robes, and an archive of books and papers which are open, by prior arrangement with the Archivist, to anyone interested in undertaking research on academical dress.

If you would like to join the Burgon Society, please visit the website www.burgon.org.uk and download a membership form. For further information, please email registrar@burgon.org.uk.

www.ingramcontent.com/pod-product-compliance
Lightning Source LLC
Chambersburg PA
CBHW060756150426
42811CB00058B/1421